PUSHMATAHA

THE FORGOTTEN WARRIOR

Thomas L. Wiley

Pushmataha 1764-1824

Also by Thomas L. Wiley

The Angels of Lockhart

The Telegrapher

Although this story is based on actual historical events, it is written as a narrative, with dialogue among the characters. Liberties have been taken. Day to day actions, interactions, and conversations, though fictionalized, are felt to be accurate portrayals of the times and characters.

INTRODUCTION

ON CHRISTMAS EVE, 1824, the *Washington Gazette's* front-page story read:

"This morning, a few minutes after 12 o'clock, Pushmataha, the principal chief of a district of the Choctaw Nation of Indians, died. He departed this life at the hotel of Mr. Joseph Tenneson in the city (Washington, D.C.) where he had been residing with other Choctaw delegates, during their late pending negotiations with the Government for the disposal of a portion of the lands of the Nation.

"This chief was remarkable for his personal courage and skill in war, having engaged in twenty-four battles, several of which were fought under General Jackson...

"Pushmataha was also a man of great eloquence. He possessed a rich and fertile imagination with a sound understanding, and was classed by his Choctaw countrymen among the first of their warriors, and was considered the greatest of their orators.

"He fell victim of the distressing malady of croup... He bore his affliction with great firmness, was conscious of his approaching end, and predicted with unusual sagacity the hour at which he would die. This prediction was literally fulfilled.

"... He gave with great composure directions to his friends and associates for the disposition of his property, recommended his family to the fatherly care of the Nation, and breathed his last amid the tears and regrets of his companions and acquaintances. Whilst living he had conciliated the friendship of all who knew him."[1]

---

[1] *Washington Gazette*, December 25, 1824.

i

AT TWO O'CLOCK ON CHRISTMAS DAY the Chief of the Choctaws was buried in Washington's Old Congressional Cemetery with pomp and circumstance fit for a national hero. Two thousand lined Pennsylvania Avenue as the Marine Band played and the big guns were fired. Andrew Jackson himself led the processional for "the greatest and the bravest warrior he had ever known."

And the United States Congress likewise honored the great chief on that dark winter day. It was the least they could do for the Red man who had literally saved the United States. Senator John Randolph of Virginia eulogized the great warrior before the Senate Chamber as "one of nature's nobility; a man who would have adorned any society." He further stated that he was "a warrior of great distinction; he was wise in counsel, eloquent in an extraordinary degree, and, on all occasions and under all circumstances, the white man's friend."

IT'S SURPRISING THAT PUSHMATAHA—a man who was so revered and honored by our nation's leaders two hundred years ago—is today virtually unknown. Outside of the Choctaw Nation few have heard of him and even fewer know the impact he had on the early years of the United States.

Names like Geronimo, Sitting Bull, Tecumseh—the great "enemies" of our nation's past—roll off our tongues with ease, but Pushmataha, "the greatest and the bravest" and "on all occasions the white man's friend," a name that was once synonymous with courage and leadership, has faded into obscurity, not even relegated to a footnote in the history books.

What happened to his legacy, his place in American history?

TO BEGIN, we must first go forward six years after his death, to the fall of 1830, when Secretary of War John H. Eaton and General John Coffee, under the direction of President Andrew Jackson, met with the leaders of the Choctaw Nation to finalize an agreement that would transfer eleven million acres of land to the United States Government. If negotiations went as planned, the United States would not only complete one of the largest non-wartime acquisitions of Native

American land in history, but the Choctaws would be giving up the last of their ancestral lands east of the Mississippi.

The proposed agreement, or treaty, was not the first between the United States and the Choctaws. It was one of many. For almost thirty years, beginning with the Treaty of Fort Adams in 1801, the United States had negotiated with the Choctaw Nation and had, through false promises, bribery, and intimidation, gained control of most of their vast landholdings which spread over Mississippi and western Alabama—land that had been promised to the Choctaws "in perpetuity" by the Treaty of Hopewell in 1786.

But the United States needed more land. The fledgling nation was bursting at the seams. Expansion across the Appalachians into the Ohio Valley and the land of the Shawnee, Illinois, and Miami had given temporary relief, but it had not been enough. The next great migration had been into the fertile subtropical Mississippi Territory— the land of the Choctaws, Creeks, and Chickasaws—and with the signing of this last treaty, the acquisition of Choctaw land would be complete.

Secretary Eaton and General Coffee were successful in their negotiations, and early on the morning of September 27, 1830, on the banks of a small stream in present day Noxubee County, Mississippi, the Treaty of Dancing Rabbit Creek was signed. According to the Choctaws, there was really no negotiations—either accept the demands of the white man or have the land taken by force.

Within two years, removal of the Choctaws to their new home in Oklahoma began. Of the sixteen thousand men, women, and children who made the six-hundred-mile journey, almost twenty-five hundred died of exposure and starvation on this, the first "Trail of Tears and Death." The Chickasaws, Seminoles, Creeks, and Cherokees would follow later.

THE STORY OF THE CHOCTAWS has, for the most part, been forgotten. Unlike the Cherokee Nation, whose Trail of Tears experience is memorialized through a popular outdoor drama, *Unto These Hills*, or the western Native Americans, whose conflicts and massacres in the late 1800s were glamorized by the rapid dissemination of information through the telegraph and newsprint and later on the screen, the Choctaws have had no fanfare. Theirs was a story of peaceful acceptance, without conflict, in a time when communication was slow. Realizing that resistance would most assuredly result in their total annihilation, the Choctaws never raised a hostile arm towards the United States.

THE LIFE OF CHIEF PUSHMATAHA paralleled those tumultuous times of the Choctaw Nation as he dealt not only with Andrew Jackson but with other greats—Thomas Jefferson, John C. Calhoun, and Shawnee Chief Tecumseh—to try to save the lands of his ancestors. From his humble beginning as an orphan, to his reputation as a vicious warrior and later a master of oratory and diplomacy, Pushmataha led his people through a time of marginal contact with the white man into an era of submission and despair—and along the way helped ensure a victory for the United States in its Second War of Independence, the War of 1812. Sadly, in the two centuries since his rise to greatness, his name, like the struggles of his nation, has faded from the memory of the American public.

THE FORGOTTEN WARRIOR tells the story of Chief Pushmataha, the Choctaw Nation, and early Mississippi following a fictitious pipe. Although the dialogue and interactions are fictionalized, the stories within the story are based on true events in history.

"A LITTLE CLOUD WAS ONCE SEEN in the northern sky. It came before a rushing wind, and covered the Choctaw country with darkness. Out of it flew an angry fire. It struck a large oak and scattered its limbs and its trunk all along the ground, and from that spot sprung forth a warrior fully armed for war. And that man was Pushmataha."

SPOKEN BY THE GREAT WARRIOR in 1824[2]

[2] Appleton's Journal. 1870. Volume 4, Issue 71. p 166.

CHAPTER ONE

THE PIPE WAS LIKE NO OTHER the eight-year-old Pushmataha or any in Coosha Town had ever seen. It was pure white and exquisitely carved, so different from the bare gray stone pipes the Choctaws were accustomed to.

"It is made from meerschaum," the Englishman said through an interpreter. "It is soft when it's first collected from the ground, allowing it to be carved with a sharp object. With time and exposure to the air, it hardens into a stone that is as white as snow and as hard as granite. This one was fashioned by artisans across the Great Waters to the east, in a nation called Italy.

"It is a gift," the Englishman continued as he presented the pipe to the mingo, or chief, of Coosha Town. "I ask for nothing in return except to abide with your people for a few days. I have come, not to trade, but to draw pictures of your rivers and towns. My king, the chief of the white man, has sent me to listen to your words. He wishes to know of your ways and of your land."

IN 1768, FOUR YEARS before his visit to Coosha Town, the Englishman, Bernard Romans, had been appointed by King George III as the principal surveyor for the Southern District of the American Colonies. Romans had spent the first three years charting the coastal waters of the Florida peninsula, and for the last year, he and his party had worked their way along the West Florida coast.

When he reached Pensacola, his mission changed. Romans' new task, with the assistance of John Stuart, Superintendent of the British Indian Department, was to complete a comprehensive mapping of the less well-known Indian territories of his district.

His fellow surveyor, David Taite, traveled north into present day Alabama to complete the task of cataloguing the Creek Nation, while

1

Romans and his crew ventured further west and north along the Big Trading Path into Choctaw Country.

For centuries the Big Trading Path had been the primary commercial route connecting the Mobilia and Creek Nations with the Choctaws and Chickasaws. No more than a path in most places, the trail originated at the great Bay of Mobile, coursed north through the fertile lands that paralleled the Tombigbee River, and then turned northwest along the Sucarnoochee River and Ponta Creek, through Coosha Town, and into Choctaw Country. From there it continued north through the Chickasaw Nation and on to the land of the Yazoos and Quapaws.

Native American Tribes of Mississippi, circa 1700. By the mid-1700s, Tunica, Natchez, Biloxi, Ofo, and Houma tribes no longer existed in Mississippi, having for the most part assimilated into the Choctaw and Chickasaw Nations.

"FATHER, MAY I HOLD THE PIPE," Pushmataha asked during a lull in the conversation between the white man and the mingo, who was also his father.

All eyes in both parties turned toward the eight-year-old Pushmataha.

Two of his friends who were standing beside him snickered at his boldness, but he ignored them. Pushmataha was a leader, or at least he thought he was.

Never at a loss for words, young Pushmataha had never been afraid to voice his thoughts. And even though his friends often teased him at his boldness, they secretly admired his gift with words and his ability to tell stories. The tales of creation and of the great warriors of the past, tales that were told by the ancients in the ceremonial lodge and around the council fires: Pushmataha would hear them and repeat them with such passion and strength that even the originators of the tales were in awe, as if they were hearing the stories for the first time.

He had always been smaller than the others of his age and would remain so as an adult, but he made up for it by carrying himself like a warrior. His face was inquisitive and determined, yet it was boyish. With age his face would remain boyish, hiding a fierceness and a power that few could equal.

"This is my son, Apushim-alhtaha, 'the sapling is ready,'" his father said as he placed his hand on the boy's shoulder. "He thinks he is a towering tree."

Pushmataha's birth name was "Apushim-alhtaha." Birth names of the Choctaws were temporary. When he was older, his name would be changed to something befitting his character.

Bernard Romans smiled at this display of humor and familiarity from the mingo. The stay with the Choctaws would be good.

The father gave the pipe to his young son as Romans looked on. The boy turned it in his hands.

"Such a magnificent work of art," he thought.

On the outside of the bowl was carved a family of deer: a buck with a magnificent rack and two does, all looking upward. When the pipe was lit and smoke left the bowl, it was as if the three were gazing to the heavens as the clouds disappeared in the sky. The stem had a slight curve at the bowl and after seven or eight inches curved outward to a narrow mouthpiece. The entire structure was finely polished and glistened in the sun. The weight was good, not light but not overly heavy. And it fit the hand perfectly.

"The carving is so detailed," the young Pushmataha thought. "A master must have labored for weeks to create it."

As the boy admired the work of art, he had no way of knowing how pipes similar to this one—thousands of them—and the tobacco that burned in them, had impacted the lives of his Red brothers to the north and east. He had no way of knowing that this aromatic leaf had become such a part of the culture of the white man that the demand was insatiable. No one had told him that to meet this demand the white man had decimated vast forests, and in their place stood cultivated fields with nothing but tobacco as far as the eye could see. He knew nothing of the fences that the white man had built. How the white man had laid claim to the land— "owned" the land—and had banished the original inhabitants. But with time, he and his Choctaw brothers would learn.

ROMANS HAD NOT BEEN the first white man to have come through Coosha Town. Pushmataha had heard tales of the past, many generations ago, when men in armor had come through killing and destroying. The ancients told of the great Tuscaloosa, Mingo of the Mobilia, who died with his warriors as they battled the evil white man called De Soto.

ON HIS SECOND JOURNEY to the New World in 1539, Hernando De Soto and six hundred Spanish and Portuguese conquistadors journeyed through present day Florida, Alabama, and Mississippi conquering the land in the name of Carlos I of Spain, while searching for rumored gold and treasure. In 1540 they were attacked in present day Alabama by the Mobilia tribe under the leadership of Tuscaloosa, the "Black Warrior." Having grossly underestimated the effects of mounted cavalry and muskets, Tuscaloosa and several hundred of his warriors were killed. (By some accounts it was several thousand.) Only twenty-two Spaniards were lost. Hernando De Soto never found his treasure and died on the banks of the Mississippi River in 1541.

The Mobilias, one of the most powerful tribes of the time, dwindled in number over the next two centuries. By the mid-1700s they ceased to exist as a distinct tribe and were assimilated into the Choctaw Nation, with whom they shared a common ancestry.

The decrease in the population of the Mobilias was not an isolated event. Most other tribes of Native Americans, including the Choctaws, experienced dramatic declines in their numbers during the sixteenth century, most likely as a result of diseases such as smallpox and measles brought by early European explorers. Later explorers, rather than finding vastly populated cities, found only isolated villages: remnants of an earlier culture that numbered in the millions. Some theorize that if not for disease, the European encounter with North America would have been similar to that with India, China, and Africa—initial conquest that later, due to the sheer number of the native populations, gave way to native independence—and subsequent cultures based on that of the original inhabitants rather than that of western Europe.

SINCE THE TIME OF DE SOTO, other white visitors, primarily traders and trappers, had come through Choctaw territory. Most of them had stayed for only a short time and then moved on. But in the past few years, a few had built lodges and stayed, some with their families, living off the land as the Choctaws did. Some had come in and opened trading posts, exchanging white man goods for beaver and deer pelts. And others had even taken Choctaw women as their wives and were living among the Choctaws as members of the Nation.

Pushmataha would later learn that along the Great Waters to the south, only three days journey from Coosha Town, the white man was settling in great numbers. In villages once inhabited by his brothers, the Biloxi and the Mobilia, the white man had built forts surrounded by great walls—walls built not to keep their animals in but to keep the Okla Humma, the "Red Man," out. Mighty canoes powered by the wind were coming and going, loaded down with goods from faraway lands.

And only five days journey to the west of Coosha Town, where his brothers, the Natchez, had lived—on the high bluffs that overlooked the mighty Father of Waters—the white man was building magnificent lodges where simple dwellings of the Red man once stood. The surrounding forests that once offered bountiful hunting grounds were being cleared and cultivated—tilled by men with even darker skin than the Red man.

The young warrior would also learn that the land that he and his forefathers lived on was continually being fought over by different nations of the white man. For generations, their land, the land that gave the Choctaws life and meaning, had at different times and under different treaties been claimed by the Spanish, the French, and the English. Soon the United States would join them.

FOR SEVERAL WEEKS Bernard Romans and his party explored the surrounding area and drew maps of the streams and rivers. With the help of the leaders of Coosha Town, he identified scores of villages and plotted their location on the maps.

Romans found the Choctaws to be a peaceful, quiet people living in small villages scattered throughout the land. The villages were connected with well-worn trails, and flow between the peoples seemed to be easy and friendly.

The Choctaws were primarily an agrarian society, cultivating small patches of corn, peas, pumpkins, squash, and sunflowers. Plum, peach, and pecan orchards also dotted the landscape. Their diet was supplemented by animal flesh: deer, turkey, fish, and bird, but for the most part theirs was a vegetarian diet.

Romans learned that the land of the Choctaws included the fertile bottomlands of the Pearl, Pascagoula, and Tombigbee Rivers and extended west to the Mississippi River, the "Father of Waters." To the south its border was the Gulf of Mexico, the "Great Waters," and to the north the Yazoo and Yalobusha River Basins and the land of the Chickasaws.

He also learned that there were three distinct districts of the Choctaw Nation—the Okla Hannali or Six Towns People, the Ahi Apet Okla or Potato Eating People, and the Okla Falaya or Separated or Long People. The districts had a loosely aligned governing structure, each with its own chief, or mingo.

The Okla Hannali, located in the southeast portion of the Nation, of which Coosha Town was a part, drew their name from their initial coalition of six clans, or iksas. The Ahi Apet Okla, also called the Okla Tannap, inhabited the northeast and cultivated potatoes as their main starch. They would slice them thinly, cure them with hickory smoke, and store them in large baskets.

The Okla Falaya, the largest district and occupying the western half of the Nation, lived in villages that were farther apart from each other and tended to congregate less often than the other districts. With the Mississippi River to the west and the other two districts to the east, defense from warring tribes was less of a problem for the Okla Falaya: thus, they could live "separated" from each other, and their distances were "long."

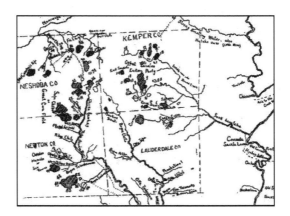

Bernard Roman's 1772 Map of Choctaw Settlements with the Counties of East-Central Mississippi Overlaid (Neshoba, Kemper, Newton, and Lauderdale Counties). Dark Areas are the Choctaw Settlements.

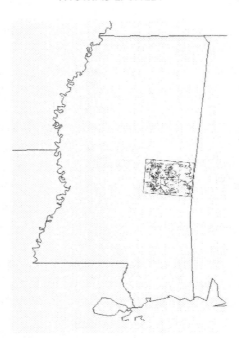

Barnard Roman's Map Overlaid on Present Day Mississippi.

HE LEARNED ABOUT the Choctaws' neighbors. To the east lived the Creeks (Muskogee) and the Alabamas, close relatives of the Choctaws and their brothers, the Chickasaws. Along with the Seminoles, they spoke languages that had a similar root, Muskogean, making communication fairly easy. But like brothers who never get along, the Creeks and Alabamas were always in conflict with the Choctaws. In most conflicts, the Choctaws tended to not be the aggressor, but when threatened, they were a fierce force to reckon with.

ROMANS LEARNED ABOUT some of the lesser tribes of the region and those that no longer existed: the Biloxi, Ofo, Tunica, Yazoo, Houma, Taposa, Chakchuima, Pascagoula, and Tiou.

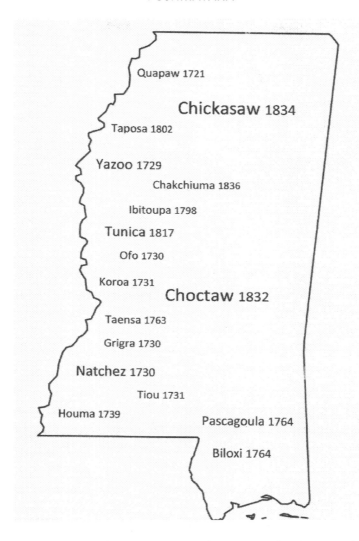

Native Americans of Mississippi and the Year the Groups Ceased to Exist as Tribes in Mississippi.

ROMANS MADE HIS CAMP just outside of Coosha Town, but the Englishman was there only to sleep. He was too busy exploring the land and talking with the elders.

One afternoon Pushmataha and several of his friends were playing stickball in a meadow when Romans happened upon them. He and his party were returning from a venture to the south and west of Coosha Town. They had been mapping out the Chickasawhay River—a moderate size stream that flowed south, joined the Leaf River to form the Pascagoula River, and then emptied in the Great Waters to the south. As he approached Coosha Town, he stopped to watch the would-be warriors at play.

"Ah, the sapling who will one day be a mighty tree!" Romans exclaimed when he recognized Pushmataha among the players.

As the Creek interpreter relayed the message, Pushmataha smiled.

Romans and his party stopped in the shade beside the meadow that served as the ball field. It was a hot day, and Romans wiped his brow with his shirtsleeve.

"I hear that boy is quite a story teller," he said to his party as he sat down. "Let's see what words of wisdom he can give us."

For several minutes, Romans watched them play. The boys used sticks fashioned with scoops at one end to pick up, carry, and then throw a small leather ball through the opponent's goal. It appeared to be a very rough sport, even for these young boys, with collisions and tackles a common occurrence.

The game finally wound down, and Romans invited the boys to join them in the shade.

"What kind of game is this?" he asked. "It seemed to be quite rough."

"It is stickball," Pushmataha replied as he caught his breath. "The game has been played since the beginning of our people: even before Chahtah and Chickasah were born. Often it is used to settle disputes between villages and between tribes. It is rough, but it is fun."

Stickball Player by George Catlin 1834.

"Tell me of this Chahtah and this Chickasah," Romans said. "I have heard their names spoken by the elders. Who were they?"

Pushmataha stood, and his eyes brightened as he began the tale of the Choque-ta's beginning.

"IN THE OLDEST MEMORY of my people, there was a time when we did not have a home. We wandered here and there until our numbers became many. Everywhere we went we carried the bones of our dead. It was a great burden, but we would not abandon the bones.

"One day, two of our people were out hunting, when they saw a glow of light on a hill in the distance. They hurried to it but found nothing. They camped nearby, and the next morning the light appeared again. It was a woman, who said, 'I am very hungry.' The two hunters did not have much food, but they gave her what they had. She ate a little of it, and then she said, 'Come here tomorrow and I will give you something.'

"The next day the two hunters returned. Where the woman had been standing, they found a beautiful plant. It was corn. They took it to our people. They learned to grow the corn, but they had to camp for a long time before it was ready to eat. Before long, some of our people began to complain that it was time to move.

"Two brothers, Chahtah and Chickasah, who were leaders of our people, heard the complaints and consulted with a hopaii about what to do. The hopaii erected a pole. He said, 'In the morning, if the pole is leaning in any direction, we must follow it to find a home.' The next morning the pole was leaning toward the rising sun. Chahtah and Chickasah gathered our people together. They started on a great journey. Each night the hopaii planted the pole, and each morning the pole was found leaning toward the rising sun. The journey lasted a long time. It was a hard journey and many died. After a while they found it necessary to go forward only one-half day, carrying the bones of the dead, and then returning for the rest of the bones.

"My people came to a great river. It was so mighty that it had to be beyond age, so they named it Misha Sipokni. They built rafts and spent many days crossing the river. Not long after crossing Misha Sipokni, they came to a beautiful stream and followed it to its source. It was time to plant the corn, so they camped for a long time. The land was abundant in game and berries and many useful plants. The corn produced a big crop. When it came time to move, the hopaii planted the pole. But the next morning the pole was found standing straight. My people rejoiced when the hopaii announced they had found their home.

"My people built a great mound, and when they saw that it was leaning, they laughed and named it Nanih Waiya. They said this mound will be our mother and we will spread from here to make our homes.

"Chickasah led the first ones out to make their homes. One evening he was smoking some tobacco and dropped some fire. When Chahtah went out to see where Chickasah had gone, he found that the fire had destroyed the trail, and he could not find him. Many years later the ones who had followed Chickasah were found again, but they had been gone so long that their speech had changed slightly. They now call themselves Chickasaws, and the ones who had followed Chahtah now called themselves Choctaws, and they became two separate nations, always living near each other."[3]

PUSHMATAHA FINISHED his story and sat back down. The white men were quiet, dumbfounded by this oration from such a young boy, an ignorant eight-year-old "savage" many would say.

Romans stood and began to clap his hands. The men of his party joined him.

"Splendid!" he said. "Young man, I dare say you would rival our great Shakespeare!"

---

[3] Birchfield, D. L. from *How the People Found a Home*. The Encyclopedia of North American Indians. 1977.

ROMANS REMAINED in Coosha Town for another few weeks, finished his mapping of Choctaw Country, and moved on, following the Big Trading Path to the land of the Chickasaws.

CHAPTER TWO

FOUR YEARS HAD PASSED since Bernard Romans had left, and Coosha Town had been quiet. An occasional white man had come through, but nothing had been as exciting as the visit by the Englishman who had traced the rivers and towns on paper.

But word had come to the Choctaws through a trader that there was unrest among the white man who had settled in the east. No longer did they wish to be led by a chief who lived across the Great Waters. Their wish was to be their own nation. Thirteen tribes had treatied, become united, and were demanding freedom from the same chief who had sent Romans to visit the Choctaws. The king had refused, and battles were being fought. According to the trader, the thirteen united tribes would most likely win, and a new nation would be formed.

The Choctaws were interested, but unconcerned. This change in power was far away. The Choctaws could not see into the future. They could not know that before their children were old, the thirteen tribes would grow and devour the land of the Choctaws, as well as the lands of their brothers, making the Choctaws, the Chickasaws, and the Creeks orphans searching for a home in a distant land across the mighty river that is beyond age.

The Choctaw continued their lives of hunting, fishing—and warring with their neighbors, the Osages, Caddos, and Creeks.

PUSHMATAHA AND HIS FATHER left Coosha Town to hunt bear. But unlike most hunting expeditions where many joined the chase, this trip was for father and son alone. With his father's help, the boy would take a bear—his first step on the journey to manhood.

At twelve years of age, Pushmataha was beginning to show signs of maturity. His shoulders were broadening and his arms were becoming strong. His voice had started to change. At one moment he would caw like a frightened crow; the other he would growl like an old bear.

"Gather your spear and bow," his father said. "We will go to the forest and seek the will of the Great Spirit."

His father placed some dried fruit and corn cakes in his totem pouch, a small leather pouch that all Choctaw men carried when they traveled. He also gathered his wampum belt, his pipe—his white man's pipe—and several leaves of tobacco.

Father and son travelled swiftly to the west through quiet meadows and thick forests of pine and oak. They soon left their own district, the Okla Hannali, and entered the district of their Choctaw brothers, the Okla Falaya.

Several times Pushmataha and his father stopped at villages inhabited by their brothers. His father greeted the leaders and sat and visited. As was the custom for all travelers in Choctaw Country, food was offered and food was accepted; the villagers expected nothing in return.

The path took them farther from home than the young boy had ever been. Pushmataha began to tire. His father's stride was long, and the boy almost had to run to keep from falling behind. His legs grew heavy and his breathing fast as he used all of his strength to keep up. He followed silently. He kept going. He would not give up. He would go until he collapsed.

Finally, the father led his son up a steep rise to what appeared to be an ancient campground perched high on a bluff and stopped. Pushmataha, who was only steps behind, eased up beside him.

Before them to the west was an expanse greater than any the young boy had ever seen. Two hundred feet below, a river rushed by—a muddy, foamy, swirling mass of water moving faster than a man could run. A half mile to the other side, partially submerged trees fought to keep from being uprooted and swept away: the banks unable to hold the waters from the rains of spring.

Even though Pushmataha's breathing was labored and his lungs ached, the vista caused him to gasp.

"What is this great water that flows endlessly to the south?" he thought. "Surely there is nothing in nature greater!"

"Before you lies the mighty Misha Sipokni, 'the river that is beyond age,' the great 'Father of Waters,'" the father told his son.

"Many generations ago our fathers crossed this river carrying the bones of our ancestors. The Great Spirit led our people to the east, giving us all the land from here to beyond the Tombigbee. It is a great land. A land that we must hold on to for all generations to come."

The father turned to his son.

"Take your bow and bring back a young deer. We will feast here tonight, and tomorrow we will go down to the river among the canebrakes to hunt bear."

When he returned with a young buck, he found the fire ready and the coals hot. His father was standing at the edge of the bluff looking to the setting sun. Pushmataha dropped his prize beside the fire and stood beside his father. The sun was low in the orange sky. Purple and pink clouds floated low above the trees, creating a barrier to the full glory of the sun. But there were breaks in the clouds that allowed golden beams of light to strike the river below. The rushing water shimmered and danced, like thousands of pieces of quartz, reflecting up a brilliant light, bright enough to cause him to narrow his eyes. Never before had he seen such a sunset, and never would he forget it.

"When I was young," the father said, "my father led me as I have led you to this place—to this same campground—to witness the greatness of the river that is below: the river that is beyond age. He had made the same journey with his father; and his father before him.

"My son, remember this place when you grow old. Show it to your children and your grandchildren."

FATHER AND SON SAT QUIETLY before the low fire as they ate. After they finished eating, the father reached into his totem bag and retrieved the white man's pipe and the tobacco. He tore off a piece of the dry leaf, crushed it in his hands, and pressed it into the bowl. With a small burning branch he lit it, taking small, quick puffs until the glow was steady. He gave the pipe to his son.

Pushmataha had never smoked the pipe before. He wouldn't smoke with the elders in his tribe until he was older; but here, just father and son, he would be a man.

Pushmataha held the pipe up and admired it. In the light of the fire the deer on the bowl appeared to dance as he tilted the pipe from side to side. In the darkness of the moonless night, father and son shared the white man's pipe. All was quiet except for the howl of a wolf in the distance and the steady hum and rush of the waters below.

The son said nothing. Words spoken this night would begin with the father.

Father and son looked up as a light streaked across the sky.

"Fichik hika, a shooting star!" the father said. "The Great Spirit smiles on us. Our hunt tomorrow will be good."

He pointed north.

"And look. Fichik issuba: the great dipper which points the way to falammi fichik, the great star of the north that does not move."

He then pointed to a bright constellation in the southwest.

"Watalhpi fichik, the stars of the seven sisters: they will soon go to bed for the summer and rest until the winter returns."

The father continued to speak of the stars and to tell great stories of the heavens—stories that Pushmataha had heard many times before. Stories that for countless generations had been passed from father to son. Ancient stories that should never be forgotten.

After a few minutes, he paused and laughed. "My son, why do I tell you these tales? You are the one who has the gift of words, not your father. I should remain silent and allow you to speak."

In a serious tone, he continued. "I have not spoken of this before, but you bring honor to your father. Even the ancients marvel at your wisdom. They tell me that someday you will be known throughout the Choctaw Nation: that you have the tongue of a leader."

The father paused and placed a log on the fire.

"But first, my son, you must become a warrior. Words without deeds are like a drum—loud but empty. When a great warrior speaks, people listen. His words are not hollow. His knife has known the blood of the enemy, and people do not take his words lightly.

"Tomorrow you will take a bear. In three springs, when you are fifteen, you will take a scalp."

Pushmataha's father stood up and tapped the pipe on his palm to dislodge the ashes and placed the pipe in his totem.

"We will talk more tomorrow," he said, "but now, we will sleep. At the first light we begin the hunt. I will take you among the canebrakes where my father led me to my first bear."

IT WAS STILL DARK when Pushmataha felt a touch on his shoulder. He had been sleeping soundly, and it took a moment for him to gather his thoughts. He raised his head and strained his eyes. His father was lying on the ground beside him. His left hand was on his son's shoulder; his right hand was holding his tomahawk.

"There is danger close by," his father whispered to his son. "Remain silent. Say nothing. You must crawl without making a sound to the edge of the clearing. Find a place to hide and do not let yourself be found. And do not come out—no matter what happens."

He squeezed his son's shoulder. "Do not disobey me."

Pushmataha quickly did as his father said. He began to move. When he reached the edge of the clearing, he found a thick bush and crawled under. He listened, but heard nothing except his heart pounding in his chest.

"What did my father hear?" he thought. "Is there a wild animal close by? Has an enemy found us?"

His father remained on the ground as if sleeping, but every muscle in his body was at full alert—poised to spring into action. He gripped his tomahawk tightly and waited.

A moment later the father heard it—the barely perceptible scrunch of a moccasin stepping on a leaf. Within seconds he heard it again, but from a different direction.

"There are at least two," he thought. "Are there more?"

"There will be bloodshed," he said to himself, "for a friend would never approach a sleeping camp at this time of night in such a quiet manner."

He stared into the moonless night but saw nothing. He again heard the soft movement of feet—many feet.

In his mind he prepared for battle.

"I am a Choctaw warrior," he thought." I have fought many times against my enemies—the Caddos, the Osages, and the Creeks—and I have always been victorious, but tonight I am outnumbered. Yet I will fight with courage and strength, even unto death. For my concern tonight is more for my son's safety than my own. My hope is that whoever is there doesn't suspect that there is more than one person camped here. The fire burned out hours ago, and the night is black. That is in my son's favor."

Pushmataha lay silently under the bush. His heart began to slow down, and he finally caught his breath. He strained to listen. There was no sound and no movement. In the darkness he could see nothing.

SUDDENLY WAR WHOOPS filled the silence. Dark figures emerged from the surrounding forest and ran into the clearing.

"What is happening?" the boy thought. It was too dark for him to see, but he heard shouts, and grunts, and cries of agony and pain.

"A battle is raging! I must get up and go to where my father is! Join in this fight!"

But Pushmataha remained still. With all of his being he wanted to get up, but he did not. He would not disobey his father.

As quickly as the battle had started it was over. There were whoops of victory in the dark, but the whoops didn't belong to his father.

"What has happened?" the young boy panicked. "My father...?"

There was movement in the camp for another few moments, then silence.

"The intruders have gone," Pushmataha thought. "I must get up! I've got to see my father! I have to know!"

He started to get up, but then reason and good judgment kept him still.

"What is done is done," he lamented. "There is nothing I can do now. I must remain cautious. It is too dark to see, and I cannot be sure that the enemy has left."

For another hour he didn't move: listening and staring into the darkness. The clearing was quiet, but he would wait until there was light.

The eastern sky began to lighten. Soon there was enough light to allow Pushmataha to see. He crawled from underneath the bush but remained in a crouched position for several minutes. There was still no movement, no one waiting to catch him off guard. He stood and slowly crept into the clearing.

He had gone half way to the burned-out fire when he suddenly stopped. His stomach began to tighten. Three men lay motionless on the ground. Two of them were Osage warriors. The third was his father.

Pushmataha knelt beside his father. Anger, greater than his sorrow, seized him. He clinched his fists and raised his face to the heavens, but he suppressed the urge to wale and cry out. There could still be danger close by.

"I will avenge the taking of my father's scalp," he thought. "My father's shilup, his spirit, will not wander for long. He will find peace. I will not only take the scalp of the one who did this, but everyone in his village. I will honor my father with my bravery."

Pushmataha looked at the two Osage warriors. They had been killed with blows to the neck by his father's tomahawk. Pride filled his heart.

"My father was a great warrior. He fought bravely, even when he knew that death was near."

The Osages had left their fallen warriors to rot in the sun or to be devoured by animals. That would not happen to his father.

"I will take my father back home," the boy said, "back to Coosha Town on Ponta Creek, for a proper burial."

Pushmataha lashed together a litter and placed his father on it. He looked around for his father's belongings. His bow and tomahawk were there, but his totem pouch and wampum belt were gone. The white man's pipe which had been in the totem was also gone. Pushmataha placed the bow across his father's chest and put the tomahawk in his own belt.

"My father's tomahawk will now be mine. With it I will avenge his death."

Pushmataha began the long journey back home, dragging the litter behind him. As he walked, his thoughts were full.

"I will return and stay for the proper time of mourning. Then I will leave my village, and will not return until I can hold my hand high with many scalps."

It would be easy for him to leave. His mother was dead. She had died when Pushmataha was young, and he had been raised by his mother's family, with instruction and correction primarily a function of his maternal aunts and uncles. In keeping with the customs of the Choctaw matriarchal society, his father had joined his wife's family, but offered little to the early rearing of his son. Pushmataha had only one sibling, a sister, who was older and already married, living in another village. He rarely saw her.

As the first day of travel wore on, Pushmataha began to tire. He had had nothing to eat since the night before, and for a spring day, the sun was hot. His father was getting heavy.

"I will not falter," he thought. "I will not rest until I am home."

He was tiring rapidly, and his muscles ached.

"Take your mind off of the heavy load and it will become lighter," he told himself as he adjusted his grip on the litter. "I must remain strong."

Late in the day he approached one of the Choctaw villages that he and his father had come through the day before. The villagers gathered around the litter, and one of the mingos said, "Your father was a brave warrior. I have known him since I was young. I will go and avenge his death."

"No," Pushmataha said. "That is for me, his son, to do."

"Then I will be with you as you travel. My hand will help carry your burden."

Pushmataha wanted to carry his father alone, but he realized that his strength was already giving out, and he would not make it home without help. He accepted the mingo's offer, and after eating, they journeyed on.

SIX MONTHS LATER the hattak fullih nipi foni, the bone picker, climbed the ladder to the funeral scaffold of the mingo. He removed the bear skin that had covered the body through the hot summer and began to clean what flesh remained off of the bones with his long, curved fingernails. When he was satisfied with his work, he wrapped the bones in a cloth, descended from the platform, and gave them to the son who was waiting below. The son carried them to the aboha foni, the lodge of bones, and placed them in a basket.

Pushmataha gathered his things—his totem pouch, his bow, and his father's tomahawk. The twelve-year-old boy left Coosha Town travelling west.

THOMAS L. WILEY

CHAPTER THREE

MOST OF THE CHOCTAW MEN had only a short distance to travel to get to the banks of the great Misha Sipokni. Almost a hundred of them, from throughout the Okla Falaya, or Separated District, had gathered for the bear hunt. They would take many bears, but the annual hunt was more than a hunt. It was the first great conclave of the spring.

Initially no one noticed the lanky young man. With so many men from different villages, it was easy for someone to slip in unnoticed. He appeared to be about fifteen. His clothing was barely more than rags, and he appeared in need of a good meal. He carried a tomahawk that was of excellent workmanship. His arrows were well made, and his bow was strong.

After the first day, it became apparent that no one knew who he was.

"Who is this young man," everyone was asking. "Has anyone ever seen him before?"

But no one approached him. In the Choctaw culture it is considered impolite to ask someone who they are, but curiosity was getting the best of them. Finally, one of the elders was appointed to talk with him.

"Young man," the elder asked, "of what village do you come?"

The young man was quiet for a moment and then answered, "Luma. 'It is hidden.'"

The old man did not like the answer, spat on the ground, and started to get up, but the young man placed his hand on his arm.

"Wise one, I ask that you not be insulted by my answer, but for now, I come from an obscure place."

"Then tell me your name."

Again, he answered in a riddle. "I am known as Hohchifoiksho, 'the nameless one.' Again, I ask that you not be offended. But I have no name."

The old man related the boy's answers to the men of the camp. Several acted indignant, but their curiosity had been peaked. Since the boy was behaving properly and was not in the way, they did not push it further. But his presence did give a mysterious air to the gathering.

The next morning the men rose early to begin the hunt. Seeing that the young man was frail, they wondered how he could draw his bow or how he could keep pace with the rest. The old man again approached him.

"Nameless One, stay at camp today," he said. "Rest and take of the food that is here. Maybe tomorrow you will have strength for the chase."

Calmly but sternly the boy said, "I have come to hunt, not to sit. When the sun sets, you will see my worth."

Several men laughed and jeered as they picked up their weapons.

"This boy not only insults us, but he is a braggart. His name shall be Ishtilauata, 'one who boasts.'"

At the end of the day, the men gathered to show their prizes and tell the stories of the hunt. For the Choctaws, the tales were almost as important as the hunt itself. Each man who had been successful in the hunt told of his battle, of how fierce the bear had been, and how he barely escaped with his life. Each story seemed to be grander and more exciting than the one before.

As the stories were unfolding, the group heard a noise in the darkness. The young boy with no name came into sight, dragging a litter on which lay one of the largest bears any of them had ever seen. Her claws were long and sharp, and her coat was thick and dark—a trophy that anyone would be proud of.

The young boy sat down in front of the fire, and as the men looked on in disbelief, he began to tell his story.

"When the chase began, I journeyed alone, for my hunt is like that of the panther, not the wolf. I rely on my own skills and not those of a pack. I traveled north and came to an ancient campground high on a bluff overlooking the river that is beyond age—a campground where a great bear had once been promised to me.

"Far below the bluff was a canebrake all but hidden and inaccessible except to the most determined. With great peril, I descended the sheer cliff and found myself in a primordial forest of ancient oaks, willows, and canes that had not felt the tread of a moccasin in a lifetime of winters. Great snakes, with girths more than that of a man's thigh, and alligators, with gaping jaws that could effortlessly swallow a man, made my steps through the low marshy ground cautious and determined, fearful that each would be my last.

"Among the many tracks of bear that I saw, there was one—that of the she-bear that lies before you—that drew my attention. Her prints and the depth at which her weight caused the ground to sink told of a beast of great size. She would be my prize, and I would not stop until she was mine.

"My search led me deep into the canebrake where a fast retreat would be impossible, and a sudden confrontation would mean certain death. Cautiously I advanced with my bow at ready.

"As I stepped into a small clearing among the cane, there she was— the great she-bear that I sought. Only ten yards before me, with her back toward me, crouched over a slain deer, tearing the flesh with her teeth and devouring it in large gulps. Her size was even more than I had imagined, as if instead of one before me there were two.

"In silence I raised my bow and with all of my might drew back. As I let go, I prayed to the Great Spirit that my arrow would be straight and true—that it would find its mark and bring instant death.

"But such was not the answer to my prayer. With a hollow 'thud' the arrow pierced the she bear's chest and tore into her lung. Instead of immediate death, there was instant rage. A roar greater than the loudest of thunder shattered the silence. She swung around and reared up. Her great paws were armed with claws as great and sharp as knives. Her mouth opened wide and her gums drew back, exposing teeth stained red with blood from the carrion she was devouring.

"Quickly I drew another arrow, and then another, sinking them into her massive chest. But instead of death there was more rage, the arrows seeming to be no more than mere darts from a blowgun, with no effect except to infuriate.

"She lunged forward, and I knew that death for me was seconds away. But instead of cowering in defeat, I drew my knife and stood my ground. I would die as a Choctaw, with no fear in my heart.

"As her massive frame came over me, blocking out the sun like a cloud full of death and destruction, I moved swiftly to my left and plunged my knife deeply into her chest. From her throat came another deafening roar, but this one was not of rage, but of pain and death, for my knife had found her heart. The massive she-bear fell to the ground and moved no more."

WHEN THE STORY ENDED, the only sound in the camp was the crackling of the fire. No one spoke; the group was captivated by this boy's fascinating tale of daring and danger. No other stories followed; no one dared to try and top his story. As the group dispersed, whispers were heard, "Who is this young man with no name? Where does he come from? Who is his father? Is he a shilup, a spirit, who has come among us?"

Each night the boy with no name returned with an even larger bear. And his story of the hunt and the kill were more glorious and more exciting than the night before. Soon the highlight of each day was not the hunt, but the boy's bear and his story. Everyone was spellbound by his stories and the passion he expressed in his delivery, but a few of the more seasoned hunters were quietly envious of the attention this young stranger was commanding.

AS THE HUNT CAME TO AN END, several of the warriors—not ready to go back to their villages—planned a raid on the Osages who lived on the other side of the river. They wished to return home with some scalps and new tales of battle. Their tales of the hunt were lacking: thanks to the young boy with no name.

As they began to enlist a party, Hohchifoiksho, "the Nameless One," was the first to come forward with his tomahawk and bow ready for battle. The warriors leading the party were incensed.

"You, braggart!" one of them said and then spat. "With your stories and tales, you think that you are a great warrior, too?"

The Nameless One was not disquieted by the response. He calmly said, "My deeds will speak for me. Tomorrow night I will hold many scalps of the enemy. I have already taken many from the Osages, but there is one that I still seek: the one who holds a white man's pipe."

THE NEXT MORNING twenty warriors gathered to cross the Misha Sipokni and venture into the land of the Osages. They lashed together rafts of cane and floated across the swift flowing river, armed for battle.

It didn't take the warriors long to find a well-worn path leading west away from the river. They traveled silently in single file, spaced ten to fifteen yards apart in case of a surprise enemy encounter. Within a few hours the war party spied a hunting party of Osages camped on a small rise. Several of the Osage men were skinning deer and bear on the banks of a stream that flowed to one side of the camp. Others were busy smoking and curing the meat. Their hunt had been successful.

The Choctaw warriors counted close to forty Osage men—two to one odds against the Choctaws. But they were not deterred. They knew that a surprise attack would give them the advantage. Their strategy would be to attack from three sides with the stream preventing a retreat of the enemy.

The leader of the Choctaw war party gathered his warriors together.

"We will divide into three groups, wait until dark, and attack. When the battle is over, each group will make its way back to the banks of the Misha Sipokni. There we will stay the night and join our brothers across the river tomorrow. We will take many scalps today. Our numbers are small compared to theirs, but this will only make our victory and our stories of battle greater. Our people will marvel at our acts of bravery. This will be a great day for the Choctaws."

As the night sky darkened, the Choctaw warriors divided and circled the Osage camp. They silently took their positions, closing in, getting as near to the rise as they could without being detected. In the light of the campfires, they could see the Osages sitting in small groups, laughing and feasting on greasy bear steaks.

They would have no time to respond. The battle would be quick and deadly.

The high-pitched sound was barely noticeable, like a lone cricket stroking his legs together, but it was followed by war cries from every direction. Choctaw warriors rushed into the camp with tomahawks held high. There were sounds of confusion and surprise, shouts of rage and anger, and cries of agony and pain.

The Choctaws were quick with their work, but within moments the element of surprise was lost. The Osages, fierce warriors known for their great deeds in battle, began to fight back. The Choctaws began to retreat: their mission had been accomplished. They had taken scalps, and it was now time to minimize their losses.

WHEN THE CHOCTAW WARRIORS gathered in the darkness beside the great river, only three were not present. One of them was the Nameless One. Someone had seen two of their party lying on the ground of the camp, their scalps being taken by Osage warriors. But the boy with no name was not one of them.

"What became of him?" one of the warriors asked. "I did not see him during the fight. Was he killed early?"

Another one snorted and said, "His is not only a braggart, he is a coward. Before the battle began and we rushed the Osages, I saw him turn and go toward the stream. We will not see him again. He is like the fakit nakni, the turkey gobbler. He makes a big noise, but when there is trouble, you only see his tail feathers."

The rest of the party nodded in agreement.

For the next several hours the Choctaw warriors told their tales of battle as they sat around the campfire. Each one who had taken a scalp raised his trophy and told how he slew his foe. Each story got bigger and grander as the night progressed.

Late in the night as the stories were being retold, one of the warriors suddenly raised his hand silencing the group. The entire group came to alert. Someone was approaching their camp. As they reached for their weapons, the boy with no name came into view.

"Ishtilauata, the braggart, has returned," one of the warriors said as they relaxed. "There is no need for alarm. We have more to fear from a chukfi, a rabbit."

The boy sat down beside the fire. "You now call me Ishtilauata, I accept that. But one day I will return the name to you. But you will not be bragging on your own exploits, but those of mine."[4]

The warriors began to laugh at this impudence coming from a scrawny, malnourished boy who did not know how to hold his tongue.

The Nameless One reached down to his belt.

"Let him laugh who tonight has taken more scalps than me." With that he held up five scalps. "No warrior is greater than Ishtilauata."

He then proceeded to tell how he accomplished his deed.

"BEFORE THE BATTLE BEGAN, I left our group. As in the hunt, I choose to fight as the panther—alone. I have honed my skills to rely on no one.

"I retreated to the stream and in the darkness crept around the rise until I was behind the enemy's camp. Silently I advanced into the camp until I was close enough that I could have easily stretched my hand and touched their backs. There I waited.

"When the signal to attack was given, my tomahawk was swift. The first two scalps were on my belt before the enemy could reach for their weapons.

"When the element of surprise was over and the enemy had armed themselves, true battle ensued. The Osage warriors were fierce and skilled with their weapons and fought bravely. Several times death for me was near, but the Great Spirit was with me. My knife and tomahawk did their deadly work, and three more scalps were added to my belt before I retreated back into the darkness of the night."

---

4 Lincecum, Gideon. *The Life of Apushimataha*, 1861, Republished as *Pushmataha-A Choctaw Leader and His People*. Introduction by Greg O'Brien. The University of Alabama Press. 2004: p. 49.

AT THE CONCLUSION OF HIS TALE, the leader stood and spoke. "Nameless One, I have misjudged you. Your bravery is beyond compare. And your elocution is that of a great leader. I have never heard so magnificent a story. Please forgive me for the insults I have thrown to you. And from this day, your name will no longer be Hohchifoiksho, 'The Nameless One,' or Ishtilauata, 'The Braggart.' We will bestow on you a battle name worthy of the great warrior that you have proven yourself to be."

"Your kindness is great," the boy humbly said, "but I request that a great name not be given to me. That honor must wait."

The boy then stood to address the group. "Great Choctaw warriors, I do not have to speak to you of honor. Without honor, we are nothing—no better than a kasheho, a barren old woman. I seek an Osage warrior who holds a white man's pipe. Until his scalp is on my belt, I have no honor."

The warriors nodded in agreement. Although they didn't know the significance of the pipe, they understood honor. They understood that this young boy had a burden that weighed heavy on his shoulders, and before he could go forward with life, it had to be lifted.

"We will honor your request," the leader said, "but your name for now will be Onssushi, "Young Eagle."[5]

The next morning as they prepared to cross the Misha Sipokni, Young Eagle said, "I will not return with you to the land of the Choctaws. When you join our brothers, take my skins and meat, divide them among those whose hunts were not successful. Let their children not go hungry."

"But yours is the choicest bear meat," the leader said in, "and your skins the thickest and greatest in number. Will you just give them away?"

"I have no use for so much. I travel with little and take what I need from the land," Young Eagle said. He then pointed west. "I will stay in the land of the Osages, until I am finished. One day I will return, and

[5] Appleton's Journal. 1870. Volume 4, Issue 71. p 167.

when I return, all of the sons of Chahtah will know me by a new name, a name filled with honor."

THE TALES OF THE YOUNG WARRIOR began to spread throughout the land of the Choctaws. "Who is this boy with no name?" "Where does he come from?" "Is he a shilup, a spirit?" "He is mighty in battle and unsurpassed as a hunter." "His words are like the sound of rain and thunder and wind." "He is on a mighty quest and will someday return."

THOMAS L. WILEY

CHAPTER FOUR

THE BOY WITH NO NAME was not seen or heard from for nearly two years. In the early 1780s he reappeared in the district of his birth, the Okla Hannali or Six Towns People, to wage war on the Creeks.

The Creeks and Choctaws had been bitter enemies since the beginning of time and battled continuously. The present excuse for conflict was an area of land east of the Tombigbee River near the Black Warrior River. Both nations laid claim to this fertile land, a dispute that would not be settled for another thirty years—not until the end of the Creek War in 1814, when Andrew Jackson, with the aid of the Choctaws, defeated the Creeks.

Warriors of the two nations met on the disputed land and began waging war. The battle dragged on for several days—no one able to get the upper hand. The Creeks were fighting from the security of a dense canebrake along the river's edge and the Choctaws were protected by the dense forest.

The stalemate was suddenly broken when a small group of Choctaw warriors made a daring charge into the Creek party, sending them into panic. The remaining Choctaws, encouraged by the sudden change of events, attacked with great force, driving the Creeks into the river where many of them were killed.

That night at the council fire, the chief asked who had led the charge that caused the rout. One of the leaders said that it was a young man whom he did not know. In fact, he did not remember seeing him among the warriors until the moment of the attack. Several others confirmed this, one of them saying that the man did not seem human. His attack was like that of a wild Koi, a panther, with no regard for his own safety. He bounded through the Creek warriors, wielding his tomahawk and war club with precision, no stroke wasted, each one claiming a victim.

The chief asked that this young warrior come to the council. When he arrived, the chief was stunned. There stood a very pleasant looking, calm young man who did not fit the image of a ruthless, fearless warrior. And even more puzzling, none of the members of the council knew who he was.

"Where are you from?" the chief asked.

"I am from Choctaw Country," The young man answered.

The chief was taken aback by such a general response. If the young man had not shown himself to be such a great warrior, he would have dismissed him. But instead, he asked, "Will you tell your name?"

"Great chief," the young man said, "I will be glad to tell the names that I am known by. I call myself Hohchifoiksho, 'the Nameless One.' A great burden was upon me, and I had vowed to be with no name until that burden was lifted. Then two springs ago I joined a hunting party among our brothers to the west. For reasons that I never quite understood, the party began to call me Ishtilauata, 'The Braggart.' At the end of the hunt, a group of warriors decided to make war with the Osages, and I gladly joined them. We took many scalps, and the leader bestowed on me the name Onssushi, 'Young Eagle.'

"When I left the group to continue my quest, I remained Hohchifoiksho, 'the Nameless One.'"

While the young man was relating his story, several of the men of the council began to whisper to each other and nod their heads. When he finished, one of them said, "We have heard tales of a boy with no name, a brave young warrior who is mighty in battle, and whose stories are surpassed by none."

"I too have heard these tales," the chief said. "Are you this mysterious one who some say is a spirit that has come to fight for the Choctaws?"

The young warrior sat silently for a moment before answering. He had also heard these tales of cunning and daring of himself as he travelled—tales that the elders were telling before council fires and stories that fathers were telling their children. He also knew that mystery made a man larger than life, and that humility shrouded in mystery spoke louder than great words. He would not diminish his mystery by telling everything.

"I can only tell my story. If you look for a spirit, look further. For I am only flesh, the same as you."

The council was amazed by this young warrior—humble and yet powerful and authoritative.

"Welcome to our council," the chief said as he reached for his pipe. "Let us celebrate today and honor the one who led us to the victory."

"I will gladly share your smoke," the young warrior said. "And I will be honored for this great council to take of my pipe."

He reached into his totem pouch and pulled out a pipe, ornately carved with a buck and two does looking up to the heavens.

The council shared the smoke and enjoyed the fellowship with this young warrior who was already a legend among the Choctaws, and who had shown himself that day in battle to be worthy of greatness.

The chief said, "I wish to bestow on you a name—a great name that you will carry with pride. But first, to help us decide, tell us where you come from. To what iksa do you belong? Who is your father? Who is your mother?"

"Great chief," the young man said, "is it my lineage that will decide my name or the deeds that I have accomplished? I ask that the council not take offense, but I ask—are my exploits not sufficient enough that parentage is necessary? Why should the man who fathered me or the woman who suckled me have any bearing on my battle name? The Great Spirit knows that I did not battle today in hopes of gaining a name, but I battled to lead my people to victory, which I will continue to do with or without a name. Until my deeds alone are sufficient, I ask that my name remain Hohchifoiksho, "the Nameless One.""

The young warrior then excused himself and left the council.[6]

---

[6] Lincecum, Gideon. *The Life of Apushimataha*, 1861, Republished as *Pushmataha-A Choctaw Leader and His People*. Introduction by Greg O'Brien. The University of Alabama Press. 2004: p. 63.

OVER THE NEXT SEVERAL DAYS the war continued between the Choctaws and the Creeks, and the young warrior with no name continued to amaze his fellow warriors with his daring and ferocity. Before long he had established himself as a great warrior, and his fame spread throughout the Choctaw Nation. Among the Creeks his name became synonymous with terror and death.

After one of the battles in which the young warrior had again shown himself to be worthy of distinction, the council met to celebrate and tell the stories of victory. The young warrior was now a regular participant in the council, and his tales of the battle were beyond compare. His feats of daring and death, though not boastful, were so exquisitely told that no one spoke after him.

While sharing the pipe, the chief said, "Nameless One, the council recognizes you as one of the greatest of all Choctaw warriors, whose exploits are like those of Tuscaloosa of long ago. And your words are those of a great leader who is destined one day to be a chief of the Choctaws. But the name you carry is not the name of a chief. And our children should not remember such a great warrior as a man with no name. I ask that you now allow us to give a name that equals your greatness. I will not ask that you make known the mystery of your birth, though this has caused great discussion among all the Nation, but instead, the council wishes to bestow a name that is fitting for your deeds in battle."

The young warrior rose to speak.

"Great chief and mighty council of the Choctaws, for many springs I have been on a quest among our enemy who live beyond the great Misha Sipokni, the river that is beyond age. As a young boy, a heavy burden was placed on me—the details of which I wish not to tell this council. This heavy burden could be lifted only with the taking of the scalp of an Osage warrior who carried a white man's pipe.

"I traveled alone through their land searching. I took many scalps in preparation for the one that would end my journey, honing my skills as a warrior, learning the art of battle and death. I also took from the land, as well as from the Osages whose scalps I carried, and learned to hunt and survive depending on no man. In my quest I ventured farther west of the Osages, into the land of the Comanches and Arapahos. I ventured onto the vast plains of grass and hunted the yannash, the great bison, who are more numerous than the stars in the sky.

"As my journey continued and the days stretched into years, doubt entered my heart. Would I find success? With so many of the enemy, could I find the one I sought? Was I on a quest with no end? My heart began to falter and the burden became unbearable. But to give up I would be as nothing.

"I vowed never to stop. I even vowed to become as nothing until my quest was over—either through success or through death. I would have no name. I wished no greatness to befall me or my deeds. When I battled and took a scalp, "No One" was the victor. When I hunted the great bear and bison, "No One" took the hide. If I died in my quest, the victor had taken the scalp of "No One."

"Several moons ago, I came upon a village of Osages. I rested in the cover of the forest until darkness fell and then crept close. As I watched in silence, the men of the village gathered around the fire to take smoke. A warrior, who appeared to be their mingo, took a pipe from his totem. It was the white man's pipe for which I searched. My heart filled with hatred and anger. I prepared for the battle that would end my journey.

"But I did not attack without warning. This battle would not be a surprise. This warrior, whom I had sought for so long and been burdened so greatly, would not die without seeing my face and experiencing my viciousness. We would fight as warriors facing each other on the battle field. He would have a chance to take my scalp, making my victory all the greater.

"I stood and walked into the village, my tomahawk in my left hand, my knife in my right. I called to the warrior, 'I have come for the pipe that you hold in your hand. But you will not give it to me. I will take it.'

"The Osage warrior stood. He was tall and muscular with fire in his eyes that spoke of many scalps on his belt. He sneered and spat on the ground. 'You are but a mangy dog. Your scalp is not worthy of my belt. But it appears that you wish death. I will make quick work of you and throw your scalp in the dung pit.'

"The Osage warrior moved quickly, lunging with his tomahawk held high. As he brought his weapon down, I swiftly moved to the right, deflecting his weapon with mine. I drove my knife deeply into his left temple, and he fell to the ground. As he lay quivering, I took his scalp, raised it high, and cried out to the Great Spirit for giving me the victory.

"My brothers, my quest is over. As you have seen many times as we council, I have the white man's pipe. My burden is lifted, and I am ready to receive a name that is fitting to me. The name that the council decides I will carry with pride."

The young warrior sat down and took his place among the other leaders.

The chief stood. "Great council of the Choctaws, again we have heard words beyond compare. Sitting among us is one destined for greatness. It is time for a name, but we will not take this task lightly. Great thought and consideration are needed. Will any of the council speak?"

The Ishtahullo, the holy man, keeper of all that is sacred, began to rise with the assistance of a warrior sitting next to him. He was one of the ancients who had sat at many councils. His back was stooped and his hands gnarled. His sight was dim, but his hearing and mind were keen. When he gained his balance and was standing unaided, he spoke.

"The Nameless One shall have a new name that befits him. His reputation is that of a great warrior, ruthless in battle, wielding his weapon with great precision. The Great Spirit has told me that his name shall be "A-pushamata-hahubi," for he is "a messenger of death, whose tomahawk is fatal in battle."

Whispers went through the council, as they quietly discussed this among themselves. After a moment, everyone nodded in agreement.

The young warrior smiled to himself. The council could not know how ironic and how fitting this name was. His childhood name "Apushim-alhtaha," "the sapling is ready," had been altered to become his war name "A-pushamata-hahubi," "a messenger of death." Names so similar in their sound yet so different in their meaning.

The young warrior bowed his head. "I accept this name with humble gratitude. From this day my name will be A-pushamata-hahubi."

CHAPTER FIVE

CHAM NAY WAS CURIOUS about the young warrior who had built his lodge in her village. "Where does he come from?" "To what clan does he belong?" she and her friends whispered as they pounded the corn into meal. They knew nothing about him except the tales of his greatness in battle and his cunning as a mighty hunter. Every few minutes, hopefully unknown to the newcomer, they would steal glances toward him as he chipped flint into small arrowheads.

THE CLASHES BETWEEN THE CHOCTAW and Creeks had begun to wane—as perpetual conflicts tend to do—and the young warrior, Pushmataha, had settled into the life of a Choctaw.

He made his home among the Okla Hannali, or Six Towns People, whom he had left five years earlier. But instead of returning to Coosha Town, he settled in Osapa Chito village, on the banks of the Noxubee, or "the River of Strong Odor," where his origin would remain a mystery.

Pushmataha was no longer the young boy who had left on a seemingly impossible quest so many years ago. He was now a man of seventeen—changed by age and hardships. With only casual contact with his former villagers, he was never recognized.

THE WARRIOR'S AWARENESS of his surrounding was too keen to miss the glances and giggles from the young maidens, but he continued to chip away as if he were alone in a vast forest. It was strange: this uneasy interest, a feeling that was foreign to him. While most of the young Choctaw boys had been busy trying to impress the maidens with their stickball, his time and focus had been filled with a quest of vengeance. But now his life was different. It was time to think about a wife.

Late in the afternoon Pushmataha took his knife down to the canebrake in the floodplain of the Noxubee. It was mid-summer, and the tall, thin bamboo shoots had hardened, ready for use. He took only the straightest and strongest for his arrow shafts. Even an almost unperceived curve in the shaft would make the weapon useless.

As he returned to the village, he heard laughter and came upon several women picking blackberries. One of them was Cham Nay. The women became quiet as he approached, but a few giggles could be heard as he walked by. Cham Nay looked up and smiled.

Cham Nay was a typical Choctaw girl of sixteen. Her hair was dark and straight and her skin the color of dark cinnamon. Her smile was pleasant and warm: her eyes dark and lively. A deerskin dress covered her healthy frame: one that was not immune to the hard work that faced Choctaw women from an early age.

"She would make a good wife," Pushmataha thought.

A FEW WEEKS LATER the young warrior made a visit to the lodge of the maiden's father. Pushmataha took smoke with the patriarch and spoke pleasantries, but the purpose of the visit was obvious to all. The young maiden sat in a corner sewing beads on a pair of moccasins. She had no expression on her face, concentrating on her work as the men conversed.

After enough time had passed to make it proper, Pushmataha picked up a small twig and tossed it at Cham Nay. The twig bounced off her head and landed in her lap. She picked it up, looked at it for a moment, and then threw it back to the waiting suitor.

Pushmataha inwardly felt a sigh of relief. The ritual had been followed, and the maiden had accepted. If she had kept the twig and left the lodge, he would have returned to his own lodge, burned it, and moved. He could not have lived in a village where everyone knew he had been rejected.

Several days later the maiden's family prepared a feast for the village to welcome this new member to their family. As was the custom, Pushmataha would now become part of Cham Nay's family, from thence forth his name would be associated with her clan. For him, it was not a loss: he was leaving nothing. But if he had had family, he would be relinquishing all material ties. Woman, the giver and keeper of life, held all that is of the earth. Man—the warrior and the hunter—the giver and keeper of death, held nothing.

SHORTLY BEFORE THE FEAST BEGAN, the women of the village planted a tall pole in the ground near the center of the village. When a signal was given, Cham Nay emerged from her father's lodge and started running toward the pole, cheered on by the women. Pushmataha, who had been conversing with several young warriors, let out a war whoop and began to chase after her. If she reached the pole, the ceremony would end, and the embarrassed young suitor would retire alone to his lodge. If he captured her before she touched the pole, the two would join the feast before joining hands and disappearing into his lodge.

Like most maidens, she made sport of her suitor and ran as fast as she could.

"She is running fast!" Pushmataha thought. "Is she having second thoughts?"

The young warrior began to sweat. Anxiety, stronger than any he had experienced while taking scalps, gripped him.

Just as Cham Nay came into reach of the pole she stopped and proceeded at a snail's pace, looking back at her pursuer and smiling. Pushmataha reached out and grabbed her outstretched hand seconds before it would have touched the pole.

The women who had been cheering her on, shook their heads for a moment as if shocked at her losing the race, but then began to laugh and cheered along with the men.

THOMAS L. WILEY

CHAPTER SIX

FOR THE NEXT FEW YEARS Pushmataha and Cham Nay lived a quiet life. The duties of each were well defined by tradition. His work was to hunt and fish and occasionally to make war. He and others of the men left for weeks at a time to make the hunt, returning with meat to supplement their primarily vegetarian diet.

Her duties were in the home. From the moment the sun chased away the darkness until it hid itself again at night, Cham Nay was busy planting, harvesting, cooking, sewing, making baskets and pottery—all the things necessary to keep her home functioning.

Soon there were children, two daughters: Isi Maleli or Running Deer, and Pis Tikio Ko Nay. When the time came for each to be born, Cham Nay left her work and disappeared into the woods alone. She returned hours later with the newborn wrapped in soft rabbit fur and resumed her household duties.

ONE DAY PUSHMATAHA and several men returned from a three-day hunt, disappointed with the results. Turkey and rabbit were plentiful and filled their baskets, but only four deer had been taken. The men commented how deer were becoming hard to find, and how the hunt was taking them farther and farther from their village. Only a few years earlier deer could be seen in the many meadows around their village, but now sightings were rare.

"What has happened to the isi, the deer?" Pushmataha asked. "Why are they so hard to find?"

"It is the white traders," one of the men said. "They want skins of the deer, and they make good trades for them."

For several years white traders had been coming into the land of the Choctaws. They opened up trading posts and offered guns, powder, metal goods, and whiskey in exchange for the pelts of deer and beaver.

For twenty pelts a man could get a rifle. For two he got a keg of whiskey. The trading posts were soon very successful, drawing Choctaw hunters from throughout the nation.

Many of the traders came for only a short time, made a fast "buck," as the dollar was soon called, and then left. But there were several who settled permanently and joined the Choctaw Nation. Louis Lefleur was one of them, opening up a trading post in the early 1780's on a high bluff overlooking the Pearl River.

LOUIS LEFLEUR WAS BORN in Mobile in 1762. His father, Jean Baptist, had been a member of the French Colonial Army at Fort Conde in Mobile. The year following Louis' birth the Treaty of Paris of 1763 was signed, ending the French and Indian Wars and transferring control of the Choctaw territory from the French to the British. Jean Baptist, not wishing to return to France, was allowed to remain in Mobile and pledged loyalty to the British.

In 1781 nineteen-year-old Louis began trading with the Choctaws, running a boat service from Pensacola up the Pearl River, carrying supplies in and deer skins out. His endeavor was so lucrative that he decided to open his own post near the Choctaw village, Chisha Foka, on the west bank of the Pearl River, and here he made his home. The trading post was very successful and soon developed into a thriving community.

Forty years later, because of its central location, Lefleur's Bluff became the site of the Capital of the newly formed State of Mississippi. The name was changed to Jackson in honor of the great General.

Louis assimilated into the culture of the Choctaws, and in 1790, following their custom, took two wives—mixed-race sisters Rebecca and Nancy Cravat—who happened to be nieces of Pushmataha. A son born to Rebecca, Greenwood Lefleur, would later change the spelling of the name to Le Flore and would become an influential chief.

Other traders, Nathaniel Folsom, James Cole, and John Pitchlynn, also assimilated into the culture taking Choctaw wives; and like the

Lefleurs, they and their sons would become important figures in the future of the Choctaw Nation.

"I MUST MEET ONE of these white traders," Pushmataha said. "See his lodge of pots and cloth. Find out what he does with so many skins."

Traveling alone and stopping only to sleep, the two-day journey to Lefleur's Bluff gave him plenty of time to think.

Before Pushmataha was born, the white man had come into the territory with goods that seemed almost too good to be real—pots that didn't crack or break like their clay ones; knives of steel that were sharper than the sharpest flint; finely woven cloth and needle and thread as thin as a strand of hair. And the most amazing of all: guns.

Initially the white man's items were a novelty. But within a few years that changed. In his short lifetime of twenty-one years, Pushmataha had seen the clay cooking pot disappear, replaced on almost every fire with a metal one. Flint knives were rarely used—the sharp rock no match for the finely honed steel. The women of the village were being seen more and more in bright colored dresses of cloth rather than their deer skins. And then the guns: even though the bow and blowgun were still being used, men were beginning to lay them aside and picking up the "sticks that shot out flames."

And with the introduction of rifles, the hunt was easier and quicker. The hunter no longer found it necessary to get close to the deer—so different from hunting with the bow. And with more skins, more of the white man's goods could be purchased. This easy killing and desire for more soon disrupted the balance of nature, decimating the deer population.

PUSHMATAHA LOOKED ACROSS the river, and on the high bluff he could see the white man's lodge. From here it looked no different than his lodge, built of logs with a roof of reeds. The only difference he could see was a tall stack of rocks attached to one side of the structure with smoke coming out of it. In a Choctaw lodge, the fire was placed in the middle and smoke escaped from a hole in the roof. In this lodge the fire was built inside these rocks.

He swam and waded across the slow-moving water and climbed the steep incline. Initially it appeared that no one was there, but after a moment, a young white man not much older than Pushmataha came out of the only opening of the lodge. He spoke to his visitor in perfect Choctaw.

"Welcome to my trading post. What can I do for you?"

"I come to talk and learn of the white man's ways," Pushmataha answered.

The trader looked surprised. "That's an interesting request. I'll do what I can to help. But first, come and partake of food. Then we will smoke and talk."

"I am called Lefleur," the trader said as they walked in. "In your tongue it is Pakanli, or The Flower."

He began to laugh. "Not much of a name for a man according to the Choctaws! But it's a respected name from where I come from. The white man carries the name of his father and doesn't take a new name when he is older like your people."

The young trader seemed very pleasant and friendly, and Pushmataha knew that they would be friends.

Pushmataha entered the low-lit lodge, and as his eyes adjusted to the darkness, he was surprised at how full the one room was. In one corner there were stacks of pots and other metal cooking instruments. Rolls of cloth filled another, and dozens of rifles were hanging from pegs on the walls. Stacked haphazardly around the lodge were barrels, some filled with gun powder and others with whiskey, as he would soon learn. Leaning against one wall were hoes and axes, their heads made of iron rather than stone. In the middle of the room were deer skins piled waist high. He guessed that there must have been several hundred of them.

The white man carved a large piece of venison off of the hind quarter roasting over the fire and handed it to his guest.

"It's a little warm in here," Lefleur said. "Let's visit outside."

As they exited the lodge, Lefleur grabbed a jug that appeared to be filled with water. The two sat down under a nearby oak tree.

"Tell me about yourself. What iksa do you belong? Where is your village?"

"I am called Pushmataha," he said as he ate. "My village is among the Okla Hannali, Six Town People."

"Ah! 'The Messenger of Death,'" Lefleur said. "Your name goes before you. You have a great reputation of bravery in battle."

Lefleur looked the warrior over from head to foot as he stroked his beard. After a minute or two of contemplation, he shook his head.

"Don't take this wrong," he said, "but I would have expected someone a little older and fiercer looking. You don't look the part of war hero."

Pushmataha was surprised by the white man's comment. It was a rather bold statement from a stranger, but then, the white man's customs must be different from that of the Choctaws. He was also humored at the comment—it was not the first time he had heard that statement and he knew it would not be the last.

"The raccoon has the manner of the rabbit. But an unsuspecting dog will lose his eyes and ears in a fight."

"Well said, my friend! Well said!" Lefleur hooted as he lifted the jug and took a swig of liquid. He grimaced, shook his head, swallowed, and exhaled loudly.

"Wow! Good stuff! This Jamaican Rum!"

"You want a swig?" he asked as he offered the Red man the jug.

Pushmataha was familiar with the white man's oka humi, bitter water, but had never tasted it. Several of the Choctaw villages had been trading quite a bit for the "water that brings happiness," but his village had not.

The warrior raised the jug to his lips and took a swallow. Suddenly he couldn't breathe. His eyes watered, and his throat was on fire. He began to cough.

"Got to take it slowly, my friend," the white man laughed as he took back the jug. "Takes a bit getting used to. But then it becomes mighty tasty!"

Pushmataha mouth and lungs finally settled down, and he was able to finish his venison. He then reached into his totem and pulled out his pipe. He lit the pipe, took a few puffs, and passed it to Lefleur.

After taking a puff, Lefleur held the pipe up, turning it in his hand as he admired it. "That's a fine-looking pipe. It looks Italian. Good quality."

Lefleur then looked over at Pushmataha as he took another puff, and in a half serious, half joking tone asked, "You didn't take this from a white man while you were taking his scalp, did you?"

"Many Osages lost their scalps for this, but no white man."

"That's good, that's good!" Lefleur said with a bit of relief in his voice. He handed the pipe back to Pushmataha. "Wouldn't want there to be any trouble between our people.

"Now, tell me what you would like to know about the white man," he inquired as he took another swig from the jug and leaned back against the tree.

"What does the white man do with so many skins?"

"That, my friend, is a very good question. In fact, you are the first of your people to ever ask me that. Most of your brothers come in with their pelts, trade for what they want, and silently leave without ever wondering what becomes of all of their work. It's good that someone is taking a little interest.

"The simple answer is I trade them, just like your people. When I have accumulated a few thousand of them, I float them down the river to the great waters to the south, and from there float them to Mobile to the east. It takes about two weeks to get there. I trade them for more goods—pots, guns, and such—and bring them back here to trade for more skins. I also trade for money: paper and gold used to barter with."

Lefleur took another sip from the jug and began to laugh. "My friend, it's getting difficult to keep up with what money is what down there. When I was born—and I was born there in Mobile—the money was the French Franc. Then the British took over and we were using the Pound. Five years ago, in 1780, the Spanish took control and brought in the Spanish Dollar. And now with that new nation to the east, the United States, entering the picture, we will probably be using their money before long."

The trader paused. "My friend, that's probably more than you wanted to know about money in Mobile."

Pushmataha silently agreed. He had no concept of what Lefleur was talking about: paper used for bartering didn't make sense.

"Let me get back to what happens to those skins. Once I trade the pelts, they are placed in a large building—a large lodge—for storage. Last time I took a load, there must have been over fifty thousand deer skins in that building. From there, the skins are loaded on a boat with sails and taken east.

"Most of the skins have been going across the great waters to the countries where the white man came from. I don't know if that will change with this new government in the picture. But that's what happens now. Once the skins get there, they are made into clothing— shoes, or white man moccasins, gloves to keep the hands warm, and coats to keep the body warm.

"So, there it is," he said as he took another drink. "That's what happens with the skins."

Pushmataha sat silently. He was amused, yet disturbed. How strange: the Choctaw wears the white man's clothes, while the white man wears the Choctaw's clothes. And such a great number of skins— fifty thousand! How can there be deer left? The Red man's desire for things of the white man and the white man's desire for things of the Red man—this was destroying the balance of life.

He wondered how many white men there were! Their numbers must be greater than the stars in the sky!

"Tell me of this new nation of white men to the east," the warrior said.

"Thirteen tribes—the British called them colonies, and the new nation calls them states—rebelled against their leaders across the water and formed their own nation. They have been fighting for the past several years, and finally, just two years ago in 1783, a treaty was signed ending the war and giving the thirteen tribes independence. They call themselves the United States of America."

Lefleur paused to take another drink, wiped his mouth with the back of his hand.

"You want to have another taste," he said as he held out the jug.

The warrior lifted the jug to his mouth, but he took only a small swallow. It burned his throat, but he did not cough.

"That's much better, my friend" the white man said. "You're learning.

"Now, a little more about that new nation—they're no older than a nitushi, a newborn bear cub, but they are already roaring like a tek, a momma bear. And they are land hungry. I hear they are already pushing toward the west, needing more land to settle.

"Last time I was in Mobile, that was a couple of months ago, there was talk that the Great Chief of the new nation wants to council with all the chiefs of the Red man. Make treaty. I haven't come across any of your people who seem to be interested, but I think it would be a good idea for the Choctaws to go. Your people need to know what's happening."

"When is this meeting with the Great Chief?" Pushmataha asked.

"Sometime later this year, but I don't know when or where. The white chief in Mobile should know. I'll write you a note of introduction if you plan to go there. He is a friend of my father's. He can give you the information."

The two continued to talk and share the jug and the pipe. Lefleur told how the white man's concept of land was so different from the Red man. The white man felt that he had to lay claim to land: he had to own it. He built fences to show his boundaries and to keep others out. Land was an object to be bought and sold.

For the Red man ownership of land was beyond understanding. The land belonged to no one; it was shared by the entire tribe. Everyone had the right to live and hunt as they wished with no restrictions from others. Yes, they defended their land from other tribes, but no one ever laid claim to land. And to sell land would be like selling air or water.

He told how he foresaw difficulties between the white man and the Red man concerning land. The two different views could not exist together.

Lefleur spoke about this new nation, the United States, which in such a short time was making a name for itself with the other nations of the white man. Their leaders were good and their laws were just, attracting many to cross the great waters to settle in their new land. And with so many coming, there was no choice for the nation but to spread to the west.

As the white man continued to speak, Pushmataha began to feel strange. It was a pleasant feeling, though, one that he had never experienced before. He began to understand why some called it "the water that brings happiness." After a while, he began to lose interest in what the white man was saying. "What does it matter?" he thought. "All will be good." He started to feel as if he were in a canoe, slowly rocking with the waves. The white man's voice became distant, like an echo across a lake. His head began to slowly spin. He was tired, but it was an amusing tiredness. He began to smile. He needed to close his eyes and go to sleep.

WHEN THE RED MAN WOKE, it was dark. The moon was bright in the cloudless sky, and the frogs and crickets by the river were calling and singing. In the moonlight he could see the white man leaning against the tree, fast asleep, snoring softly with his arm wrapped around the jug.

Pushmataha's head ached and his stomach felt tight. He slowly got up and walked to the edge of the lodge where he had seen a bucket of water. He splashed his face. Never had he slept a sleep like that. The sleep was deep, like death, but the sleep did not rest him or refresh him. He lay down on the ground and went back to sleep.

THOMAS L. WILEY

CHAPTER SEVEN

PUSHMATAHA LEFT EARLY the next day, traveling southeast. Lefleur had given him a paper to present to the commander in Mobile. It would take five days to reach Mobile and then another three days to return to his village. As he traveled, his head began to clear and he pondered what he had been told.

"The Choctaws must learn more about this nation that had settled in the east," he thought. "How powerful are they? How many are there? Is this new nation a friend of the Choctaws, or is it an enemy that threatens to take her land? Should the peace pipe be shared, or should they be met in battle and driven away?"

Pushmataha knew that the Choctaws must go and meet the new leader of the white man—understand his intentions. In Mobile he would learn about the council and take the information to his leaders.

MOBILE HAD BEEN FOUNDED in 1702 by the French as Fort Louis de la Louisiane and served for several years as the capital of the French territory. In 1723 a brick and stone fortress replaced the woodened one and the name changed to Fort Conde, which guarded the Bay of Mobile for almost one hundred years. In 1763 the British took control of the fort and change the name to Fort Charlotte in honor of George III's wife. In 1780 the Spanish, as allies of the United States in the Revolutionary War, captured Mobile during the Battle of Fort Charlotte and changed the name to Fort Carlota. In 1813, the area came under the control of the United States.

Mobile was named after the Mobilia, or Mauvila, tribe, close relatives to the Choctaws. Little is known of them. Their place in history relates primarily to their leader, Tuscaloosa, the "Black Warrior," who battled De Soto in 1540. Tuscaloosa and several hundred of his warriors were killed, no match for the guns and armor of the Spanish soldiers. By the time the French settled the area in the early 1700's, the Mobilia tribe was not a distinct tribe and consisted of only a few hundred families. By the mid 1700's the tribe no longer existed, most likely having assimilated into the Choctaw Nation.

THE WARRIOR HAD NEVER SEEN a large white settlement. In fact, Bernard Roman's party that had visited when he was eight was the largest gathering of white men he had ever seen. He had heard tales about the white man's village on the great Bay of Mobile. For several years leaders of his nation had regularly traveled to Mobile to discuss trade relations and had returned telling of hundreds of white men and their families and of a great stone fortress. But Pushmataha was not prepared for what he saw.

The village appeared to covered several acres. Hundreds of lodges were scattered about with white men working, talking, and laughing. In the center of the settlement was a huge fortress with stone walls twice as tall as a man—walls that would be impossible to scale. Men with guns stood guard at the entrance, preventing anyone from entering.

As he looked around, he thought, "The white man cannot be taken lightly."

Pushmataha handed the paper to one of the men at the gate, was taken in, and was soon introduced to an older man who looked over the paper and smiled. He began to talk, but the words had no meaning. After a few minutes, a white man entered the lodge, spoke to the older man, and in Choctaw spoke to Pushmataha.

"Our chief welcomes you and hopes that young Lefleur was well when you left him."

"His health was good," Pushmataha said, "but his eyes were heavy and his stomach sour from oka humi."

The interpreter spoke to the older man, who appeared to be the chief, and both men began to laugh. "It sounds like the wilderness hasn't changed Louis at all."

"Now, the letter states that you represent the Choctaw Nation and wish to know about the great council that is to be held with the United States. We are not governed by the new nation: we are Spanish. But our chief knows of the council and will be glad to give directions."

The older man unrolled a large paper and began to point and talk. On the paper were lines drawn that represented rivers and streams, similar to what Bernard Romans had drawn when Pushmataha was a child. The interpreter related the information. He pointed to a river that flowed into the Tombigbee just above the Bay of Mobile—the Alabama River. He traced the Alabama up stream, then northeast along the Coosa River through Creek country into the mountains... He continued to relate to the young warrior the route he should take.

The white chief wrote on a paper and handed it to Pushmataha.

"When you arrive in that area, show this to any white man and he should be able to give you directions. Hopewell Plantation in South Carolina is a well-known place."

The Council would take place in the moon of Hash Haponi or the month of cooking, which was four moons away. The distance was far, four hundred of the white man's miles, and would take nearly one moon to get there.

AT THE END OF THE REVOLUTIONARY WAR, the United States began experiencing tremendous growth. Expansion into lands occupied by the natives to the west was inevitable. Realizing the almost certain unrest and violence that would occur, an invitation was sent to the tribes to treaty. The plan was to come up with boundaries and conditions which were acceptable to both sides.

Treaties had already been signed a year earlier with the northern tribes—the Iroquois, Delawares, and Wyandots—and now the United States hoped to treaty with the southern tribes—the Cherokees, Creeks, Chickasaws, and Choctaws. The meeting was to take place at Hopewell Plantation in October 1785.

Hopewell Plantation, located in the western most part of South Carolina, was the home of General Andrew Pickens, hero of the Revolutionary War, now a U. S. Representative in the Congress of the

Confederation. He and Colonel Benjamin Hawkins, Senator from North Carolina, were commissioned to meet with the southern tribes and come up with an agreement—to treaty.

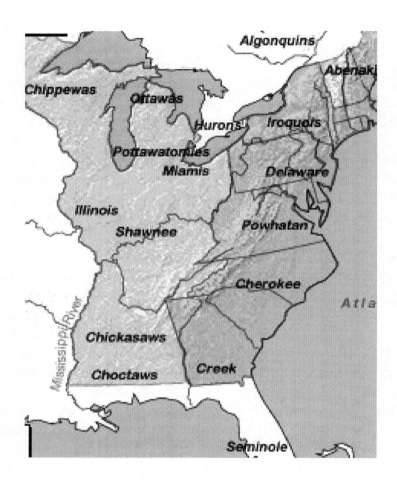

Major Native American Tribes East of the Mississippi at the Time of U.S. Independence—1783

AS PUSHMATAHA TRAVELED NORTH along the Big Trading Path toward his home, he thought of how the diversity of the Choctaw Nation sometimes made negotiations difficult. There was no one chief of the Choctaws. Each of the three districts had its own chief. But even these three leaders held only nominal power over the village chiefs, or mingos. Decisions, for the most part, were made by consensus in council. The size and participation of a council was determined by the villages or districts that would be affected and often didn't involve the entire nation.

This type of governance was good in that it was a true democracy: everyone having an opportunity to voice his opinion, but it made important decisions affecting the entire nation more complicated. Another difficulty: in negotiations with a Choctaw district, the other party would often not realize that he was dealing with only that district and not the entire Choctaw Nation.

UPON RETURNING, Pushmataha presented his information to the chief of the Six Town District, Pooshemastubie. A call went out to all three districts, and a council convened. Seated closest to the inside of the circle were the chiefs and leaders; the lesser mingos and younger warriors were seated behind them.

After the pipe was passed, the meeting began. Fanchimastabe, chief of the Okla Falaya or west district, was first to speak.

"Great Council of the Choctaws, news has come to us of a council to be held far to the east with a new nation of the white man. As this council knows, we have treatied with many nations of the white man in the past. When our grandfathers were children, the French came trading for skins and pelts. Many of them settled along the great waters to the south and on the Misha Sipokni, the river that is beyond age, where our brothers the Natchez once lived. Unlike the Natchez, who tried to drive the French away and are now no more, we lived in peace with the French and benefited from their trade. And then only twenty winters ago, when I was young, a new nation, the English defeated the French and became our friends, trading with us no different than the

French. Now another nation, the Spanish have come, replacing the English. Only one winter ago, we treatied with their chief in Mobile. He has promised us peace and continued trade.

"Now we are told that another nation wishes to treaty, but they are far away. Their land does not even border ours. The Creeks and the Cherokees are between our nations. I find no need to put in danger our relations with the Spanish."

When he finished, many nodded in agreement. After a moment, Pushmataha stood to speak.

"Great Council, Fanchimastabe, the chief of the Okla Falaya, has spoken words that are true. He is a great and wise leader, and I—one who has little knowledge and understanding of the ways of the white man—do not wish to speak a differing opinion. But in my limited knowledge, I sense that this new nation is not to be brushed off so quickly. I agree that they are far away. But they are growing fast. The Cherokees and Creeks feel the breath on their necks. Their lands are already being settled and claimed by this nation. They have no choice but to treaty, yet they will begin talks at a disadvantage. Will we do the same? Will we wait until they are building lodges on the Tombigbee or Noxubee Rivers before we meet with them?

"I do not propose to break ties with the Spanish. Their trade is good and necessary. But will we have only one white friend at a time? We should meet with this new nation and hear their words. If their words do not benefit the Choctaws, a treaty will not be accepted."

The council felt that Pushmataha's words were good, and a delegation was chosen to make the journey east to meet with the Chief of the United States.

OVER ONE HUNDRED WARRIORS, including Pushmataha, made the journey. Chiefs from all three districts were represented: Mingohoopoie and Yockehoopoie of the East, Taboca and Yockonahoma of the West, and Pooshemastubie of the Six Town District. Fanchimastabe, of the West, who was considered the patriarch and most influential chief of the time, did not go. It was felt that he was too old to make the long journey, especially with winter approaching.

Accompanying the delegation were interpreters, John Pitchlynn and James Cole.

JOHN PITCHLYNN NOT ONLY PLAYED a major role as interpreter at Hopewell, but he translated for every treaty and almost every major meeting between the Choctaws and the United States for over fifty years. Born on board a ship off Puerto Rico in 1764, the same year as Pushmataha, Pitchlynn grew up among the Choctaws. His father, Isaac, a Scotsman, was an officer in the British Navy who served as a liaison to the Choctaws.

On one trip into the Choctaw Nation, he took his young son, John, with him. While there, the elder Pitchlynn died. Apparently the two had traveled alone, and John was left to live among the natives. He assimilated into the Choctaw culture, and later married two mixed-race sisters, Rhoda and Sophie Folsom, daughters of Ebenezer Folsom. John's sons, John, Jr., Peter, Silas, Thomas, and James, later played major roles as chiefs during and after the Choctaws' removal.

John Pitchlynn was well respected and trusted by the Choctaw Nation. The name bestowed on him by the Choctaws was "Chatah It-ti-ka-na"— "The Choctaws' friend." (Many feel that great orations of the future chief, Pushmataha, were made even greater by the spellbinding presentation of his ever-present interpreter, John Pitchlynn.)

INSTEAD OF THE ANTICIPATED one-month journey, it took two months for the delegation to reach Hopewell Plantation. While traveling through Creek country, they were attacked by a raiding party, who took most of their supplies and their horses. Also, winter came early with heavy snows, making travel slow. The party—exhausted, cold, and famished—finally arrived at Hopewell on December 26.

When the Choctaws arrived, they learned that negotiations between the United States and the Creek and Cherokee Nations had been underway for almost two months. In fact, the Cherokee negotiations had concluded a month earlier with terms of the treaty satisfactory to both parties. Negotiations with the Creeks, however, were not successful. The Creeks rejected the boundaries laid out by the new nation and left without an agreement. The Chickasaws had yet to arrive, but would finally appear and would find the terms satisfactory.

AFTER SEVERAL DAYS OF REST and recovery, the Choctaws were ready to talk, and a council was called. Following Choctaw custom, the pipe was passed before any talk began.

General Pickens, the ranking United States official, spoke first. "We are honored that the Choctaw leaders have traveled so far and under such conditions. We look forward to an amicable relationship with our new friends."

Yockonahoma of the western district, who had been chosen as spokesman for the Choctaws, responded. "We are humbled and honored to meet the Great Chief of the white man. Your nation is young yet news of its greatness and the wisdom of your leadership have traveled far."

Pickens suddenly realized that the Choctaws thought that he was the President—a misunderstanding that he had to correct, and one that he hoped would not jeopardize the proceedings. He stood and rubbed his chin, as if searching for the right words.

"I am a chief among the white man," Pickens said, "but I am not the Great Chief. He is not here. Though he had every intention of meeting with our new friends, he was unable to make the journey. Duties in Washington demanded his presence there, and he sends his regrets. In his stead he has sent Colonel Hawkins and me. We are both capable representatives and have been given authority to negotiate on his part, as if he were here."

The Choctaws were disappointed but understanding. They would treaty with those sent by the Great Chief.

WHAT THE CHOCTAWS WERE NOT TOLD was that there was not a "real" Chief of the new nation. At the time, the United States was being governed by the Articles of Confederation and Perpetual

Union—a federation style of government with the thirteen states united and yet retaining their sovereignty and independence. The governing body was the Congress of the Confederation with the "Presidency" rotating yearly. In fact, while negotiations with the Red man at Hopewell were taking place, the leadership changed: in November 1785 Richard Henry Lee of Virginian rotated off as president and John Hancock of Massachusetts rotated on. Not until the United States Constitution was ratified in 1788 would there be three branches of government with a President as the executive branch. George Washington would take office as the first "real" President, or Great Chief, in 1789.

AFTER SEVERAL DAYS OF MEETINGS and discussions, a treaty between the United States and the Choctaws was agreed upon and signed on January 3, 1786. The Choctaws left very pleased with the results. Boundaries for their nation were set with no land ceded by the Choctaws. No citizen of the United States would be permitted to settle on Choctaw land and violators would be punished. And trade negotiations with the new nation were established that seemed very beneficial to the Choctaws.

NONE OF THE RED MEN who met at Hopewell Plantation— Cherokees, Creeks, Chickasaws, or Choctaws—could foresee that these treaties were not permanent. This was but the first of many that over the next fifty years would be made, broken, revised, disputed, and ignored until the Red man could no longer build his lodge on the lands where the bones of his ancestors were buried.

THOMAS L. WILEY

CHAPTER EIGHT

OVER THE NEXT FEW YEARS, the Choctaw Nation was quiet. Trade relations with both the Spanish and the United States developed, and trading posts were established by both nations in the land of the Choctaws. The competition between these two, vying for the business of the Red man, was quite beneficial. It ensured a good rate of exchange for their skins and pelts.

The Choctaws were rapidly becoming more and more dependent on the things of the white man. No longer were the Choctaws seen wearing clothes made from the skins of animal. All clothes were cotton and wool, the material purchased with the skins they once wore. Fish hooks, sugar, flour, rakes, hoes, plows, nails, saws, hammers, pots, pans, cooking utensils, and numerous other trade goods of the white man became common place in all villages. Guns became the preferred weapon for hunting and warring.

Pushmataha and the other men continued their life of hunting, but found that the hunts were becoming even longer and more widespread. Pushmataha soon realized that the bow was becoming obsolete, and even though he realized the impact that the gun was having on the balance and stability of nature, he laid down his weapon of old and traded pelts for the weapon of the white man. Otherwise, his hunts would never be successful.

IN 1786 THE SPANISH EXTABLISHED a trading post on the Tombigbee River, Fort St. Stephens, a two-day journey from Pushmataha's village. Shortly after that, the United States built one at Mussel Shoals on the Tennessee River, but Pushmataha continued to make visits to his friend on the Pearl River and enjoy smoking the pipe and drinking the oka humi, "bitter water," under the oak tree.

"MY FRIEND," Lefleur said as he took a swig from his jug, "I've been thinking. It's hard to believe, but I've been here going on nine years. I've done mighty well. But I'm missing something. I think I need some companionship. It's time for me to take a tekchi, a wife. In fact, I've got my eye on two of the daughters of a trader who lives in the Ahi Apet Okla district of your nation. Jean Cravat is his name; he's a Frenchman. Do you know him?"

Pushmataha puffed on his pipe and laughed. "Yes, I know Cravat. His wife, Nehomtima, is my sister."

FOR ALMOST THIRTY YEARS, Jean Cravat had lived among the Choctaws. He had left Pensacola following the Treaty of Paris in 1763 when the British took control of the fort from the French. He settled among the Choctaws, working as a translator and trader. He eventually married Nehomtima and was adopted into the tribe. Two of their children, the interests of Lefleur, were Rebecca and Nancy.

"WELL, ISN'T THAT SOMETHING!" Lefleur said as he scratched his beard. He took a swig from his jug and chuckled. "If I marry one of them, why, we'll be related!"

Pushmataha grunted and reached for the jug.

"Cravat visits here fairly often and usually brings his daughters," Lefleur continued. "Those girls must be in their late teens. I'm surprised neither one has been taken. They both would make a pretty good wife. Problem for me is—I don't know which one to ask."

Pushmataha puffed on his pipe. "Why take only one? Take both."

"Take two wives?!" Lefleur asked as he took another drink. "Well, I don't know about that. That's not the way the white man does it. Only one at a time for them."

"You now live among the Choctaws," Pushmataha said. "Why should you not follow the ways of your new tribe? To have two wives is good. If you take only one, you deprive the other of a man."

A BYPRODUCT OF WARFARE was an oversupply of women. The constant warring and fighting between the Choctaws and the Osages and Creeks left many more women than men. For centuries, the solution was bigamy, which had become an accepted practice among many tribes of the Red man. Surprisingly, there never seemed to be jealousy between the wives. But then, there was no time for jealousy. There was too much work to bicker.

"I have two wives," Pushmataha said.

"My friend!" the white man exclaimed. "You surprise me!"

AFTER FIVE YEARS with only one wife, Cham Nay, Pushmataha had taken another wife—Immayahoka. Immayahoka was of mixed race. Her father was James Cole, an English trapper, who had settled in the area in the 1760's and had taken a Choctaw wife, Shumaka. Cole had accompanied the Choctaw delegation to Hopewell in 1785 as an interpreter, and while on the journey, he and Pushmataha had become friends. Shortly after returning to Choctaw country, Cole gave his daughter, Immayahoka, also called Rebecca, to Pushmataha as a wife. Pushmataha and Immayahoka had three children, two girls, Betsy and Martha, and a son Haschalahurtibbi, who was later called Johnson.

In every respect, mixed-race children, such as those of Cravat and Cole, were Choctaws—reared by their Choctaw mothers and families with little influence by their white fathers and the white man culture. The children spoke Choctaw, thought Choctaw, and lived Choctaw. Even among the full-blooded, fathers were present but took a minor role in instruction and discipline, which for the boys was relegated to their maternal uncles. Only when the boys were older was there teaching by the fathers—teachings of hunting and war.

"WELL, IF YOU SAY it's good, I guess I'll have to try it out." Lefleur said. "But if I find two is too many, you, my friend, may find yourself with three, or even four, wives!"

The white man and the Red man continued to visit and share the pipe and jug, discussing the affairs of their land.

"My friend," Lefleur said, "the market economy is working well for your people. They are learning the art of commerce and business and are beginning to make competition work to their benefit. Since the United States started trading with them, I've had to lower my price on goods. If I don't, the pelts are packed up and traded elsewhere.

"I've been instructed by the company I trade with, the Panton, Leslie and Company, to be as accommodating as possible and to not lose the business. Panton and Leslie are feeling the effects of competition not only among the Choctaws, but among the Creek, Chickasaws, and Alabama tribes. That new nation, the United States, is mighty aggressive.

"Panton, Leslie and Company, in case you don't know, is English. When the Spanish took over a few years ago, they continued working with Panton and Leslie because they already had the trading relationships established with the Red man."

Lefleur began to laugh as he lifted the jug. "My friend, it strikes me as funny. Here I am, a Frenchman about to marry a Choctaw, working with an English company, which has contracted with the Spanish Government, wanting me to be competitive with the United States. If that's not complicated, I don't know what is.

"There's another thing that concerns me, though, and I don't know if it's due to the competition or not: your people are bringing in less of the deer skins than they did a few years ago. Also, I'm getting a lot more fox, rabbit, and beaver than I used to. Those are good but not as valuable. Also, there is more bees' wax being traded."

Pushmataha took a puff on his pipe and handed it to the white man.

"The deer in the land of the Choctaws will soon be no more," he said. "Even now we travel far to the west, across the Misha Sipokni, into the land of the Osages and Caddos to hunt the deer, and the hunts now last many days. In council two moons ago, Fanchimastabe, chief of the Okla Falaya, grieved as he spoke. He is old and wise, and he sees beyond our time. In a dream he saw the end of the hunt. No more were the Choctaws in the forests hunting the bear and the deer. The warriors were in meadows surrounded by fences, feeding cattle and hogs.

"Several members of the council spoke against him, saying: 'He is an old man. His dreams are nothing. We will hunt as our fathers have hunted since the time of Chahtah and Chickasah.'

"I listened as they spoke and said nothing. I desired to believe their words, but in my heart, I too began to grieve. The hunt has changed. We no longer kill for food and clothes, but for trade. In many ways the trade is good for the Choctaws. The goods of the white man are welcomed. They are superior to what the Choctaws make. But the doe cannot bear enough fawns to replace the killing, and soon there will be no more. What will the Choctaws do when there are no more skins to trade? Will he go back to the old ways of stone axes and clay pots? Or will he learn the ways of the white man—learn to raise cattle and hogs, and learn to plant like the farmer? This he must do, or he will have nothing."

"My friend," Lefleur said, "You sound too gloomy, and I hope you're wrong. My livelihood depends on those skins. But time will tell."

CHAPTER NINE

IN 1790 A STICK BALL GAME was held between the Choctaws and the Creeks. It was a game that ended in bloodshed.

Along the lower Noxubee, where the river joined the Tombigbee, the land was marshy. Many beaver made their homes in the wetland and among the small tributaries that flowed into the two rivers. This land was of little importance until the past few years when, as the deer population decreased, beaver pelts took on a greater importance in the trade with the white man. Both the Choctaws and the Creeks laid claim to this area, and several conflicts had occurred among hunting parties. Tensions were high and rising.

To try to resolve the issue peacefully, chiefs from both nations met at council. After much deliberation, the leaders decided that a game of stickball would be the deciding factor. For both nations, stickball was a time-honored way of resolving minor conflicts: a binding arbitration based on skill on the field. The winner would have exclusive rights to the land and the beaver.

A time was set two moons away for the game, and the field of play was selected: a meadow on the banks of the Noxubee River, just north of Shuqualak Creek. Word went out to both nations telling of the great event, and for two weeks before the appointed time, members from the far reaches of the two nations gathered in anticipation. By the time the game was played, several thousand people were camped in the surrounding forest.

Pushmataha was there, not as a player, but as one of the observers. He was now twenty-six, and he had never developed the skill of the game. His youth—a time when most boys were perfecting their throws and catches—was spent alone on a quest beyond the Misha Sipokni.

On the night before the game, excitement filled the air as the two teams, the best of both nations, prepared to meet in a battle of strength and skill. Both nations celebrated and danced late into the night in anticipation of their team's victory. Dressed only in breechcloths, the players painstakingly painted their bodies with bright colors and adorned themselves with feathers of eagles and hawks and tails of raccoon and panther. They shouted and sang and beat their chests, ready to take on the challenge that dawn would bring.

Long before the sun rose in the east, the spectators gathered at the meadow: the Choctaws on the west side of the playing field and the Creeks on the east. No one spoke. Everyone listened.

Faint chanting was soon heard in the distance to the north and to the south. The spectators strained their eyes as the voices grew louder and louder. From the dimly lit forest, seventy-five players appeared in each direction, advancing rapidly, running in perfect order and in perfect rhythm. The crowd began to cheer and shout.

The two teams advanced to the middle of the field, and the order and rhythm suddenly disappeared as the two teams mingled together— laughing, jeering, and taunting each other. Abruptly, there was silence as each team retreated to their end of the field. Each player took his two ka-puch-a, ball sticks, and waited. A Hopaii, holy man, from each tribe walked to the center of the field, chanting a blessing on his respective team. The ball was thrown, and the game began. Suddenly the silence was broken with shouts of "Hokli! Hokli!"— "Catch! Catch!"—and "Falamochi! Falamochi!" — "Throw! Throw!"

The game was rough, much rougher than the usual stickball between villages. The pride of two nations was at stake. There were few rules of conduct, and injuries were great. Some most likely would result in lifelong scarring and disability.

The game was long, lasting from the rising of the sun until its setting. There were no breaks, no time for the teams to rest. The only rest was for those injured too seriously to continue to play. Individual players stopped momentarily to take water or a little food and were back in the game. The sun beat down, and the day grew hot, but none complained. They were warriors—Choctaw and Creek.

The game was close, one of the closest games that any had seen. For hours they played with the lead changing hands numerous times. Finally at the end of the day, the Creeks were victorious, winning with a goal in the last moments of play.

A game that is a rout is humiliating, but a game that is close is often harder to accept. Individual shame and frustration emerge as players consider 'what if' and 'if I had only…' One of the young Choctaws, distraught at losing and upset at the exuberant celebration of the victorious Creek, shouted an insult at one of the Creek players. The Creek player, in retaliation, shouted back that the young Choctaw was a poor loser, no better than an old woman, and threw a petticoat on him.

The insults were too great, and suddenly the two players were at each other's throats, engaged in a fight to the death. In a matter of seconds, the two teams were fighting, using their sticks and bare hands as weapons. Warriors on the sidelines, unable to stay out of the melee, joined in. Tomahawks, knives, and war clubs appeared out of nowhere. Pushmataha was among them, reeling his tomahawk with precision.

The battle was fierce and bloody. Before order could be regained, dozens of young Choctaws and Creeks lay dead and dying on the ball field.

The chiefs on both sides were distraught at this sudden deadly turn of events. This gathering was to have been peaceful, not an excuse for killing. The small patch of land was not worth the cost and suffering. Council was called and the nations met together. The leaders voiced shame for the actions of their people and chastised the participants. The loss of life was so unnecessary—many of the finest young men of each nation lay dead on the field, and many more were maimed.

Many who participated lowered their faces and voiced regret for their actions, but not Pushmataha. The Creeks were his enemy and the enemy of the Choctaws. This would never change. He knew that the conflict between the two nations, which began long ago in the days of

Chahtah, would never end. He would mourn the loss of his Choctaw brothers, but the death of a Creek was never to be lamented.

The dead were buried in the meadow where they fell. The council had decided this would be a better tribute to the slain young men, rather than having each one taken back to his village for burial.

The families wailed and cried as their sons and brothers were laid to rest, and for days both nations stayed and mourned. Gradually they dispersed, and the meadow became silent. For the next forty years, until the last treaties were signed and both nations moved to the west of the Misha Sipokni, Choctaws and Creeks alike made pilgrimages to the banks of the Noxubee River to mourn their dead—to the place forever to be known as 'Nan Anusi Hashuk Abasha,' 'the Meadow of Mourning.'

At council, both nations agreed that neither would claim the marshlands of the Noxubee or the tributaries where the beaver abounded. Neither nation would hunt in the land or trap in the waters out of respect and reverence to those who had died. Strangely, within a few years of the great ballgame, the beaver disappeared. None were found within miles of the area. Their homes were vacant, and their dams untended. The hopaii said there was too much death for them to stay.

Most likely, though, the disappearance of the beaver was a natural phenomenon—related to a famine that gripped the land of the Choctaws.

SUMMERS WERE ALWAYS HOT and dry in the land of the Choctaws, but the abundant rains that fell in winter and spring seemed to be enough to water the fields of corn and squash and to nourish the orchards of peaches and plums. The dryness of late summer and fall was actually welcomed as the fruits ripened, ready for harvest. Following the harvest, the coolness of winter would descend with her cloudy, wet days until spring again appeared with her heavy rains.

But in 1793, there were no spring rains, and summer came early. The land was unusually hot, and the dirt was dry as gun powder. The corn stalks, at first stunted by the lack of rain, were soon scorched by the unrelenting sun. The peaches, growing no larger than muscadines, fell to the ground. Even the pecans trees, usually resistant to the lack of water, failed to give fruit.

The drought not only affected the crops but also the deer, the fox, and the raccoon. The meadows were bare of grasses, and the land was cracked and parched. Deer, rarely seen before the drought, were nowhere in sight.

With the drought, the dependence of the Red man on the white man and his trading posts increased significantly. Unable to produce his own food, the Choctaws found it necessary to purchase flour, sugar, corn, and other staples from the Spanish posts at Fort Stephens and Lefleur's Bluff and from the American post at Muscle Shoals. With a lack of skins and pelts, purchase was on credit, a trading practice that the Red man did not yet understand—debt was incurred and it was calculated in dollars.

In 1794, the Spanish opened another trading post on the Tombigbee River just a few miles north of where it was joined by the Black Warrior River and less that a day's journey from Pushmataha's Village. Fort Confederation, or Fort Confederación as it was called by the Spanish, was built on the ruins of Fort Tombigbee which had been vacant for sixteen years. Initially built in 1735 by the French, Fort Tombigbee had been used as a base during the Chickasaw Wars and then as a post for trade with the Choctaws, Chickasaws, Alabamas, and Creeks. After the treaty of Paris in 1763, the British took control, renamed it Fort York, but abandoned it after only five years. Sixteen years later, in response to the famine, the Spanish rebuilt it and named it Fort Confederación.

With the opening of Fort Confederación, the Spanish appeared to have the upper hand in trade with the Choctaws—even though the trade was built on credit which could not possibly be repaid. Superficially, this trade relationship would seem to be either foolish or benevolent, but it was neither. The Spanish and their agent, Panton, Leslie and Company, had a bigger reason for allowing the indebtedness—land. If the Choctaws were steeped in debt, the only way to repay it was to give up their land. But a year later, in 1795, the plans of the Spanish abruptly changed.

CHAPTER TEN

"MY FRIEND, IT'S GOOD to see a few deer skin for a change." Lefleur counted thirty skins on the back of the packhorse. "I was afraid my business was going to dry up and blow away, same as the weather."

He and Pushmataha unloaded the skins and stacked them on the floor of the lodge. Even though Fort Confederación was closer, Pushmataha continued to make the three-day trek to the bluff on the Pearl River to trade with his friend. Over the years the two had developed a close friendship—also, they had even become related by marriage.

Since the last visit, Lefleur had gained weight. At age thirty-six, he now carried a large belly, the result of good cooking from his two wives and his ever-present jug of oka humi. His chest had also grown thick, and with his bushy black beard, he looked like a bear in clothes rather than a white man. With the little energy he used to carry the skins into the lodge, he broke out in a sweat.

"Trade has been picking up, now that we're out of the drought," Lefleur said as he wiped his neck and forehead with a cloth. "My friend, I don't think I've ever seen anything so wonderful as the day the rain started to fall, and I'm sure the Choctaws feel the same way. Why, even the bees have gotten back into the business of making honey. One of your red brothers brought in three gallons just this morning. Gave him a good price for it, too—honey's selling really well in Mobile."

The white man laughed as he grabbed his jug and the two headed outside. "I told that fellow my hat was off to him and anyone else foolish enough to collect honey. I haven't found anything worth what it takes to rob a hive. Why, if having honey depended on me, there wouldn't be any. There's nothing worse than a bee sting!"

Pushmataha pulled out his pipe and filled it with tobacco. "The white man's skin is too thin, and his spirit is too weak. When I was a boy, my friends had a game. We played it many times. We would hit the nest of wasps, bees, or hornets—made them really mad—and we would stand still. The last boy to run was the bravest and was declared warrior and chief."

"The bravest!" Lefleur said as he sat down under the oak and lifted the jug. "I would call him the dumbest! There are a lot better and more fun games to play than 'stir up the hornets' nest.' Tell me, my friend—the great warrior—how did you fair in the game?"

"Pushmataha never won," the Red man said as he puffed his pipe.

Lefleur hooted. "Why, you old fake!"

The two shared the pipe and jug, catching up on what was going on in the world of the Red man and the white man.

"Those are good looking skins you brought in," Lefleur said. "The deer in Okla Hannali, Six Towns, must be rebounding fairly well after the drought."

"No," Pushmataha answered. "Even with abundance of rain, we see no deer near our village. I return with these from a hunt in Osage country. We still find many deer across the Misha Sipokni."

"I'm sorry to hear that they're not rebounding," Lefleur said. "That's not good for my business. But something has happened that I'm afraid is going to affect my little trading post even more. The United States has taken control of Choctaw land."

Pushmataha didn't understand. "What do you mean 'taken control?' There has been no battle. There has been no council, no treaty. No one has taken our land. The land belongs to the Choctaws."

Lefleur scratched his beard. "Push, my friend, it's a little difficult to explain, but I will do my very best.

"First, for the past fifteen or so years, ever since they declared their independence from Britain, the United States has been claiming that the land of the Choctaws is theirs. Now, don't misunderstand me; the land still belongs to the Choctaw Nation—it's still yours: that was agreed upon at Hopewell ten years ago in 1786. It just means that the United States wanted it to be part of their country, under their control, but still belonging to the Choctaws—if that makes any sense. Now, the Spanish didn't see it that way. They said Choctaw land was theirs.

"As you know, both nations have been acting like they own the place: trying their best to establish good trade relationships with the Choctaws, to become your friend—building trading posts and such."

Lefleur took a sip from his jug, snorted, and then continued. "I know that I'm a little biased—since I've been working with the Spanish—but it seems to me that they've done a better job of it. They really stepped in during the drought and helped prevent a lot of Choctaws from starving.

"Well, a few years ago the Spanish got themselves into a bit of trouble back home across the great waters to the east. It all started with a revolt among the French. It's been called the 'French Revolution.' The French rebelled against their king and took over the government."

Pushmataha shook his head and thought, "The white men are never satisfied. They fight among themselves worse than the Red man."

"Three years ago, in 1793, Spain, as well as almost every country in Europe, got involved in the conflict and declared war on France. In no time the Spanish were in deeper than they should have been, and all of a sudden, the United States was breathing down their necks about this land over here. Not only were they pressuring them about the land, but they also wanted to work out a deal about the great river to the west, the Mississippi, or the Misha Sipokni as you call it. The Spanish in Natchez and New Orleans were not allowing the United States to navigate down the river.

"My friend, you probably don't realize what navigation of that river will do for the United States. People by droves are moving west of the Appalachians into the Ohio and Cumberland Valleys. Even now there are over a hundred thousand citizens of the U.S. living in Kentucky, Tennessee, and Ohio. Why, Kentucky and Tennessee have already become the fifteenth and sixteenth states, and they say that Ohio is not far behind. A water route into those states will open up trade like nothing we've ever seen.

"Well, a treaty was signed last year between the United States and Spain, called the Treaty of San Lorenzo, which set the southern boundary of the United States and opened up the river to navigation. The Spanish had no choice but to sign it. They knew that if they didn't sign it, there was going to be war—which they could not afford.

"The boundary that they agreed on is about a hundred miles south of here. It stretches from the state of Georgia on the east to the Mississippi River on the west: along a line that the white man calls the 31st parallel. Anything north of that line belongs to the United States. Within a couple of years, the Spanish are required to be out and give up all their holdings. They will have to give up Natchez, Fort Confederation, Fort St. Stephens, and even my little trading post here. They still have Pensacola, Mobile, and New Orleans, but with the way things are going, I wonder how long that will last.

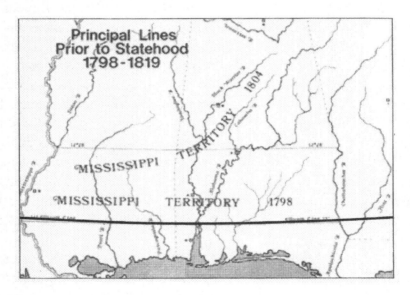

31st Parallel *makes up the North-South Boarders between Present day Mississippi and Louisiana, and Alabama and Florida*

"Since I'm French and not Spanish," Lefleur continued, "I'm hoping to work out a relationship with the U.S.: stay here and keep my trade relationships with your people going. But time will tell."

Pushmataha puffed on his pipe as he listened to his white friend. He wasn't sure what to think of this new development. He and his people had learned that competition was a good thing. With each country, there had been ups and down in the trading relationship. When trade with one wasn't beneficial, they would load up their goods and go to the other side. Often, to sweeten a deal, the traders would throw in gifts and extras to keep the Red man happy.

At different times over the past couple of years, leaders of the Choctaws had traveled to Natchez and Mobile to work out trade agreements with the Spanish and to Nashville to do the same with the United States. And contrary to what Lefleur thought, the United States was becoming easier to deal with and was giving the best trades. The Spanish, at times, seemed a little too sure of themselves. But Pushmataha still liked dealing with his friend, and as long as his post was open, he would come back.

Both sides had also introduced buying on credit, a practice that appeared good on the surface but was about to come back and haunt the Red man.

Pushmataha was also concerned about the expansion of the United States into the lands north.

"One hundred thousand white men now settled in those lands," he thought, "and more coming in all the time. How could that be? Why, there are no more than twenty or twenty-five thousand people in the entire Choctaw Nation!

"Will the white man soon need more land? Will he venture south? Even now, the Chickasaws, our brothers to the north, are seeing their lands in Tennessee taken over by farms and villages of the white man. With the new development—the land of the Choctaw Nation becoming a part of the United States—will settlement in our land be inevitable?"

Lefleur took another swig of his oka humi. "Well, my friend, if I have to close my post, I'm not sure what I'll do. Trading is all I know."

"If you close your post, you can come live with your wives' people. Become a Choctaw."

"Me? A Choctaw!?" Lefleur burst out laughing. "Why, I'm too fat to be a Red man! And besides, my skin is too thin, and my spirit is too weak!"

CHAPTER ELEVEN

THE TRADE OF PELTS and skins did not affect every animal in that land of the Choctaws. The wild boar, or razorback, continued to survive and flourish. And even in the worst of droughts and famines, his numbers increased.

The boar is not native to the Americas. His smaller cousin, the peccary or javelina, is indigenous to the southwestern deserts and mountains, but no other pig-like animal was found in the Americas until the introduction of the hog by the Spanish in the sixteenth century. Christopher Columbus supposedly released domestic swine in the West Indies on his second voyage to the Americas in hopes of providing a future food source, and De Soto was reported to have brought several hundred with him on his travels through the land of the Creeks, Choctaws, and Chickasaws. Through the years, other white men brought with them hogs as a source of meat, and many either escaped or were intentionally released in the wild.

Unlike the cow, the hog needs very little from man to survive. He eats everything and anything—roots, plants, grubs, insects, nuts, acorns, fruit, carrion, and animals that it kills. Even a rattlesnake or moccasin will become a meal if he slithers too close to a hog pen. Early settlers often allowed the swine "free range," letting them wander as they wished and running herd only when it was "hog killing time."

A strange thing happens to a hog when it is in the wild. Within a few generations, he becomes truly wild. He reverts to his pre-domestic form, with thick muscular front and hind quarters and tusks as sharp as razors. He becomes very aggressive, especially if threatened. For short distances, he is faster than a horse; and in a fight, he is more deadly than a bear. With a well-placed blow of his tusk, he will disembowel his foe or tear the flesh from his bone.

Truth be known, the American boar is not really a boar—he is a feral hog. The first true wild Eurasian boar from previously undomesticated stock was not introduced to the Americas until the late nineteenth century. Not as large or as vicious as a true boar, the feral hog is still a fearsome animal.

Three things ensured the American boar's survival while other animals were disappearing at the hands of the Red man for trade with the white man. First, the sow is a prolific reproducer, capable of mating at eight months of age and giving birth to four to ten young twice a year. Under favorable conditions, a pair can easily become thirty-two in a little over two years.

Second, its hide is worthless. The hair of a boar is coarse, and the skin thick. The bristle on the back of his neck makes a good hairbrush, but otherwise the only use of the skin is "crackling," a not so healthy snack made by deep frying small strips of the tough hide.

Third, before the introduction of the gun, killing the animal was difficult and dangerous. Arrows tended to enrage rather than kill these compact, muscular beasts. And even with the gun, the shot has to be well placed, preferably the head, to bring him down.

"I HAVE A GOOD VIEW from here," Tushtallay said as he eased around the tree and took aim. "One shot and he will be dead."

The three hunters, Pushmataha, Tushtallay, and Tenetchenna, had been tracking the boar all morning. Even before coming upon him in the canebrake, they knew that he was a large animal. His hoof prints were massive, and the large holes in the ground where he had rooted gave evidence of great power and strength in his shoulders.

Pushmataha did not like hunting boar. He hated the taste of pork. When he was a child, the Choctaws despised the meat. "Swine and chicken are dirty animals—not fit for consumption. They eat dirt and refuse. Let the white man eat them, but not the Choctaws." But times had changed. With the deer gone, pork had become one of the few available sources of meat.

There was no honor in killing a swine. Even though the boar was a fierce animal and difficult to kill, it was not the same as killing a bear or a panther. Those were majestic, proud animals, not grunters in the dirt. And hunting the boar was dangerous. Enraged or wounded, he was unpredictable and deadly.

"He has moved," Tushtallay stated as he lowered his gun. "I still see him, but the shot is no longer good. I will get closer."

"Take care that your aim is good," Tenetchenna said. "There is no room for error."

The canebrake was small, only twenty yards wide and forty yards long, running alongside a dry creek bed. On the opposite side and to the rear of the brake was a steep embankment, making the only way out where the three men stood.

Pushmataha shook his head. He did not like this setup; it was too dangerous. Each man had a gun—three shots. The muskets had to be reloaded at the muzzle after each shot, taking more time than the boar would give if the aim was not true. And Tushtallay was the only one with a good view of the beast. Pushmataha could only see his rump.

The boar was rooting in the dirt, eating grubs among the roots of the cane—either oblivious to their presence or ignoring them. It would be best to leave him now and not take a chance.

"It is too dangerous," Pushmataha said. "Let us hunt for boar elsewhere. The risk of disaster is too great."

"No," Tushtallay replied. "I have a good view now. It will be easy." He then began to laugh. "And besides, I am tired of eating corn. My mouth longs for the taste of smoked ham."

Pushmataha thought about the times he had seen the white man hunting boar. He didn't like most of his hunting techniques, but when dealing with this beast, the white man was better and smarter. He used hounds to track and flush him out. Hounds instinctively knew how to draw the beast into the open, surround him, and take nips at his rump, distracting him and giving the hunter ample time to take careful aim. Sometimes, though, the hounds were caught off guard or got too close, and the result was a nasty and sometimes fatal encounter with six-inch razor-sharp tusks. But better a dog than a man.

Pushmataha instinctively looked around for the nearest tree that would support his weight.

Tushtallay eased closer with his gun to his shoulder. He took careful aim and slowly squeezed the trigger. In the fraction of a second between the click of the hammer on the flint and the discharge of the gun, the animal turned abruptly. The musket ball grazed the side of his head and lodged in his shoulder.

The boar squealed and spun around. He bolted in the only direction he could—straight toward the three men. There was rage in his eyes as he charged. Pushmataha and Tenetchenna raised their muskets. There was no time for careful aim. The beast would be on them in seconds. They fired, but neither ball slowed him down. Pushmataha dropped his gun and lunged for the branch of a nearby tree and swung himself high out of reach of the screaming animal. Tenetchenna did the same, but Tushtallay was a fraction too slow. He grabbed the branch of the nearest tree, but as he began to pull himself up, the boar with his four tusks reached his leg, tearing the flesh from his calf. Tushtallay let out a scream as he lifted himself up and out of the reach of another swipe of the tusks.

For over an hour the three men stayed in the trees, unable to get down. Tushtallay pressed his hand against the open wound to stem the bleeding but with only moderate success. Blood dripped down his leg and onto the already bleeding boar.

The boar circled the trees, squealing and grunting. Tushtallay became weak, but there was nothing he could do. He had to cling to the tree. To fall would be instant death by the tusks of the enraged boar. Pushmataha and Tenetchenna could only watch. For them to come to his aid would be suicide.

Finally, the boar tired of the stand-off, slowly retreated, and disappeared. Pushmataha and Tenetchenna dropped to the ground, but before aiding his brother, Pushmataha reloaded all three muskets. He would not risk a surprise attack if the animal returned. Tenetchenna reached up and helped Tushtallay out of the tree. He was too weak to stand. Half of the calf muscle was gone and he had lost a lot of blood. He would survive, but he would never be able to run again.

As the two men dragged their weakened brother on a litter back to their village, Pushmataha had time to reflect. He was disturbed and felt shame for his wounded friend. To be wounded by a bear, or even killed, there was honor. But to be crippled forever by a swine—there was no honor—only shame.

What was becoming of the Choctaw people—reduced to killing pigs to live? How could this have happened? Who was to blame? Was it the white man? Was it the Red man? It was both. The white man had come with a thirst for skins that could not be quenched, and he offered goods that the Red man wanted. The Red man had a hunger for the goods of the white man that could only be satisfied with more skins. The result had been wealth and prosperity for the white man and loss of honor and indebtedness for the Red man. That was not good.

Pushmataha worried that things would get worse. But he had no way of knowing that the Choctaws would not only lose their honor, but they would also lose their land.

THOMAS L. WILEY

CHAPTER TWELVE

AFTER THE TREATY OF SAN LORENZO in 1795, the Spanish did not immediately leave. There was a transition period in which the reins of control were passed. The trading posts were straightforward. The American agent would show up, go over the books and inventory, and the Spanish agent would leave. Natchez was different. Being the only settlement of any size, Natchez and her changeover was a little more complicated. Also, there was the survey of the boundary that had to be completed.

In 1797 Andrew Ellicott traveled to Natchez to expedite the transition of power and to begin the survey. Ellicott, a surveyor by trade, was also known for his studies in astronomy and mathematics. During the Revolutionary War he was commissioned an officer and rose to the rank of Major. In 1784 he was instrumental in establishing the Mason-Dixon Line, the boundary between Virginia and Pennsylvania. From 1791 to 1792 he worked closely with Pierre Charles L'Enfant on the plans for the District of Columbia and eventually completed the plans when L'Enfant was dismissed by President Washington. Ellicott also taught Meriwether Lewis surveying techniques in preparation for the Lewis and Clark Expedition in 1803.

For four years beginning in 1797, Ellicott worked with the Spanish Commissioners in Natchez, New Orleans, and Mobile to survey the 31st Parallel, which soon became known as "Ellicott's Line."

Ellicott's Stone: the only known remaining stone marking the 31st Parallel. It is located thirty miles north of Mobile.

When Ellicott arrived in Natchez, Spanish Governor Gayoso de Lemos was still in residence, diligently working out the agreement between the two governments. Immediately upon arrival, Ellicott demanded that the Stars and Stripes be hoisted over the town—not a good idea according to Gayoso.

"I understand your desire to hasten the influence of your government," Gayoso said through his Spanish-English interpreter, "but we need not rush it. There may be repercussions. As you can see, we no longer fly the Spanish flag, but to raise your flag at this point— that is not a good idea. There is still a significant amount of misunderstanding, especially among the Choctaws. They need to get used to your presence."

"Misunderstanding? Well, I'm the one who doesn't understand," replied Ellicott. "There have been no problems reported from the posts to the east along the Tombigbee River. The American flag has been flying there for almost two years, and the Choctaws seem indifferent to the change."

"You have to appreciate the dynamics of the Choctaw Nation," Gayoso continued. "There is no one leader, no one authority to deal with. There are essentially three separate districts, each functioning autonomously. The two districts to the east along the Tombigbee have been dealing closely with your government for years; but around here, the Okla Falaya are more comfortable working with the Spanish— even though they have been known to pit our countries against each other over trade. They do not quite grasp the changes in governmental control."

"Well, the savages will just have to get used to it," replied Ellicott, who was known for his arrogance and pushiness.

THE NEXT MORNING THE STARS and Stripes was raised, and as Gayoso had predicted, there were repercussions. Rumors, most likely fanned by some of the Spanish, began to run through the surrounding Choctaw villages that the United States had come to claim their land and drive them away. The Choctaws worked themselves into a frenzy, and soon a group decided to take matters into their own hands.

Ellicott's group had camped outside the fort, and within hours of the hoisting of the flag, the Choctaws began to approach their camp with weapons drawn. Thankfully Gayoso intervened and prevented any conflict. Gayoso, along with Ellicott, met with the Choctaw leaders and eased their fears, reassuring them that the United States had no desire to take their land.

The rumors, however, were not totally unfounded. In 1801, only four years later, the Treaty of Fort Adams—the first of many treaties of secession—would be signed, transferring the lands around Natchez from the Choctaws to the United States Government.

IN THE FALL OF 1797, Fanchimastabe, the chief of the Okla Falaya, and several men of his district traveled to Muscle Shoals to trade. Fanchimastabe was now old, but he was still very wise and influential among his people—and he was a shrewd trader. For years he had pitted the Spanish against the United States and negotiated deals that seemed to always be in the Choctaws' favor. It was also understood that special gifts were to be bestowed on him at the end of the trade—a horse, a few extra blankets, a barrel of whiskey—something to let him know he was special. The traders knew that he was very influential, and if an unhappy Fanchimastabe told his people to trade elsewhere, they would.

When the group arrived, there were the usual greetings and the smoking of the pipe. Finally, Fanchimastabe and the agent began to negotiate. The American trader, who in the past always bent over backwards to please the chief, would not budge. Take the going rate or take nothing at all. And a further insult—there were no gifts—not even a pint of whiskey.

Fanchimastabe took offense, and through the interpreter he let his feelings be known. It did no good. The white man just shrugged his shoulders and smiled. The chief, who had wielded his influence for so long, felt his power suddenly leave him. It was as if his blood had instantly drained from his body. What was he to do? There was no bargaining power. There was no longer the threat to trade with the Spanish—they were gone.

The old chief settled for what he could, and like a whipped dog with his tail between his legs, left the post. Within a few months he was dead. Some say he died of old age, but most say he died of humiliation.

SIX MONTHS LATER, on April 7, 1798, a law was passed by the United States Congress that further changed the future of the Choctaws. The Territory of Mississippi was formally incorporated, ushering in an unprecedented migration of settlers from the east. Boundaries of the Territory were: to the east, the State of Georgia; to the west, the Mississippi River; to the south, the 31st Parallel, or

Ellicott's Line; and to the north, latitude 32°28'—the level at which the Yazoo River Flows into the Mississippi River (present day Vicksburg, Mississippi).

The most shocking and disturbing aspect of the Mississippi Territory: there was not a single square mile of the territory that was not part of the Choctaw, Chickasaw, or Creek Nations. And even though the Treaty of Hopewell twelve years earlier had forbidden the white man from settling in the land of the Choctaws, he descended like a swarm of locust.

Mississippi Territory 1798, by Nathan Glick, c. 1802-1809.

THOMAS L. WILEY

CHAPTER THIRTEEN

"WHOA! JEN! WHOA BESS!" Jonathan Grafton shouted as he pulled back on the reins. The two mules stopped and stood motionless as he unhooked the plow. It had been a long, hard day, and darkness was rapidly descending.

Across the field, two dark figures were bent down side by side, dropping cotton seeds, one by one, into furrows and gently covering them with dirt.

"Mo!" he yelled. "Time to quit. You and Zip come on."

Jonathan looked around and smiled. One more day like this and the planting should be finished. He was very pleased with his progress that spring, and he was even more pleased with what he had been able to accomplish in only three years.

THREE YEARS EARLIER, Jonathan and his wife, Janet, had left their home in South Carolina to journey west and seek their fortune. The decision to leave the comfort of civilization and go into the wilderness had not been easy, but it was the only decision that had made sense to them.

Born in Ireland in 1760, Jonathan had come to America with his family as a young child. Within a few years of arrival his father had become a very successful tobacco planter, providing a very comfortable life for his family. But when Jonathan was twenty-two, his father died, leaving the plantation to Jonathan's older brother. For several years, he and his brother had worked together, carrying on the success that his father had started. Jonathan married his childhood sweetheart, Janet, and they soon started a family.

After a few years, friction began to develop between the two brothers, and Jonathan realized the two of them could no longer work together. And a bigger consideration: the land he worked would never be his; it would never belong to his children. It was time to think not only about his future but about the future of his family.

He considered purchasing land in the area, but the cost was high. Then he heard about a place where money seemed to be growing on trees—the Mississippi Territory.

"JONATHAN," JANET SAID as she removed the dishes from the table, "tell me what's on your mind."

Dinner had been quiet. Their children, James, Elizabeth and Mary, had eaten earlier and were already in bed. Janet had waited to eat with her husband, a practice she did almost every night during this time of the year. It was harvest time in Virginia, and Jonathan rarely got home before dark.

"Oh, I'm just thinking," was Jonathan's response as he sat there, staring at nothing.

"That's obvious," his wife said. "You haven't said three words since you got home."

Jonathan stood up and walked to the mantle where his pipe and tobacco stayed. After he lit it and took a couple of puffs, he sat down at the table again.

"I was in town today and heard another man talking about it again. And I can't get it off my mind."

Janet cringed. Jonathan didn't have to say what "it" was. She knew. In fact, all he had talked about for weeks was "it"—the Mississippi Territory.

"Jake Stewart received a letter from his brother last week. Says he's doing really well. Cotton grows like a weed in Mississippi. He says the soil is rich beyond compare, and the bolls are as big as a fist. He's making a fortune with the yield he's getting. And there's more land than people know what to do with—an endless supply of fertile earth just waiting for the taking. All a man needs to make it rich is a strong back and a will to work." Jonathan paused for a moment. "Jake's thinking about joining him."

Janet didn't respond. She continued to take care of the dishes. She had never encouraged him in his talk about Mississippi. She had been so afraid that one day he would say...

"Janet, I think we should go. I feel it in my soul that that's where we are supposed to be. We can go there and start a new life for us and our children. There is nothing here for us."

Janet remained quiet, but she wanted to shout at him. "What do you mean 'There is nothing here for us'? You're wrong. There's family and friends. There's home and church and community. Are we to leave everything that we know and hold dear, travel a thousand miles into the wilderness, start from nothing, and probably never see our families again?"

But Janet didn't say anything. Even though she hated the thought of leaving, even though her stomach felt like it was going to give way at the thought, she knew deep in her own soul that her husband was right. She had prayed for weeks that God would tell her otherwise, but He had not. Instead, He had told to her, as plainly as if He had spoken aloud to her, to follow her husband's dream. She began to cry.

Jonathan eased up beside her and placed his arm around her waist. "We'll find a new life. It will be a good life where the land is ours and will belong to our children when we are gone. If we stay here, our children will have nothing. It's time to build a life for them."

SIX MONTHS LATER, in the spring of 1790, Jonathan and Janet loaded their wagon with their three children and as much supplies as Jen and Bess could pull, bid their families good-bye, and left. He also took with him Moses and Zipporah.

"Mo" and "Zip," were gifts from his brother. Mo was a black slave, but to Jonathan he was like a brother. They were the same age and had been best playmates while growing up. The closest white family to the Grafton plantation had been ten miles away—a two-and-a-half hour walk—making play time with boys of his own race an occasional occurrence. As they grew older, their roles changed—they became master and slave—but their friendship remained.

Mo and his wife, Zip, were good workers, and when Jonathan was making preparations to leave, he asked his brother if he could purchase the two slaves and their two children. His brother was kind enough to give them as a departing gift.

Jonathan joined a caravan of other fortune seekers as they traveled along the Wilderness Road through the Appalachians. They crossed Moccasin Gap, traveled along the Clinch and Powell Rivers, and passed over the Cumberland Gap into Kentucky and Tennessee. As they traveled, they heard tales of how Daniel Boone had blazed the trail almost twenty-five years earlier, fighting off hostile Cherokee and Shawnee warriors along the way.

The trip through the Appalachians was uneventful, so unlike stories that Jonathan had heard of earlier travelers. There were no attacks by the Red man as had occurred just a few years earlier when one hundred travelers were attacked and killed in the Cumberland Gap. There were no robbers or bandits waiting to pounce on unsuspecting pilgrims.

Times had changed, and now thousands were making the journey into Tennessee, Kentucky, and Ohio. But travel was hard and accidents and break-downs were a constant worry. The road was being improved to allow easier wagon travel, but the upgrades were slow and would not be completed for another six years. Still travel was much better than in the early days. Thirty years earlier the journey on the Wilderness Road would have taken twice as long and would have been by foot and pack horse or mule—no wagon could have made the two-hundred-mile trip. When the upgrades are finally completed, travel will not be much different that back east.

THE TEAM CONTINUED WEST along the Cumberland River to Nashville, where Jonathan was lucky and found a fur trader preparing to float his goods to New Orleans. Having built his keelboat a good bit larger than needed, the trader had been looking for other merchandise to carry and was more than willing to ferry Jonathan and his family, as well as Jen and Bess, to Natchez.

The river trip took four weeks, floating north on the Cumberland River, joining the Ohio River until it flowed into the mighty Mississippi. The rivers were high due to the recent spring rains, but again, travel was uneventful. They arrived in Natchez in early July 1798 after four months and twelve hundred miles of travel.

NATCHEZ WAS JUST BEGINNING to boom when Jonathan and Janet arrived. Several thousand people occupied the area and hundreds were coming in every year. Jonathan was surprised to see several substantial homes occupying choice areas of the town: Jesse Greenfield's 'Cherokee,' Daniel Clark's 'Hope Farm,' Connelly's 'Tavern,' and Girault's 'Richmond Hill.' But the most impressive was 'Concord,' the home of former Spanish Governor Gayoso. It was a large sprawling home set on a hill two miles out from town. Jonathan thought to himself, "One day, my family will live like that."

The first order of business for Jonathan was to inquire about purchasing land. One of the governmental agents laughed and said, "Just go find some land that doesn't belong to someone else, and it's yours."

The Graftons settled about six miles north of Natchez in a community that would be called Pine Ridge and began to carve out a plantation from the virgin oak and pine forest. After building two log cabins, one for Jonathan and his family and the other for Mo and his, the two men took on the monumental task of clearing the land.

But truth be known, they didn't "clear" the land. Time would do that. Two-hundred-year-old trees aren't "cleared" easily by two men. The towering oaks were "ringed"—a one-inch-wide strip of bark was removed from around the trunk, causing the tree to die. It would be years before the trees would rot and fall, but without leaves, the trees allowed plenty of light to reach the ground for the cotton.

Now, after three years, he had accomplished much more than he had ever imagined. He and Mo had cleared fifty acres, harvested bumper crops of cotton for two straight years, and had laid claim to another five hundred acres of land. Cotton was selling at an unbelievable thirty-seven cents a pound. (This is equivalent to $2.81 a pound in today's dollar. Compare this to today cotton which sells for about seventy cents a pound.) Within the next year, his plan was to purchase a few more slaves to help work the land. The future for Jonathan and his family looked bright.

A FEAR THAT JONATHAN HAD from early on was the Red man. In South Carolina, he had had very little exposure to the Native Americans, but in Mississippi that was not the case. The Choctaws significantly outnumbered the white man in and around Natchez, especially when Jonathan first arrived. They were seen in town, on the roads, even in the forests. Over the past three years the numbers of white men had increased significantly, but the Choctaws were still ever present.

For the most part, Jonathan's fear and concern of the Red man was the result of petty vandalism. He would come out in the morning and find his fences torn down and his cows and hogs scattered. The garden and cotton would be trampled with horse hooves. With time, this started happening during broad daylight. When approached, the culprits, usually young men in their mid to late teens, would laugh and jeer as they rode off.

Other farmers experienced this same "foolishness," as they called it, but the settlers did nothing about it. There was a fear of reprisal. These were savages known for killing, and there were a lot more of them than there were white men.

And an even bigger, more overriding concern of the settlers was that the land belonged to the Red man and not to them. Even though the United States quietly encouraged settlement and cultivation of the land, in reality they were squatters, and according to the Treaty of Hopewell in 1786, the Choctaws had every right to forcibly remove them from the land. Instead, the Red man used harassment to make his feelings known.

Jonathan had not known about these problems when he first arrived, and now that he was settled, what was he and his family to do? He, like the other "land owners," petitioned the government to take the land from the Red man and give it to them.

"MISTER JONATHAN! MISTER JONATHAN!" Mo shouted as he ran down the road toward Jonathan. "They're at it again! But it's much worse this time. It much worse!"

Jonathan had taken the day to go into town and was on his way back home when Mo approached. Planting was done, and it was time to take care of some business. Cotton prices were at an all-time high, and he was making deals with merchants who wanted to purchase his harvest, even though it was four months away. Purchasing "futures," as they called it. Also, he was looking into buying lumber to begin construction of a permanent home. He had promised Janet that this would be the last year she would spend in the log cabin.

Jonathan spurred his horse to a gallop and was home in less than three minutes. Janet was standing with the three children at the door of the cabin.

"We're okay," she said between tears. "No one was hurt."

The front door of the cabin had been ripped from the hinges. Jonathan rushed in to find the cabin ransacked with the table and chairs turned over and dishes everywhere. He ran back outside to find a breathless Mo standing there.

"Mister Jonathan, there wasn't nothin' I could do," he said as he panted." They were here and gone before I could get to your gun."

"Mo, it was probably good you didn't. The door can be replaced, but you can't. I'm just glad no one was hurt."

"They messed up the barn too," Mo said, looking down at his feet. "They killed Jen and Bess. They're just a bunch of savage heathens!"

Jonathan found the two mules lying in their stalls dead with gunshot wounds to the head. One cow and three hogs had been wounded with arrows. They were still alive but would have to be put down.

Rage filled him. He wanted to get his gun and go after the savages—kill every single one of them—but he knew all that would do was get himself killed. He calmed himself and went back to the cabin to comfort his wife and family.

There seemed to be no recourse for the settler at this point: no way for justice to be served. The agent in Natchez recommended restraint. The Choctaw Nation was very powerful, and the United States Government had little authority over them. Thankfully, there had been no deaths and no physical harm. In simple acts of vandalism, the government had taken a "hands off" policy. To try to bring these renegades to justice in the legal system would open up too many issues. Only when the land legally belonged to him, would he really have a case.

Jonathan, along with thousands of other settlers, vowed to do all in their power to push the government as hard and fast as they could to make the land theirs.[7]

---

[7] Jonathan and Janet Grafton are buried six miles north of Natchez at Pine Ridge Presbyterian Church, the oldest Presbyterian Church in the Old Southwest, established in 1807.

CHAPTER FOURTEEN

"WELL, MY FRIEND," Lefleur said as he shook hands with the Red man and then slapped him on the shoulder, "it's good to see you. I've been missing you. How long has it been? A year, eighteen months?"

The Frenchman grabbed a jug, and the two headed outside to the shade of the oak tree. He laughed as he sat down. "Why, for all I knew, your scalp could have been hanging on the belt of some Osage or Creek warrior."

Pushmataha sat beside him and pulled out his pipe. "Even though I am no longer a youth, I am still strong in battle, and I take scalps rather than give them."

"Glad to hear that. And, my friend, you may be getting older, but you still have the same innocent, boyish face that you had the first time I met you. Why, you don't look like you would know the difference between scalping and shaving!"

"The Red man knows nothing of shaving," Pushmataha said as he stroked his bare chin and looked at his friend's bushy beard, "but this Red man does know a thing or two about scalping."

Lefleur let out a hoot and lifted his jug. "Well said, my friend! Well said! And from your reputation I would say your words are quite accurate. And you are right about getting older. Let's see... It's 1801. That makes me almost thirty-eight, and I don't think you're far behind me."

Pushmataha heard giggles and laughter behind him. He turned to see several children coming out of the log cabin next to the trading post, running toward Lefleur.

"Inki! Inki! (Papa! Papa!)," they shouted.

Lefleur set his jug aside and took several of them in his thick, hairy arms.

"What do you think of my younguns?" he asked. "Aren't they a good-looking bunch?"

Pushmataha counted them. Nine children, and the oldest couldn't have been older than ten and the youngest could barely walk. Their skin color varied greatly from dark brown to pale white, and hair color from straight black to curly blond.

"Once Nancy and Rebecca started having them, I wanted more," the Frenchman said as he tussled with several of them. "And my quiver is not full yet. Ho-ke-hoke is about to have another one any day now. I guess you didn't know I took a third wife, did you? Ho-ke-hoke—she's full-blooded Choctaw. She and the other two get along really well."

Lefleur began to laugh. "I've tried to keep at least two of them with child at all times, but it hasn't quite worked out." (Lefleur would have sixteen children who reached adulthood. With the high child mortality of the time, he was probably more successful that he let on.)

After a few minutes Lefleur shooed them away. "You children run along so I can visit with my friend."

The youngest was the last to go.

"This one's Greenwood," Lefleur said as he patted the bottom of the eighteen-month-old and ushered him along.

Lefleur and Pushmataha shared the jug and pipe for a while, making small talk and catching up on what was happening.

"I had a group of surveyors come through a year or two ago," Lefleur said. "They stayed for close to two weeks, camped around my post, making day trips to the east and west, setting the northern boundary of the Mississippi Territory. The children enjoyed all the excitement, but I didn't think they would ever leave. They spent more time drinking my whiskey than setting the markers. But it worked out okay. The government picked up the bill.

"Well, when they finally set the marker on the Pearl River—lo and behold, I couldn't believe it!—they set the boundary a mile south of here. My post is not even in the Territory! I'm in Georgia!"

The northern boundary of the Mississippi Territory had been set at 32°28' because Georgia had laid claim to all the land north of 32°28' and south of the State of Tennessee. In 1804, this large area of land was reluctantly given up by Georgia and became the northern part of the Mississippi Territory.

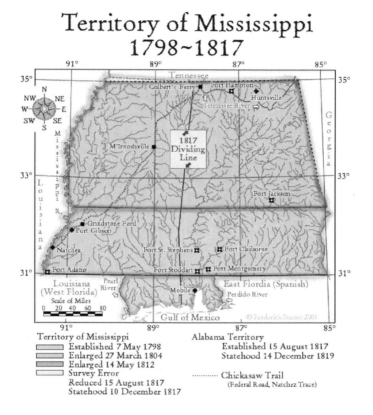

Mississippi 1798-1817

THE TWO CONTINUED TO TALK, but Lefleur sensed that Pushmataha's visit was business and not social.

"My friend," Lefleur finally said, "tell me what brings you here. I see that you have nothing with you to trade, and I know you didn't come all this way just to sit in the shade."

Pushmataha puffed on his pipe. "Tell me of this council that is to happen at Fort Adams."

FORT ADAMS HAD BEEN CONSTRUCTED by the United States Government two years earlier on the Mississippi River at the 31st Parallel. Located thirty-eight miles south of Natchez, it was the southernmost landholding of the U.S. on the Mississippi and served as the port of entry into the United States for five years. With the Louisiana Purchase in 1803, that function was moved to New Orleans, and the fort was abandoned. The story "The Man without a Country" by Edward E. Hale was set at Fort Adams.

LEFLEUR SHOOK HIS HEAD. "Push, my friend, a lot has been happening in Natchez over the past few years. I was there on business a few months ago and was surprised at how it had built up. With the area no longer controlled by the Spanish, people are coming in by the boatloads. Why, there are now over seven thousand people living in and around the town, up from less than two thousand ten years ago. And as you well know, Natchez is not the only place where the white man is coming in. In your area, along the lower Tombigbee, I was told there are close to twelve hundred people settled in."

Pushmataha was well aware of the large numbers that had settled to the south of Fort St. Stephens. And recently a few had settled farther north on the Tombigbee River, causing great concern among his people.

"Cotton is really taking hold around Natchez," Lefleur continued. "For a while the crop was tobacco, but now it's cotton. They say the rich Mississippi land is perfect for it, and the yields are two to three times what it is in Virginia and the Carolinas. And they came up with a machine about eight years ago, a cotton gin is what they call it, which makes the process of separating the fiber from the seed easier. Now everyone seems to be getting into the business of cotton.

"The demand for those white blossoms is insatiable. They can't grow enough of it. It's kind of like the deer hides—an endless demand. But unlike the deer, which can't reproduce fast enough to keep up, the cotton just needs more land—land without trees. The forests around Natchez are disappearing faster than a puff of smoke, and fields are stretching as far as the eye can see. And everywhere one looks, black slaves, planting and hoeing. I was told that there are close to two thousand slaves in Natchez and more coming all the time.

"And the influx of settlers doesn't appear to be slowing at all. In fact, it's escalating. The newspapers back east are printing stories that would make one think that Mississippi was the Promised Land, flowing with milk and honey, just waiting for the taking. Well, what they find isn't milk, but it's still white—cotton—and it's a whole lot more valuable."

The Frenchman paused for a few moments, took another swig from the jug, and quietly spoke.

"Push, my friend, the government wants your land."

Pushmataha already knew this to be true, but his heart still sank.

"That's what the council is about," Lefleur continued." They want the Choctaws to agree to give up the land around Natchez. The government wants to let the white man claim it as theirs. Their rational is that the land's not being used by the Red man anyway, so why should it not be claimed by them."

"Not 'used'?" thought Pushmataha. "What does he mean: it is not 'used'? The Choctaws have for centuries 'used' the land—hunted the deer, the bear, and the panther; gathered nuts and acorns from the hickory, pecan, and oak trees; collected wild honey from the hives of the bee. Yes, it has been 'used,' but now, no more. The land is now devoid of all but the cotton."

"The white man sees land differently than the Red man," Lefleur continued. "If there's not a fence around it or a deed to it, it's his for the taking. He doesn't understand the concept of the land belonging to the land. For him land is meant for the axe or the plow.

"And Push, my friend, I don't think you have any choice but to give in. The settlers are settled in, and they are not going to move—unless the government makes them, which I don't think will happen. If you try to fight, your people will not win. The Choctaws will disappear like the Natchez."

Pushmataha was well aware of what had happened to his brothers, the Natchez. Seventy years earlier, in 1729, the Natchez tribe attempted to drive the French from their land and attacked Fort Rosalie, located in present day Natchez, killing over two hundred French settlers and taking over three hundred women and children captive.

The Natchez did not understand the power and wrath of the white man. Within a few years the tribe no longer existed. Some were sold into slavery and shipped to the Caribbean, others assimilated into the Choctaw and Chickasaw cultures, but most were exterminated.

"And the raids that your young men are doing, tearing down fences and killing livestock, isn't doing anything but making the white man push harder."

Pushmataha was aware of the raids. These young bucks were frustrated. Their land was being taken away, and their fathers' way of life was rapidly disappearing. The hunt—the source of not only food but of honor—had disappeared. The dear and bear were gone. With the raids these boys were trying to find honor and pride, but the result was only destruction and more frustration.

"There is another thing that the United States wants to do," Lefleur said. "They want to develop an overland road connecting Natchez with Nashville, Tennessee. Their plan is to use the old Chickasaw Trail, improve it, and make it capable of wagon travel. The Chickasaws have already given their permission to begin work in their land, and the United States wants permission from the Choctaws, too. I understand that it is to be called the Natchez Road."

The Chickasaw Trail, originally a collection of animal trails running through present day Mississippi and Tennessee, had over the centuries become a major trade route for the Natchez, Choctaw, Chickasaw, Yazoo, and Creek nations. Only a path in most areas, the trail ran for over four hundred miles from Natchez to Nashville. Initially called the Natchez Road by the white man, it was later named the Natchez Trace.

Pushmataha sat in silence. A wagon road through his nation would be devastating—like a beaver dam with a breach: once the water begins to flow, it is almost impossible to stop. But what was the Red man to do?

"As well as I can see it," Lefleur continued, "there's not much the Choctaws can do but agree. My advice would be to deal with the United States as best you can, get as many concessions as you can. Come away from the negotiations with at least something."

Lefleur looked over at Pushmataha. "Who's going to do the negotiations for the Choctaws?"

Pushmataha knew that was to be a problem. There was no one chief of the Choctaw Nation. Fanchimastabe, who had for years been the best negotiator, had died, and Apuckshanubbee had replaced him as chief of the Okla Falaya. Would he have the skill to deal as his predecessor had done? There was Mingo Poos Coos, chief of the Okla Tannap—a great warrior but he was old, and his mind was not as strong as it once had been.

"The Choctaws need a strong leader," Lefleur said. "Someone with a gifted tongue and a sharp mind. Someone who will know when he is being taken advantage of. Push, my friend, from what I hear, that leader would be you."

Already, there had been those of the Okla Hannali who had approached Pushmataha, wanting him to become chief to deal with the white man. Even Tuskona Hopia, the present leader of the Okla Hannali, had offered to step down and let Pushmataha assume the lead. But he refused. He would go to the negotiations and actively participate, but Tuskona Hopia would still be chief.

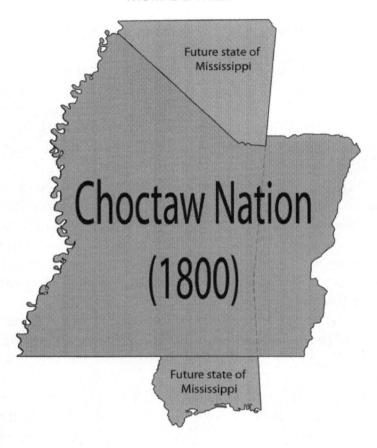

Choctaw Nation 1800

IN DECEMBER, THE TWO PARTIES met at Fort Adams to hammer out an agreement—to treaty. General James Wilkerson, commander of the Fort presided. Benjamin Hawkins of North Carolina and Andrew Pickens of South Carolina, familiar faces from the Treaty of Hopewell fifteen years earlier, negotiated for the United States. Representing the Choctaws were a number of chiefs and mingos from the three districts. Mingo Homastubby, who would soon replace the aging Mingo Poos Coos as chief of the Okla Tannap, was chosen to be the spokesman.

Before negotiations got underway, Homastubby made a plea to the gathering. "We came here sober, to do business, and wish to return sober and request therefore that the liquor which we are informed our friends have provided for us may remain in the store."[8]

Alcohol had been, and would continue to be, a problem for the Choctaws. The Red man as a whole seemed to suffer from the abuse of and the addiction to oka humi, or 'bitter water.' Whether it was a natural inborn weakness or whether it was a product of despair and hopelessness, alcoholism was rampant. Moderation in drink was not a concept, and drunkenness seemed to be the goal whenever liquor was present.

The white man took advantage of this. In all manner of negotiations, whether it was a simple trade of skins or a complicated governmental treaty, the presence of liquor made the proceedings go quicker and the decisions easier—usually to the benefit of the white man.

Homastubby's request was honored, but it most likely made no difference in the outcome. At the end of negotiations, the scales tipped heavily in the white man's favor.

The Treaty of Fort Adams was signed on December 17, 1801, and the Choctaws ceded the land around Natchez to the United States Government. This was not a small area—2,641,920 acres. From the Mississippi River on the west, it extended east for approximately fifty miles, and from north to south it comprised the entire width of the Mississippi Territory (the southwest corner of the present State of Mississippi).

Within the Treaty was the provision for the improvement and widening of the Chickasaw Trail, or Natchez Trace. Also, construction of trade establishments, or 'stands' as they were known, would be allowed along the route for the convenience of travelers and adventurers.

In return, the Choctaws received instruction from the commissioners on how dependent the Choctaws had become on the

---

[8] Lewis, Anna, *Chief Pushmataha-American Patriot*, 1959, Exposition Press, p. 48.

United States government, and until he learned how to make a living like the white man, he would remain dependent. The benevolent 'White Father' wished to send teachers to instruct the Choctaws on the ways of the white man.

In tangible payment, the United States gave to the Choctaws 'the value of two thousand dollars in goods and merchandise, the receipt whereof is hereby acknowledged; and they further engage to give three sets of blacksmith's tools to the said nation.'[9]

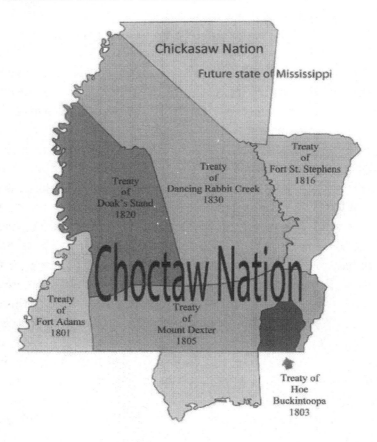

Treaties with the Choctaw Nation from 1801-1830

---

[9] Treaty of Fort Adams, 1801.

CHAPTER FIFTEEN

PUSHMATAHA WAS MOMENTARILY STARTLED when the large clock against the far wall chimed. He had been lulled by the rhythmic ticking as he and the other chiefs waited silently outside the President's office. The chime had suddenly brought him back to awareness. He and the other two chiefs, Homastubby and Apuckshanubbee, and the interpreter, John Pitchlynn, had been waiting for well over an hour to meet with the "White Father."

A man opened the door and spoke. Pitchlynn responded, and the man closed the door.

"It won't be long," Pitchlynn said. "The President will be ready to see us in a few minutes."

Pushmataha once again looked around the large room and down the long spacious hall, amazed at the President's home. "Such an impressive and ornate lodge," he thought. "The white man, or at least his leader, lives very well."

The President's Palace, or "The White House" as it would later be called, had been completed four years earlier in 1800 according to plans approved by President Washington. He left office three years before completion and never had the pleasure of living there. The second President, John Adams, got the honor, but only for his last few months of office. Thomas Jefferson was the first to be able to call it home, living there for his entire eight-year term.

EXCEPT FOR THE SHORT INTRUSION by the President's secretary, there had been complete silence in the waiting area. None of the men had spoken. All were too anxious and apprehensive, wondering why they had been asked to come fourteen hundred miles to meet with the President.

A lot had happened since the treaty was signed at Fort Adams three years earlier. The designated land around Natchez had been vacated by the Choctaws. The Natchez Trace had been completed, ushering in a stampede of settlers. Stands were springing up all along the Trace like mushrooms after a rain. At one time or another, there were over forty stands in existence between Nashville and Natchez.

Two other treaties had been agreed upon between the Choctaws and the United States. The first one, the Treaty of Fort Confederation, was signed in 1802, clarifying the eastern boundary of the Choctaw Nation. This was the first treaty that Pushmataha signed, or at least the first he left his mark on. Tuscona Hopaii was still chief, but Pushmataha was becoming more a part of the dealings with the white man. With the "clarification," the Choctaws lost another fifty thousand acres, ceding a tract of land north of Mobile. The Choctaws received nothing in return.

A year later at Hoe Buckintoopa, a treaty was signed ceding even more land north of Mobile—853,760 acres along the Lower Tombigbee and Chickasawhay Rivers.

There had not been agreement on this cession among the leaders of the three districts. In fact, the Okla Hannali and Okla Falaya chiefs had refused to sign it. Only the aging Poos Coos and Alatala Hooma, a lesser chief, were the principal signers of the treaty. Without asking any questions, General Wilkinson took the two signatures as a binding agreement for the entire nation. In return for their signing, Poos Coos and Alatala Hooma each received 'fifteen pieces of shrouds, three rifles, one hundred and fifty blankets, two hundred and fifty pounds of powder, two hundred and fifty pounds of lead, one bridle, one man's saddle and one black silk handkerchief.'[10]

Also occurring in 1803 was a purchase by the United States that would have a monumental impact on the growing nation—the Louisiana Purchase. In 1800, New Orleans and the vast territory to the west of the Mississippi were transferred from Spanish to French control in the Treaty of San Ildefonso. Shortly after taking office in

---

[10] Treaty of Hoe Buckintoopa, 1803.

1801, Thomas Jefferson began negotiating for the purchase of New Orleans from the French. He gave instructions to his envoy, Robert Livingston, to offer up to $10,000,000 to the French government for the city. Negotiations at first failed, but two years later, a cash-strapped Napoleon Bonaparte offered not only New Orleans but the entire 828,800 square miles of the territory for $15,000,000—a deal that the President could not refuse.

The Choctaws could not know the impact that this purchase of land would have on their future—it gave the United States a place to move the Choctaws when they were finally banished from the land where they had lived since the days of Chahtah and Chickasah.

IN EARLY 1804, SILAS DINSMOOR, the Choctaw agent, called a council of the chiefs of the three districts. He had very important information from the White Father in Washington.

The council was held at Fort St. Stephens on the Tombigbee River. The chiefs attending were familiar faces, but in new roles. The leadership which had been stable for so many years had changed. Fanchimastabe of the western Okla Faya, the most able and shrewd leader of the Choctaws for decades, had died a few years earlier and was replaced by his nephew, Apuckshanubbee. The aging Poos Coos of the Okla Tannap or eastern district had died only a few months before, leaving the leadership to Homastubby. Tuscona Hopaii of the Okla Hannali had recently stepped down at the insistence of his tribe members to allow the forty-year-old Pushmataha to lead the lower or Six Town District. Pushmataha had been showing himself to be a very gifted speaker and able negotiator.

THE USUAL FORMALITIES AND THE SMOKING of the pipe preceded the business at hand. As was his custom at all gatherings, Pushmataha lit his own pipe and passed it among the members.

When the pipe came to Dinsmoor, the pipe paused. Dinsmoor lifted it to eye level and admired the workmanship.

"This is a fascinating piece of art," he said through the interpreter. "It appears to be Italian."

As he passed it back to Pushmataha, he asked, "Where did you get this?"

Pushmataha did not speak for a moment but then replied, "It was a gift."

"Well, it was a very fine gift. A man would give a lot to have a pipe like this."

The Red man did not tell the agent that many had given their lives because of this pipe.

Dinsmoor finally stood to begin the meeting.

"Esteemed leaders of the Choctaws, the White Father of our nation has asked that I meet with you to bring to your attention a matter that disturbs him greatly. In fact, it is of such importance that he wishes you to meet with him personally at his home in Washington. He states that it is not a matter that can be settled through letters or through emissaries. A discussion with him personally is imperative."

He paused as the interpreter relayed his words. He casually glanced at the faces of the leaders of the Choctaws, who remained expressionless. But he knew that confusion and surprise must be raging through their thoughts.

"We will make arrangements for you to travel to see him as soon as possible."

Dinsmoor then sat down.

The chiefs remained silent. After a moment, Pushmataha stood to speak.

"We, the Choctaw Nation, are flattered that the White Father thinks so highly of us and regards us in such esteem that he would want to council with us in his home. A man of his importance must be very busy with the affairs of such a great and mighty nation. That he would pause to give us council is humbling."

Pushmataha turned toward the other chiefs and spoke to them. Each one nodded in agreement.

"We will do as he wishes. Such a request by the leader of the United States cannot be refused. We will travel to his home to council with him."

Pushmataha paused a moment. "But a meeting of such mystery is certain to cause concern among our people. To quiet rumors and to calm our people, is the very capable agent allowed to tell us the purpose of the meeting?"

Dinsmoor again stood. He stroked his chin as he paced, appearing to be deep in thought. Finally, he said, "I am able to relate that it concerns the debt that the Choctaws owe to a British trading company."

Pushmataha and the other chiefs were well aware of this problem. As the deer skin trade suffered and the Red man had less to offer, Panton, Leslie and Company, at the request of the Spanish, continued to supply the Choctaws with goods on credit. In return for this "benevolence," the Spanish allowed the British company to continue trading throughout the Spanish territories. The Spaniards had not done this out of benevolence themselves; they understood that debt meant dependence, and with dependence there was the opportunity of land acquisition.

Over the years the Choctaws had accumulated significant debt—$46,000—and once the Spanish were gone, Panton, Leslie and Company began pressuring the chiefs for payment—an impossible task. Recently the company had approached the United States, requesting that the government allow the Choctaws to give land as payment.

This development initially concerned the President greatly, but with further thought, he realized that this was an opportunity that may never come again. Settlers were pouring into the Mississippi Territory, and there was an escalating need for more land. The United States would acquire the land and pay the debt for the Choctaws.

The only obstacle to the plan was convincing the Choctaws that this was in their best interest. With a little persuasion, the President felt that the Choctaws could be led to believe that the White Father loved his red children and was willing to go to great lengths to help with the debt that they had incurred.

A FEW MONTHS LATER Homastubby, Apuckshanubbee, and Pushmataha boarded a ship in New Orleans. Not only did the three chiefs make the voyage, but a fairly large group of mingos and women joined them. Not accustomed to the white man's food, the delegation brought the women to prepare their food.

The voyage was terrifying. The confines of the ship, the expanse of water, the land so far away, and the ever pitching and rolling of the sea was more than these land loving people could stand. The Choctaws rarely learned to swim and usually stayed away from water. There was no need to swim. The rivers and streams that coursed through their lands were either small or forded easily in shallow areas. The only river of size was the Mississippi, which was crossed on rafts.

When the delegation finally arrived in Washington, their host did what politicians do best—they wined them, dined them, and flattered them. Before they got down to business there were banquets and speeches and gifts and plenty of liquor. Speeches were made to the delegation telling of the importance of the Red man, especially the Choctaws, to the future of the new nation, and how their presence in the Nation's Capital was such an honor and privilege.

Speeches were made by the chiefs with Pushmataha leading the way. Pushmataha was a very gifted speaker. His mannerisms, his intensity, and his delivery were spellbinding to his listeners, even when they could not understand a word he said. When translated, his speeches were even more amazing—poetic, with descriptions and imagery that captivated the listener. Soon this savage with the silver tongue was the talk of the town.

THE PRESIDENT'S SECRETARY OPENED the door again. "The President is ready to see you."

As the chiefs and the interpreter entered, the President stood and greeted them with a handshake, a custom the Redman had become used to.

"Come in. Come in," Mr. Jefferson said. "Thank you so much for agreeing to visit with me. I have been looking forward to our meeting for quite some time. Please have a seat."

The three chiefs took seats in front of the desk. John Pitchlynn, the interpreter, remained standing.

"I hope that your journey and your stay thus far have been to your liking. Is there anything that has not been satisfactory?"

"Your village and your home are most impressive and your hospitality is beyond reproach," Pushmataha, who had been designated spokesman, answered. "But there is one thing. With the power that you possess, would you be so kind as to calm the sea for our journey home?"

Mr. Jefferson began to laugh. "I may have some powers, but I'm afraid that I will have to leave that request to Congress."

After a few minutes of pleasantries, the President stood and pushed his chair back. He began to pace behind his desk, his hands clasped in front of him and his face staring at the floor. He stopped and looked up at the Choctaw delegation.

"Gentlemen, a situation has been brought to my attention that is of utmost importance and has the potential of destroying the good name of my friends, the Choctaws."

The President paused as the interpreter relayed the message.

"When an agreement is made between two parties, whether they are men or nations, it is imperative that both parties involved abide by the stipulations of the agreement. To do otherwise is a breach of trust. I assume that we both would agree that good relationships depend on trust, and without trust there is anarchy, chaos, and conflict.

"Now, at times a party to an agreement, for whatever reason, is unable to uphold his end of the contract, and a very difficult situation is suddenly thrust upon him."

The President again paused.

"My friends, in regards to Panton, Leslie and Company, the Choctaws now find themselves in such a situation—unable to pay their debts, unable to uphold their end of the contract. Some would say that this failure was due to uncontrolled and unanticipated circumstances beyond the power of the Choctaws—or the power of any man for that matter. Others would say that it was due to inattentiveness, poor judgment, greed, and even treachery. But you might say there was greed and poor judgment by only a few and not the Choctaw nation as a whole."

"We know of no greed or dishonesty among our people in dealing with the traders," Pushmataha said. "There may have been poor judgment and misunderstanding, but not dishonesty."

"It does not matter," the President responded. "What is done is done. The task at hand is to remedy the situation and make it right. And I must say that this debt is not only a burden for the Choctaws, but it is a burden for our nation as a whole. It is causing difficulties and lack of trust with our trading partners. The only way to make the situation right is to pay the debt."

The President reached down and picked up a paper from his desk. He reviewed it for a moment, shook his head, and looked up.

"The amount at hand is substantial: $46,000. I surmise that the Choctaws do not have it. In fact, I would suspect that the Choctaws have very little in money, and what money they do have is spread over the entire nation, hanging on the necks of warriors or buried in jars under lodges. There would be no way to collect even a fraction of what is needed."

Mr. Jefferson placed the paper back on his desk.

"After much consideration and discussion among our leaders, we wish to come to the aid of our brothers. We are willing to pay the debt, but there must be something given by the Choctaws in return. If we did not demand this, how could we require payment from anyone else who happens to find himself in debt?

"Now, the question is what can the Choctaws give in return?"

The President paused and began pacing again, appearing to wrestle with his own thoughts. He stopped and exhaled deeply.

"One thing that the Choctaws do have is land. In fact, that's about the only thing that the Choctaws have that is of value in the eyes of the white man. We are willing to use the land as payment for the debt."

"Take more of our land?" Pushmataha asked.

"Yes, but only an amount that would be equivalent to the debt. The exact size of the transaction will need to be determined."

Pushmataha and the other chiefs spoke among themselves. "Our land? All the Choctaws have is land. The white man has already taken much of it. Does he now demand more? Will this ever stop? If our people continue to give away our land, we will have nothing. What will we then do? But what choice do we have?"

Pushmataha spoke. "What you propose requires great thought and discussion. We wish to council among ourselves before arriving at a decision."

"Very well," the President said. "Take as long as you need."

THREE DAYS LATER the delegation again met with the President. The chiefs had come to an agreement. The United States would be allowed to purchase land and use the proceeds to pay off the debts of the Choctaws. The delegation also requested that a few other stipulations be taken into consideration.

The President was pleased. The next step was to determine the exact conditions of the treaty.

When negotiations were finished, the chiefs had agreed to cede to the United States 4,142,720 acres of land, extending from the Natchez district eastward to the boundary of the Creek Nation, which included the fertile lands of the lower Tombigbee watershed. This was twice the amount of land that had been ceded in the Treaty of Fort Adams, and gave the United States the lower one fourth of the Choctaw Nation. In return, the United States agreed to pay $50,500, of which $46,000 went to pay the debt to Panton, Leslie and Company, $2,000 was to reimburse claims by settlers for 'depredations committed on stock,' $2,500 to be paid to John Pitchlynn for his services as interpreter, and $500 each to the three chiefs—'in consideration of past services in their nation.' Also, an annuity was established, whereby the Choctaw Nation would receive $300 in goods each year, and each chief would receive $150 annually during their continuance in office.

The treaty was not signed in Washington. Although the conditions were set and all parties were in agreement, the chiefs felt that this was of such importance, that it was only prudent and just to return to their people and present the terms to the entire Choctaw Nation before affixing their mark, or 'X', to the document.

IN THE FALL OF 1805, a general council of the Choctaws was called to meet on Mount Dexter in Pushapukanuk in Choctaw Country, (near Macon, Mississippi). Word was sent throughout the land that the talk was of utmost importance and would impact the entire nation. For several days before the meeting, the Choctaws gathered at the appointed place, and soon there were hundreds camped in the surrounding forest.

On the chosen day, the sky was clear—a proper day to council. In the coolness of the early evening, the Choctaws gathered on the mount. Traditions of old were followed as the greater chiefs took their places along the inner circle. The lesser chiefs and mingos sat in the outer circles. Others in attendance took their places behind them. When darkness had descended and the stars had begun to show themselves, the council fire was lit. The pipe was passed, and all became quiet. Pushmataha rose to speak.

"Council of the Choctaws, I bring news from the White Chief in Washington, but first endure with me as I tell a story.

"LONG BEFORE THE DAYS of our grandfathers, there was a bird with a song beyond compare. He was a small bird, but his song was like a ray of light peaking from the clouds after a morning rain. Although the bird was tiny, he was strong. His wings were like the wind, beating faster than the eye could behold. And yet, he was frail, for his food was limited. Unlike other birds, he did not eat the insects of the air or the grains of the field. His nourishment was the nectar of the flowers. From flower to flower he would go sipping the sweetness, singing his song for all to hear. And when he sang his song, the animals would pause and watch, for the flowers were more beautiful because of his singing. All were happy.

"One day a creature entered the forest who desired the flowers of the field. He made a treaty with the small bird. 'If you will bring to me the flowers of the field, I will feed you. I will give you nectar. No longer will you have to forage in the fields and hunt for the flowers. Here, taste my nectar. You will see that it is good.'

"The tiny bird tasted the nectar and it was pleasing. He began to gather the flowers of the field and deliver them to the creature. He drank of the nectar. He was happy.

"But soon the flowers began to disappear as the tiny bird gathered more and more. The animals of the forest began to complain. 'Where is the song that we have listened to and where are the flowers that we have loved? This is not good.' But the tiny bird did not listen.

"A time came when a famine covered the land, and the flowers refused to grow. The bird had nothing to give. The creature said, "I will continue to feed you, but one day I will desire something of you. The bird, being hungry, agreed.

"Finally, the day came where the creature demanded payment. 'In payment of your debt, I demand your song.'

"'Please do not take my song,' the tiny bird pleaded.

"'You have nothing else of worth to me,' the creature said. 'There are no flowers for you to gather, nothing else for you to give. No, I demand your song.'

"'But if you take my song, I will have nothing.'

"The creature thought for a moment. 'I will have pity on you. Your song I will still take, but in its place I will leave a small voice—a hum—that others will hear only when all is quiet. The hum will be of your wings and not of your throat. And if you stop to rest, the hum will disappear.

"The creature then reached out and tore the song from the throat of the tiny bird, staining it red as blood for all to see. The song of the tiny likunklo, the humming bird, was no more."

PUSHMATAHA PAUSED AND BOWED his head. After a moment, he raised his face to the heavens and breathed deeply before lowering his eyes to his fellow warriors.

"Council of the Choctaws, I speak tonight with anguish in my heart. My voice trembles with the words that I bring from the White Chief in Washington. I come as the tiny bird whose song has been ripped from his throat. The words I speak are not good, only a hum, but it tells of what is necessary.

"The sons of Chahtah need not be reminded that they are a proud people who live by honor. In the past, the warrior found honor in the forest, hunting the deer, the bear, and the panther. He lived and hunted where he wished and was subject to no one. In battle he found honor, fighting the Creeks, the Osages, and the Caddos. To kill in battle, there was honor, and to die in battle, there was honor. The Choctaw also found honor within his heart—his character and dignity were beyond reproach."

Pushmataha paused. No one spoke. All remained silent.

"The Choctaw now finds his honor and integrity in jeopardy in the eyes of the white man. For many winters, the Choctaw traded skins for the white man's goods. The trade was good and the Choctaw was proud of his power to barter. But with the passage of time, when the skins became scarce and the ground became parched, he found himself at the mercy of the white man. The white man said, 'Take the goods. You may repay me later.'

"As with the tiny bird, the day has now come when payment is due. The white trader demands that what he is owed be repaid. But the Choctaw has no ability to repay. The deer are no more. The Choctaw has nothing of value to the white man—except land. The White Chief in Washington is willing to pay the dept for land.

"The decision now is what will the Choctaw do? Will he sell his land for his debt, or will he refuse and leave his debt unpaid? The chiefs of the Choctaws have met in council, and I now give their thoughts. The debt must be paid. If the Choctaw refuses, he disgraces himself and becomes a stench to the white man. What is more important to the Choctaw—his land or his honor?

"Not all of the land of the Choctaws will be given. He will still have much land to call his own, and the White Chief in Washington gives his word that no more land will be taken. The debt will be repaid, and the Choctaws can start new."

THE TREATY OF MOUNT DEXTER was signed on November 16, 1805, but was not presented to Congress for approval until early 1808. Mr. Jefferson was concerned that implementation of the treaty could interfere with negotiations with Spain over Mobile, Biloxi, and Pensacola. But the delay had little effect—except to make Panton, Leslie and Company and the Choctaws uncomfortable. There was too much conflict and unrest in Europe and on the high seas for this to be of concern.

THOMAS L. WILEY

CHAPTER SIXTEEN

SETTLERS CONTINUED TO POUR into the Mississippi Territory, some arriving by boat, and many coming overland by the Natchez Trace. From 1800 to 1810 the non-native population of the territory increased dramatically from 7,600 to 31,306. With the addition of the "Georgia Territory" to the north in 1804, the Mississippi Territory over tripled in size, comprising almost the entire future states of Mississippi and Alabama. All of this "new land" was Choctaw, Chickasaw, and Creek.

Most of the new arrivals settled around Natchez and the lower Tombigbee watershed, but some were venturing into the more remote, unsettled areas. A few stopped along the Trace, carving homes and farms out of the wilderness, often on land claimed by the Choctaws and Chickasaws. These illegal settlements were causing great concern among the Red man.

"MY FRIEND, I'M SORRY I missed you the last time you were here," Louis Lefleur said as he sat down under the oak with his jug. "It's been kind of busy—trying to run this post and my stand on the Trace. I was there for several weeks making sure everything was running well."

In 1810 Lefleur opened a stand ninety miles north of his post on Lefleur's Bluff. Initially known as the Frenchman's Camp and later shortened to French Camp, the trade establishment was fairly substantial with an inn that could accommodate a good number of travelers.

"I'm considering closing the post here and moving everything up there. That endeavor is becoming more profitable and needs my attention."

"The white man is always busy," Pushmataha said as he took a swig from his friend's jug and then pulled out his pipe. "Busy trying to make a buck."

"Well, when there are sixteen children to raise and educate, I have to do what I can. I've sent several of them off to school for an education." Lefleur laughed. "As you are well aware, there seems to be a lack of schools around here. I just sent my eleven-year-old, Greenwood, to Nashville. He's living with John Donley. You know him, don't you?"

Pushmataha was familiar with him. A few years earlier Donley had contracted with the U.S. Government to transport mail between Nashville and Natchez and had become a well-known and anticipated visitor at all the stands along the Trace. It amused Pushmataha how the white men seemed so excited when Donley would leave them small folded pieces of paper.

"Donley has agreed to look after him while he is in Nashville," Lefleur continued. "Greenwood's a smart one. I look for him to do great things in the future."

On one of his stops at French Camp, Donley had been so impressed by the son of the proprietor that he offered to take the young boy under his wing and help arrange for his education in Nashville. When young Greenwood arrived at the Donley home, "our little brave," as he was affectionately called by the family, could not speak a word of English. He spent six years with the Donley family, fell in love with his daughter, Rosa, and brought her back to Mississippi as his bride.

"My children are also getting an education," the Red man said. "At the school in Fort St. Stephens, they learn the white man's words and numbers."

"That's good," the Frenchman said. "It will do them well in the future. Now, how about you, my friend? When are you going to learn English? I have never heard you utter a single word in English, French, or Spanish. Maybe *you* need to attend their school for awhile."

Pushmataha snorted and puffed on his pipe. "This sheki, buzzard, is too old to learn a new song."

"Nonsense, my friend," Lefleur laughed. "You're only forty-seven. Why, most of you Red men live to be a hundred, that is, if you don't get yourselves killed in battle or drink yourselves to death."

I like my tomahawk and my jug," the chief replied.

Lefleur took a swallow and hooted, "I know what you mean, my friend."

He took another swallow, pursed his lips and exhaled. "Good stuff, this French brandy. So much better than the American ale or the British grog. But I'm afraid that when I run out of my supply, that will be it. I won't be able to get any more—what with all the trade restrictions and embargos that are going on."

The white man looked over at the Red man and asked, "Have you been hearing about all the conflicts going on with the British and Spanish and French."

Instead of saying that he was a little remiss and neglectful in staying abreast of international policies and conflicts, Pushmataha simply said, "No."

"Well, it looks like the Americans may be pulled into it, too," Lefleur said.

"My friend," the Frenchman continued, "here's what I have been able to piece together. As you are probably well aware, the French and the British have been at war, fighting each other, for at least the past twenty years. Why, some would say they have been fighting each other from the beginning of time, and I would say they are about right.

"After the French Revolutionary Wars settled down, a man named Napoleon took over France and ultimately crowned himself emperor seven years ago in 1804. He then started trying to take over all of Europe and has been doing a pretty good job of it.

"The United States has tried to stay neutral in all of this conflict, trading with both the French and the English, but a few years ago the British put up an embargo, not allowing American ships to get to France. As you would expect, this has riled up the leaders in Washington, as well as the merchants who were shipping their cotton and tobacco to France."

Lefleur paused and lifted his jug. "That's why my brandy may run out, so I'm a little perturbed myself.

"The Spanish have sided with the British on the embargo, so things have been pretty strained.

"Another thing that started happening that has upset the U.S. was the impressment of sailors. With all the war going on, the British have expanded their navy from about a couple of hundred ships to over six hundred, requiring the services of a lot of sailors. To fill the need, the British have started searching U.S. merchant ships and taking British born sailors— "impressing" them into service. It doesn't matter to them that these sailors are naturalized U.S. citizen, they take them anyway. They have even been taking natural born Americans who couldn't prove they weren't British born.

"Something even closer to home, my friend, the British have been stirring up the Red man in the north against the United States. With the expansion of American settlements into Michigan, Illinois, and Wisconsin, the British have been telling the natives that they need to revolt, push the Americans into the ocean. They have even been supplying guns and ammunition. Word is that the Shawnee, headed by Tecumseh, are trying to form a confederation of all tribes to war against the United States."

The Frenchman took a swig from his jug and continued.

"I also hear that the Spanish in Mobile, Pensacola, and Biloxi are trying to stir up things from the south, encouraging the Creeks and the Choctaws to war with the Americans."

Pushmataha was familiar with the Spanish influence to the south, but that did not concern him near as much as the tales he had heard about the Shawnee chief, Tecumseh—one of his own race—fanning the flames of battle. There were even rumors that Tecumseh was coming to Chickasaw, Choctaw, and Creek country to persuade them to join the confederation.

Tecumseh's visit did not stay a rumor for long. Only a few months later in the summer of 1811, a council was called. Tecumseh, the great chief of the Shawnee, had arrived and wished to council with the Choctaws.

CHAPTER SEVENTEEN

TECUMSEH, OR "SHOOTING STAR," was born in the Ohio Valley about the same time as Pushmataha. At age eleven, his father was killed at the battle of Point Pleasant in 1774, the only major battle in Lord Dunmore's War. Over the next eight years his family was forced to move at least five times due to attacks by the colonial and American armies.

Understandably Tecumseh's hate for the white man, especially the Americans, was great. He had also participated in the Northwest Indian War that ended with the Treaty of Greenville in 1795 and the cession of much of present-day Ohio to the United States.

For several years Tecumseh and his brother Tenskwatawa, "the Prophet," had been gathering support among the tribes that inhabited the north and old northwest: the Iroquois, Fox, Miami, Mingo, Ojibway, Ottawa, Kickapoo, Delaware, Mascouten, Potawatomi, Sauk, and Wyandot. The United States was encroaching on their land, stealing their hunting grounds through treaties and promises. The Red man was being pushed farther and farther west. It was now time for the Red man to unite and fight back—drive these interlopers from their land—drive them back to the mountains to the east and even into the ocean beyond.

The Prophet had promised victory. The Great Spirit had given him supernatural powers to protect those who followed his call and death to those who opposed him. His magic was strong. He could make circles in the ground that entering would bring instant death to his enemies.

For several weeks Tecumseh, the Prophet, and twenty Shawnee warriors traveled from village to village in Choctaw country, presenting their case for joining the confederation. He was a very gifted orator, and with his capable interpreter, Seekabo, Tecumseh stirred the hearts of a people who were seeing their rights trampled. He encouraged them to come to the council and join him as he led the war against the land-hungry Americans.

The council took place in Molasha Town, home to Homastubby, chief of the Okla Tannap. Several thousand Choctaws gathered as the council fire was lit. Pushmataha and Apuckshanubbee, as well as most of the lesser chiefs, mingos, and warriors of the nation, were present. No one wanted to miss this—one of the greatest councils in all Choctaw history.

The pipe was passed, and all were silent. Tecumseh and his warriors in ceremonial dress danced the war dance of the Shawnee. Eagle and hawk feathers adorned their heads, and on Tecumseh, long flowing feathers of the crane swayed as he danced. The steps were deliberate, depicting greatness and power in battle and the conquest of the foe.

When the dance was complete, the Shawnee warriors and the Prophet took their seats. Tecumseh remained standing, his back to the council, gazing upward into the dark sky. Moments passed. The warrior raised his hands and shouted, "To the Great Spirit of all that is, the maker of the birds of the air, the fish of the waters, and the animals of the earth, I speak now, revealing to these brothers the vision that you have given me. May my words be as sharp as the knife and as true as the arrow."

He lowered his arms and turned around slowly. Through Seekabo, his interpreter, he addressed the Choctaw Nation.

"Tecumseh, chief of the Shawnee, stands before the Choctaws in great humbleness. I address you as my brothers, united in the distant past by fathers who were once one, of the same blood and the same shilup, or spirit. The Choctaws are a great nation, known throughout the land as brave and discerning. You are slow to anger, but your wrath is great. Your words are true, and your deeds are beyond question. That is good.

"It is not necessary for me to tell you that there is great concern among the Red man. Our freedom has been trampled and is near death.

If we do not act, all will be lost. I plead with you to heed my words and join your brothers in retaking what is ours.

"Once our grandfathers—and even our fathers—hunted the buffalo, the deer, and the bear where they desired. They built their lodges and their fires on the plains, along the streams, and in the forests with no regard to boundaries. Then the white man came, claiming the land as his own. He deceived our fathers and took their freedom. No longer could they hunt and live as they pleased.

"Like our fathers, we are misled with treaties and promises. The Americans continue to take our lands, pushing us farther from our homes, banishing us from the sacred places of our forefathers. We have been reduced to poverty. Our children go hungry. Our young men have no pride and turn to vandalism and whiskey.

"Be not further deceived—the goal of the Americans is extermination—complete annihilation of our people. If you doubt me, look to the past.

> "'Where today are the Pequot? Where are the Narragansett, the Mohican, the Pocanet, and other powerful tribes of our people? They have vanished before the avarice and oppression of the white man, as snow before the summer sun... Will we let ourselves be destroyed in our turn, without making an effort worthy of our race? Shall we, without a struggle, give up our homes, our lands, bequeathed to us by the Great Spirit? The graves of our dead and everything that is dear and sacred to us?   I know you will say with me, Never! Never!...
>
> "'Sleep no longer, O Choctaw in false security and delusive hopes...... Will not the bones of our dead be plowed up, and their graves turned into plowed fields?'[11]

"Will the Choctaw and the Shawnee vanish too? Who will save us? I submit we must save ourselves, or we will be no more."

---

[11]Turner, Frederick W, *The Portable North American Indian Reader*, 1974, p 247.

Tecumseh paused to look into the faces of his audience. Everyone remained silent.

"There is hope," he continued. "Alone we can do nothing, but as a unified confederation, the Red man is strong. Many of our brothers to the north have heeded the Great Spirit's calling and have joined our cause. I come now to you, my brothers to the south, asking you to join, creating a force that extends from the wilderness of the north to the Great Waters to the south. We will make war on the United States. United we can stop them. And not only will we stop them, we will drive them back. Instead of being destroyed, we will destroy.

"My brothers, the white man is in conflict. The British and the Americans will soon be at war, and there is no better time than now to strike. The British are our friends and vow to help us. They do not desire to take our land like the Americans: they only want our trade. The British promise to give us aid, to supply us with weapons, and to even fight beside us to destroy the Americans."

Tecumseh pulled his tomahawk from his wampum belt and lifted it high.

"Now is the time to lift your tomahawk and your war club with your brothers and fight. Let the war whoop of the Choctaw warrior be heard throughout the land. I ask you to unite with us as we make war and take back our land. Together we will restore the honor and dignity that has made the Red man great."

As Tecumseh sat down, he was pleased with his oration. With the help of the Great Spirit, his words had been good. The council had remained silent while he spoke, as was the custom, but the look in the eyes of the Choctaws let him know that he had stirred their hearts and had surely won them over. He waited to see if there would be a rebuttal.

Several of the Choctaw chiefs stood and spoke, giving their opinions of the points that the leader of the Shawnee had made. The majority spoke in great support of his words; a few were more apprehensive.

While others spoke, Pushmataha remained silent; his thoughts were on the words of Tecumseh. Much of what the Shawnee said was true, but did he really believe that the Red man could defeat the Americans? Did he not understand the power and sheer numbers of the Americans? Could such a federation annihilate the white man, or would it result in the complete extermination of the Redman. To begin such a war— there would be no other end.

Finally, it was time for Pushmataha to speak. He rose and approached the center of the council. All eyes were fixed on him, for the Choctaws knew that greatness would be spoken. The words of Pushmataha were held above all others.

With authority and firmness, he began his speech as the Choctaws had done since antiquity.

"O-mish-ke! A numpa tillofasih ish hakloh!"
"Attention! Listen you to my brief remarks!"

"It was not my design in coming here to enter in a disputation with anyone. But I appear before you, my warriors and my people, not to throw in my pleas against the accusations of Tecumseh but to prevent your forming rash and dangerous resolutions upon things of highest importance through the instigations of others. I myself have learned by experience that it is unwise to engage in any enterprise just because it is new. Nor do I stand up before you tonight to contradict the many facts alleged against the American people or to raise my voice against them in useless accusations. The question before us now is not what wrongs they have inflicted upon our race, but what measures are best for us to adopt in regard to them; and, though our race may have been unjustly treated and shamefully wronged by them, yet I should not for that reason alone advise you to forgive them, though worthy of your commiseration, unless I believed it would be to the interest of our common good. We should consult more in regard to our future welfare than we have in the past. What people, my friends and countrymen, were so unwise and inconsiderate as to engage in a war of their own accord, when their own strength, even with the aid of others, was judged unequal to the task? I well know causes often arise which force men to confront extremities, but, my countrymen, those causes do not now exist. Reflect, therefore, I earnestly beseech you, before you act hastily in this great matter, and consider with yourselves how greatly you will err if you injudiciously approve of, and inconsiderately act upon, Tecumseh's advice. Remember the American people are now friendly disposed toward us. Surely you are convinced that the greatest good will result for adopting and adhering to those measures I have before recommended to you...

"It is inconsistent with your national glory and with your honor, as a people, to violate your solemn treaty; and would be a disgrace to the memory of your forefathers to wage war against the American people merely to gratify the malice of the English.

"The war, which you are now contemplating against the Americans, is a flagrant breach of justice; yea, a fearful blemish on your honor and also that of you fathers and which you will find if you will examine it carefully and judiciously, forebodes nothing but destruction to our entire race. It is a war against a people whose territories are now far greater than our own, and who are far better provided with all the necessary implements of war with men, guns, horses, and wealth, far beyond that of all our races combined and forebodes nothing but destruction for our entire race. Where is the necessity or the wisdom to make war upon such a people? Where is our hope of success? It will be but the beginning of the end that terminates in the total destruction of our race. And though we will not permit ourselves to be made slaves, or, like inexperienced warriors, shudder at the thought of war, yet I am not so insensible and inconsistent as to advise you to yield cowardly to the outrages of the whites, or willfully to connive at their unjust encroachments; we should not yet have recourse to war, but send ambassadors to our Great Father in Washington, and lay before him our grievances, without betraying too great eagerness for war, or manifesting any tokens of pusillanimity. Let us, therefore, my fellow countrymen, form our resolutions with great caution and prudence upon a subject of such vast importance, and in which such fearful consequences may be involved.

"Heed not, O my Countrymen, the opinions of others to such an extent as to involve your country in a war that destroys its peace and endangers its future safety, prosperity, and happiness. Reflect, ere it be too late, on the great uncertainty of war with the American people, and consider well, were you to engage in it, what the consequences would be. Be not deceived with illusive hopes.

"Remember we are people who have never grown insolent with success, or become abject in adversity; but let those who invite us to hazardous attempts by uttering our praise also know that the pleasure of hearing has never elevated our spirits above our judgment... Nor do we found our success upon the hope that the enemy will certainly blunder, but upon the hope that we have omitted no proper steps for our own security. Such is the discipline which our fathers have handed down to us; and by adhering to it we have reaped many advantages. Let us, my countrymen, not forget it now... It is indeed the duty of the prudent, so long as they are not injured, to delight in peace.

"Many are the schemes, though unadvisedly planned, which turn out successfully; but more numerous are those which, though seemingly founded on mature counsel, draw after them a disgraceful and opposite result... Listen to the voice of prudence, O my countrymen, ere you rashly act. But do as you may, know this truth, enough for you to know, I shall join our friends, the Americans, in this war."[12]

Tension filled the air as Pushmataha finished and took his place among the council. During the oration, Tecumseh saw his victory slowly slipping away—the fate of his own words in the balance. As Pushmataha took his seat, Tecumseh leaped forward to the center of the circle, raised his tomahawk, and defiantly shouted.

"All who will follow me raise your tomahawks in the air! Share with me in the victory over the white man!"

The sky filled with tomahawks as warriors shouted and raised their hands. Tecumseh glared at Pushmataha, a defiant sneer on his face.

As the Shawnee took his place, all eyes turned toward Pushmataha, who suddenly sprang to his feet, let out the war whoop of the Choctaw, and leaped to the center like the panther that he was. He threw his tomahawk in the air and shouted.

"All who will follow me to victory and glory in this war lift your tomahawks to the sky!"

Again, the air filled with tomahawks as warriors whooped and shouted.

The numbers were divided almost in half. Pushmataha knew that to leave the situation as is would mean civil war. This cannot be allowed to happen. The Choctaws cannot leave council divided. A decision must be reached, even if it is to follow Tecumseh.

Discussion continued. All agreed that it had to be settled, and many suggestions were brought forth on how to resolve the situation. Finally, it was decided that the decision would be left to an aged holy man who lived some distance away. This Choctaw seer was trusted by

---

[12]Cushman, H. B., *A History of the Choctaw, Chickasaw, and Natchez Indians*, 1899, Edited by Angie Debo, 1962 p. 253.

all. His judgment would be good and would be influenced by no man. All agreed to abide by his decision.

THE NEXT NIGHT COUNCIL MET. There were even more in attendance than had been the night before. But the audience was one— the aged holy man. The only two men to speak were Tecumseh and Pushmataha. All others remained silent.

When the orations were complete, the ancient seer slowly rose with the assistance of a warrior beside him. He walked slowly to the center of the council. All were silent, the air thick with anticipation. He raised his hand and spoke.

"The Choctaws shall assemble here tomorrow when the sun sleeps. Build a scaffold, and under the scaffold, fill the space with tender wood. Bring a heifer, free of blemish and two years of age. Tomorrow the Great Spirit will decide."

Again, council met. As everyone watched, the calf was slain, his skin removed, and his body placed on the scaffold. The fire was lit, and the seer spoke.

"Choctaw Nation, prostrate yourselves on the ground facing the scaffold. Remain until I speak."

All in attendance did as the seer instructed. The holy man wrapped himself in the fresh skin and began to chant and pray. This continued until the alter was totally consumed, and the fire was almost out. The aged prophet stood and threw off the skin.

"Osh Hocheto Shilup anumpulih. Wakayah ahma Een anumpa hakloh." "The Great Spirit has spoken. Rise and His message hear."

The council rose and circled close around the seer. He pointed upward and shouted.

"The Great Spirit tells me to warn you against the dark and evil designs of Tecumseh, and not to be deceived by his words; that his schemes are unwise; and if entered into by you will bring you into trouble; that the Americans are our friends, and you must not take up the tomahawk against them. If you do, you will bring sorrow and desolation upon yourselves and our nation. Choctaw, obey the words of the Great Spirit."[13]

THE DECISION WAS FINAL. All left the council in one accord. The Choctaws, under the leadership of Pushmataha, would support the Americans when war came.

The next day Pushmataha traveled to Fort St. Stephens and met with the United States agent to the Choctaws, George S. Gaines. Rumors had been trickling in over the past few days concerning the council with Tecumseh, and the Americans had been apprehensively waiting to hear the outcome. Pushmataha relieved their fears as he pledged his support, and the support of the Choctaw Nation, to the United States.

Word was also passed on to John Pitchlynn, interpreter for the Choctaws who was also agent to the Chickasaws. With his influence and the message of Pushmataha's wholehearted support for the United States, the Chickasaw nation pledged their support to the Americans. The Cherokees also informed their agent, Colonel Return J. Meigs, that they would side with the Americans. General Hawkins, agent to the Creeks, was not as fortunate with his people. It seems that Tecumseh had not finished.

While Pushmataha traveled to St. Stephens, Tecumseh journeyed to the Creek nation, where he found fertile soil for his message of hate and destruction of the Americans. The Creeks would join Tecumseh's confederation, pledge to fight with the English, and drive the white man from their land.

Several months after Tecumseh's visit, in the spring of 1812, the Creeks wished to council with the Choctaws. The purpose of the meeting was to try to sway their ancestral enemy to reconsider and join forces with them against the United States. The Creek leaders were convinced that with their persuasion, the Choctaws would reevaluate their commitment to the Americans and change their minds. They asked for a council with the Choctaws to plead their case. Again, Pushmataha held sway, preventing a reversal of the earlier decision.

---

[13] Cushman, H. B., *A History of the Choctaw, Chickasaw, and Natchez Indians*, 1899, Edited by Angie Debo, 1962 p. 259.

At the council Pushmataha not only maintained the Choctaws' resolve, but he also sought to change the hearts of the Creeks and tried to persuade them not to take up arms against the Americans. He warned that to do such would result in annihilation of the Creeks. There would be no mercy from the Americans, and there would be no mercy from the Choctaws.

As he left the council with the Creeks, he also warned his own people. The Choctaw chief emphatically stated, "If any Choctaw joins forces with the Creeks to fight against the Americans and lives to return, he will be put to death."

Pushmataha was true to his word. Thirty young warriors under the leadership of Illi Shuah, "Dead Stink," joined forces with the Creeks. Only six returned from the war, and all were executed.

"MY FRIEND," THE FRENCHMAN SAID as he and Pushmataha shared the pipe and jug, "I shudder to think how delicate the situation was. If the Choctaws, Chickasaws, and Cherokees had joined the Shawnee and the Creeks against the Americans, the result would have been a war between our races that would make Armageddon look like child's play. The Mississippi Territory, as well as the entire continent, would have been bathed in blood. The Choctaws and Chickasaws would have massacred the whites, and in retaliation, the United States would have exterminated the Choctaws and Chickasaws. My friend, you did a great service to your people and my people."

Pushmataha sat quietly, puffing his pipe. He knew that there would still be war, and that the words 'massacre' and 'extermination' would be on the lips of both the Red man and the white man for years to come.

THOMAS L. WILEY

CHAPTER EIGHTEEN

ON DECEMBER 16, 1811, THE EARTH SHOOK. The ground split open as it heaved and rolled. Terrified inhabitants of New Madrid, a small village on the Mississippi River one hundred and twenty miles north of Memphis, were shaken from their beds and fled into the dark as their log cabins collapsed. The steep bluffs of the river crumbled, dropping massive amounts of dirt into the water. The resulting tidal-like waves surged north, making the river appear to flow backwards. Streams made new paths as beds were clogged with silt and dirt; new lakes were formed while old ones disappeared. Massive trees that had stood for hundreds of years were uprooted in the relentless quake.

Damage to buildings was reported as far away as Charleston, South Carolina. In Washington, D. C., newly laid sidewalks cracked, and in Boston, Massachusetts, church bells rang as steeples swayed.

Over the next six weeks there were thousands of lesser aftershocks and three quakes of magnitude similar to the first; the last one was on February 7, 1812.

IN THE OHIO VALLEY, Tecumseh and his brother, the Prophet, gathered with their followers. "The Great Spirit has given us a sign," the Prophet said as he held his hands to the sky. "The world shakes at the power and might of the Shawnee and his brothers of the confederation. It is time for us to take up arms and destroy the white man. We will be victorious and drive him beyond the mountains to the east."

Along the Coosa River, William Weatherford, the mixed-race chief of the Creeks—"Red Eagle" as he was known among his people—met in council with his warriors. "The Great Spirit is with us. The earth trembles with anticipation as the Creeks prepare to annihilate the white man. Prepare yourselves. Many scalps will hang from your belts in the days to come."

In the small settlements along the lower Tombigbee, the Americans worried. "Is this an omen from God? Is evil about to descend upon us? We must prepare ourselves for the worst."

CHARLES JUZAN'S TRADING POST and Inn was located on the Noxubee River only a few miles from Pushmataha's home. A few years earlier, the French trader had opened the post, taken a Choctaw wife, and assimilated into the Choctaw culture. His wife, Phoebe, was Pushmataha's niece, daughter of his sister, Nehomtima, and her husband, Jean Cravat, and also the sister of Louis Lefleur's two wives.

Pushmataha frequently visited Juzan's post, sharing a drink or two, smoking his pipe, finding out what was going on in the white man's world. He still traveled on occasion to visit with his good friend, Louis Lefleur, who was spending more and more time at his post on the Natchez Trace rather than at his establishment on the Pearl River.

On August 31, 1813, Pushmataha and Juzan were sitting on the porch, fanning their faces and discussing world affairs. It had been a hot summer, humid and sticky, weather that was conducive to nothing but visiting and drinking.

A man on horseback approached at galloping speed and rapidly dismounted, almost as out of breath as the horse. He handed Juzan a paper.

"There's been trouble," the man breathlessly exclaimed. "At Samuel Mims' place. The Creeks attacked yesterday. Killed several hundred people, even women and children. I haven't been there, but they say it's a horrible sight. Mr. Gaines at Fort St. Stephens has sent me to notify the governor of Tennessee and Andrew Jackson in Nashville. This paper gives authorization for you to give me a fresh horse. I need to be on my way as fast as I can."

Pushmataha cringed. He knew the place well—Fort Mims is what it had recently been called, located a hundred miles south of Juzan's post and about thirty miles north of Mobile. But it wasn't much of a fort at all—just a stockade—an acre of land surrounded by a hastily built wall of logs buried vertically in the dirt. Samuel Mims' house, barn, and several other buildings were in the middle of it, serving as the command post for Major Daniel Beasley.

Pushmataha knew this would happen. A month earlier, several Choctaw scouts had heard rumors that there was likely to be an attack by the Creeks on the fort, but the warning had been brushed off by Beasley and also by General Flournoy in Mobile.

A YEAR EARLIER ON JUNE 18, 1812, the United States had declared war on Britain. Most of the action thus far had been in the northeast and along the Great Lakes. In August 1812, Ft. Mackinac on Lake Huron had been lost to the British. Six months later in January 1813, the Americans were again defeated by the British in the Battle of Frenchtown, where Tecumseh's confederation slaughtered sixty-eight wounded prisoners in the Raisin River Massacre. In April the Americans finally got an upper hand and won the Battle of York, taking control of the Great Lakes. On the ocean, the USS Constitution, "Old Ironsides," was showing her worth with the defeat of HMS Guerriere.

In the south, the Americans seized Mobile from the Spanish in April 1813 and set up their southern military headquarters there. Otherwise, there had been little activity in the Mississippi Territory, except for the Creeks.

For most of the year following Tecumseh's visit, the Creeks had been quiet with only isolated incidents of attacks and killings of white settlers. But tensions began to rise in early 1813 when reports came that a settlement in the Ohio Valley had been massacred by the Creeks. Suddenly attacks were on the increase.

Within a few months hastily built stockades similar to Fort Mims were springing up along the Tombigbee and Alabama Rivers. Then on July 27, a Creek war party was attacked at Burnt Corn Creek by a white militia led by Colonel James Caller and Sam Dale. The Creeks were returning from Pensacola after having received ammunitions and supplies from the Spanish and English. Initially it appeared to be a rout by the Americans, but the tide turned with an overwhelming victory by the Creeks. The Battle of Burnt Corn Creek was the morale boost that the Creeks needed, resulting in more daring raids on the poorly defended white settlers. Rumors began to circulate that the Creeks were meeting with the Spanish in Pensacola, who, with the aid of their British allies, were supplying them with more weapons and ammunition.

Suddenly settlers were abandoning their plantations and crowding their families and slaves into the stockades.

"MAJOR BEASLEY HAD NO BUSINESS commanding that fort," the man said as he waited for his new horse to get saddled. "He had no military experience. I hear he was a lawyer from Natchez who wanted to play soldier. His good friend, General Claiborne, used his influence to get him the command. And to make it worse, most of his men were Mississippi Militia, not trained soldiers."

With the war raging in the north, there were no regimental soldiers to spare. The Mississippi Territory, for the most part, had to rely on volunteers for protection. Even Andrew Jackson's thirteen hundred soldiers who finally put an end to the Creek uprising were all Tennessee Volunteers.

"Reports came out that they couldn't even close the gates to the stockade," the man continued. "It rained a few days before the attack and sand had washed up against it. No one bothered to do anything about it. They say Beasley didn't even have sentries posted. And to make things even worse, the day before the massacre two slave boys reported that they saw Red men in the forest with their faces painted. A scouting party went out to check it out and didn't see anything. The Major had those two boys whipped for lying."

The man took a sip of water. "It gets even worse. Half the soldiers were drunk when the attack happened—a fresh shipment of rum had just made it to the fort the day before. Report is that Major Beasley was drunk himself.

"But sober or not, I'm not sure they had a chance. The estimate we hear is that there were at least a thousand Creek warriors who attacked.

"I've got to be on my way," he said as he mounted the horse. "We're hoping that Governor Blount of Tennessee will call up their militia, send them and Jackson down here to give us a hand."

After he left, Juzan and Pushmataha sat back down on the porch.

"I hate to hear that—such a tragedy," Juzan said. "I'm glad we are too far away from the Creeks to have to worry."

Pushmataha sat quietly. The War of the Creeks, which he knew was going to happen, had started. It was time for the Choctaws to get involved.

"I will go to Fort St. Stephens," he finally said. "I will offer my people to help protect the white man. Our warriors are ready."

THE NEXT DAY PUSHMATAHA RODE to Fort St. Stephens and met with the George S. Gaines, who had been in charge of the trading post there for the past six years.

"We're not really sure the number of casualties at this time," Gaines said somberly. "Our scouting team says it looks like close to four hundred—men, women, and children. It's a horrible sight."

The white man doesn't know war like the Red man, Pushmataha thought. For the white man, there is the bullet or bayonet, then death. For the Red man death is vicious and ugly. There is the tomahawk, the war club, the knife—the butchering and the scalping.

"There are a few slaves among the dead," Gaines continues, "but it appears that the Creeks took most of them with them. I would suspect there were a hundred to a hundred-fifty slaves taken. There may have been some women and children taken too, but at this time we don't know." (In later battles the Creeks used these black slaves as human shields.)

"And this morning we got word of more attacks," Gaines said. "Yesterday two families near Fort Sinquefield were massacred— Abner James and Ransom Kimbell's families. They had taken refuge at Kimbell's house when the attack occurred. Fourteen were killed— clubbed to death and then scalped. I hear that six escaped. Four were in the woods nearby when the attack occurred and made their way to the Fort. The other two, a woman and her baby, were found in the house alive. She had been beaten, scalped, and left for dead." (Sarah Merrill survived the attack and scalping, and died fifty-six years later in 1869.)

"We don't know what to expect from the Creeks," Gaines continued. "There could be attacks at any time, and we don't have the manpower to resist. Fort Sinquefield, as well as all of the other forts along the Tombigbee and Alabama Rivers, are preparing for the worst." (Unknown to the two, at that very moment Fort Sinquefield was under attack, led by mixed-race Chief Prophet Francis. The settlers were able to repel the attackers, losing only two men.)

"The Choctaws will fight for the white man," Pushmataha said. "I have hundreds of warriors ready."

"I would gladly accept your offer, but I don't have the authority. I'm a civilian official. That authorization has to come from General Flournoy in Mobile. I'll go with you to help him understand how much we need your help."

THE NEXT MORNING GAINES, Pushmataha, and several Choctaw warriors began the four-day journey to Mobile.

"I haven't met this new commander," Gaines said as they traveled. "He's new. He arrived only five months ago, and I hear that he doesn't understand how things work in this part of the country."

In March 1813 General Thomas Flournoy had replaced General James Wilkinson as commander of the military forces in the Mississippi Territory. Like Major Beasley of Fort Mims, Flournoy had been a lawyer in Augusta, Georgia. When war was declared, he was commissioned a brigadier general in the United States Army and initially coordinated military activities in Georgia. Unlike General Wilkinson, General Flournoy had no experience in dealing with the Red man, especially the Choctaws. He did not understand the intricacies of the relationship and the importance of their alliance.

SHORTLY AFTER ARRIVING in Mobile, Gaines and Pushmataha were ushered into General Flournoy's office. The General was sitting at his desk, busy at work with his face buried in a stack of papers. He was a rather rotund gentleman, so unlike most men on the frontier. In the heat of early September, he was without his coat, and his shirt was drenched in sweat; his buttons were tight, barely holding in his large stomach.

When the two walked in, Flournoy continued to read for a moment, shaking his head—the stress of his job appeared to be causing him to perspire even more than the heat. Mobile had been seized from the Spanish only four months before, and even though the takeover had been peaceful without a shot being fired, the paper transitions had been time-consuming and tedious. There was the constant fear that the Spanish, with the help of the British, may try to take back the city at any time. And now, the Creek uprising and massacre, which he had not thought would happen, were causing him great concern, stressing his meager supply of soldiers and weapons.

The General looked up at Gaines, giving no notice to the Red man standing beside him. "Mr. Gaines, so glad to meet you," he said as he stood and shook hands with the white man. "You have a great reputation in the frontier. I hear that you know more about what is happening in this area than anyone else."

George Gaines was quite knowledgeable of the Choctaws. In 1805, at age twenty-one, he had been appointed factor to Fort St. Stephens, in charge of trade with the Choctaws. He had dealt fairly with the Red man and had enjoyed a good, trusting relationship with them which lasted until their removal in the 1830's.

"Tell me what you hear from Fort Mims," Flournoy asked.

"I haven't been to the fort personally," Gaines said, "but what I hear, it's horrible. Women, children, babies—no one was spared. Burial has not begun. Everyone is too busy trying to fortify their own." (It would be three weeks before a burial party undertook the grim task of caring for the dead.)

"In this heat, the bodies..." Flournoy shook his head and wiped his brow. "Blasted savages!"

"Just before we left," Gaines continued, "I got word that there were a few who escaped. Several people have been showing up at different posts."

151

"Good," Flournoy replied. "Hopefully we can get a better idea from them as to what happened."

"I took the liberty to send a note to the governor of Tennessee and to General Jackson," Gaines said. "Hopefully we will get some support from them."

"Glad you did," Flournoy said as he wiped his brow again. "If you had waited to get my permission, it would've meant at least an eight-day delay. And as you know, I don't have the manpower to police and protect the entire frontier."

"That's what brings me to see you," Gaines said. "I want to introduce you to Pushmataha, Chief of the Choctaws. He has come to offer his nation's services in protecting the settlers and fighting against the Creeks. He can have hundreds of his warrior ready within days."

Flournoy barely glanced at the chief as he came from behind his desk.

"If that is the purpose of your trip, I'm afraid you and your friend have wasted your time. I have no intention of enlisting this savage, or any other for that matter, to fight the battles of our government. My responsibility, Mr. Gaines, is to keep these savages from fighting, not to invite them to join in. We don't need another group of renegades on the warpath—no matter who they're supporting."

The General threw his hand up. "Do these savages think of anything but war?"

He shook his head, walked back around his desk, and sat down.

"You can tell your friend that as long as I'm in command, there will be no help from him or any other savage who happens to come along wanting an excuse to scalp and butcher."

Gaines was taken aback by the General's response—and glad that Pushmataha had never learned English. It was very obvious that Flournoy had no idea who this chief was or the influence that he had on the stability of the Choctaw Nation.

Even though there had been no translation of the conversation, Pushmataha realized that things were not going as planned. He began to speak: his words translated by Gaines.

"If I may be permitted, I wish to address the able chief of the Army of the United States. My purpose today is not to force my services upon the general, but I do hope that my words will enlighten him on the desires and spirit of the Choctaws. The relationship between my people and United States has been good. We are as brothers who have never raised arms against each other.

"When my brother's heart is heavy, mine is also burdened. Today my people mourn with the white man for those who were slain at the home of Samuel Mims. But I also mourn personally, for many who perished there were my friends—both Choctaw and white—who had taken shelter to escape the Creeks.

"This is a deplorable act that the Creeks have done—a deed that cannot go unpunished. The Creeks have been our enemy since the days of our forefathers and we will gladly join to avenge their violence. We know how they fight. We know their ways. We can be of great use in battle.

"Furthermore, and the most important, the spirit of war among my people is great. Our young warriors have prepared for battle. They are ready to fight. I now petition you that the question is no longer will they fight, but whose side will they join. I have held them back as long as possible with promises of joining the Americans and fighting the British, Spanish, and Creeks. But if I return with the message that the United States does not want their services, I will no longer have the power to keep my people from violence. Many will join the Creeks and fight against you."

Following Pushmataha's speech, Gaines added his own words. "General, I implore that you reconsider and take the chief's offer. I see no other choice. To refuse will mean almost certain death to hundreds along the Tombigbee and Alabama Rivers. We cannot protect ourselves. There are not enough forces, and as you know, they are spread too thin. Fort Mims will only be the beginning of the carnage that will take place."

General Flournoy rubbed his forehead. "Mr. Gaines, my mind is made up. We do not need the services of the Choctaws. We will manage. We can anticipate help from Tennessee within a few weeks..."

"But..." Gaines interrupted.

"No," the General said, "We will do it ourselves. And besides, once you let these savages start fighting each other, there would be no stopping it. We would have absolutely no control over what happens—it would be total anarchy."

"Sir, you underestimate the leadership of Pushmataha."

THE RIDE BACK TO FORT ST. STEPHENS was quiet, both men in deep thought. Pushmataha was concerned with how the message would be received by the Choctaw Nation. He knew that his leadership was in the balance. What could he say or do that would prevent his young warriors from revolting? They were too ready for war to listen to reason, no matter how logical the argument. Pushmataha remembered those days of his own youth when the reason to fight was to fight. There was no thought of the future.

And for these young warriors, there were few chances of war. Unlike the days of his youth and the days of his forefathers, the nations were no longer in perpetual battle. The ability to prove oneself in battle, to become a real warrior, was disappearing—the result of the "civilization" of the white man. They longed to experience the glory of war, either in victory or in death, which their ancestors had known for generations.

But he would hold strong and not waiver. He would not go back on his word and fight against the United States. To do so would mean total annihilation of his people. It was a war that could not be won, and he could not be a part of it.

Gaines was also worried, but it was about the survival of the white man in the Mississippi Territory. The concern now was not only of attacks from the Creeks, but also from the Choctaws. No white settlement could withstand their combined onslaught, with or without the aid of General Jackson and the Tennessee Militia. Hopefully the Choctaws could be placated, at least until Jackson arrived. Surely, he would see the importance of a Choctaw alliance and override Flournoy's decision. Jackson was a fighting soldier, not a desk soldier.

When Gaines and Pushmataha arrived at Fort St. Stephens, an anxious crowd of Choctaws and white settlers had gathered in anticipation of the report from Mobile. None suspected that the offer that Pushmataha had given had been refused. Both men feared what the response would be.

Here along the Tombigbee, the white man and the Choctaws had learned to trust each other. They depended on each other, traded with each other, and shared life. Intermarriage had become very common, blurring the racial barriers. Now, word was to be delivered that could possibly tear these bonds apart.

The two men dismounted, and after greetings, Pushmataha addressed the crowd.

"MANY MOONS AGO, when the animals spoke—before the Great Spirit took their words and gave them to man—a fox came to a stream. The rains had been heavy. The water was swift and high, flowing over sharp rocks and forming great whirlpools before disappearing as a waterfall and crashing to the boulders below. As the fox approached, he saw his friend, the bobcat, clinging to a branch in the middle of the stream. The waters were rising, soon to overtake his friend and sweep him away.

"'Bobcat,' the fox yelled over the loudness of the flowing water, 'how did you get yourself in such a predicament? You have always feared the water and never learned to swim. I am surprised to see you there.'

"'What does it matter how I got here,' the bobcat replied as he clung tightly to the branch, 'I am in trouble and will be swept away if no one helps me.'

"'I will help,' the fox said. 'Reach for my hand, and I will pull you to the bank.'

"The bobcat eyed his friend with suspicion. 'No. Another bobcat who is my brother will come by soon, and he will save me. I will wait for him. I do not need your help.'

"The fox was surprised at the bobcat's words. He looked in all directions, as far as he could see, but he saw no one. The water was now at the bobcat's waist and rising, pulling hard to tear him from his hold.

"'Your brother is not near and soon it will be too late. Let me help you.'

"'No. I will wait.'

"'But why?' the perplexed fox asked.

"'I do not trust you. You do not wish to help me. You wish to devour me.'

"'You are mistaken,' the fox cried out. 'We have always been friends. We have walked together and hunted together. We have feasted at the same table and shared the same lodge. Have I ever tried to harm you in the past? Why do you suspect me of treachery today?'

"'The fox is sly,' the bobcat said. 'He waits for a time when I am at a disadvantage. Then he forgets our friendship.'

"'No, you are wrong.'

"The water was now at the bobcat's shoulders.

"'Reach for my hand! Or you will most surely die!'

"'No. I had rather risk death, waiting for my brother, than to use your help.'"

Pushmataha paused and surveyed the crowd. In the eyes of the Choctaws he saw perplexity and anger. In the eyes of the white settlers there was panic and fear.

As Pushmataha was about to speak again, a man on horseback approached the crowd at galloping speed waving a letter high above his head. He dismounted and handed the letter to Gaines.

"This is a message from General Flournoy," he said. "I had hoped to catch up with your party before you reached Fort St. Stephens."

Gaines read the letter and sighed in relief. "The General has reconsidered. He wishes to enlist the aid of the Choctaws in protecting our settlements and in battling the Creeks."

As the crowd cheered, Pushmataha raised his hand and shouted, "Sia Hoka!" "This is good!"

AFTER PUSHMATAHA AND GAINES had left Mobile, several of the seasoned officers had met with the General and were able to convince him that his decision was foolish. The Choctaw Nation was a powerful force in the area and their alliance was imperative. Without them, the defense of the frontier would be almost impossible, and the possibility of the Choctaws fighting against them was unthinkable. Pushmataha was known throughout the Territory as a man of utmost integrity and could be trusted to lead his people to the benefit of the United States.

IT WAS NOW TIME FOR WAR. Following the traditions of old, council was called for the entire nation to be apprised of the situation. The Choctaws must be united. There could be no dissention. Soon several thousand Choctaws gathered, including the chiefs of the other two districts, Homastubby and Apuckshanubbee. After the smoking of the pipe, Pushmataha rose to speak.

"The English people across the water have provoked the war with our good father, the President. The English agents for many moons have poisoned the minds of the Northern Indians, persuading most of them to aid in the war against our Virginia friends. Emissaries of the Northern tribes have been amongst us, but they have made little impression; however, they have succeeded in persuading the Creeks to go to war. Many of our friends of the Tombigbee have been murdered by them. Fort Mims over the river where some of our friends gathered has been destroyed and several hundred persons killed...

"President Washington advised us long ago not to engage in war; he advised us to remain quietly at home tending to our peaceful occupations, as he would always be able to fight his battles. But what man and warrior can be idle at home and hear of his friend being butchered around him? I am a Choctaw, and I am a warrior.

"I will not advise you to act contrary to the advice of our good father, but I will go and help my friends. If any of you think proper to follow me voluntarily, I will lead you to victory and glory."[14]

Suddenly every man and boy was on his feet, raising his tomahawk and shouting, "I will follow Pushmataha. I, too, am a Choctaw and a warrior."

"Sia Hoka," the chief replied. "This is good."

---

[14] Leftwich, G. J., *Colonel George S. Gaines and Other pioneers in the Mississippi Territory*, Publications of the Mississippi Historical Society, Vol. I, Centenary Series, 1904, p 442.

CHAPTER NINETEEN

"WELL, IT'S GOOD to finally meet the great chief of the Choctaws," General Jackson said through his interpreter as he shook hands with Pushmataha. "I have heard nothing but great things about you."

In early October 1813 Andrew Jackson and a force of thirteen hundred Tennessee Volunteers had left Nashville. Governor Willie Blount had commissioned a force of twenty-five hundred, but Jackson could not wait until the full contingency had been enlisted. It was time to get going and put a stop to this uprising. He would show the Creeks, as well as every other tribe of the Red man in the country, the price of revolt.

ANDREW JACKSON, WHO WOULD later become the seventh President of the United States, was born in 1767, the youngest of three boys to Scots-Irish immigrants. His father died a few weeks before his birth, leaving his mother to fend for herself and her three small children in the wilderness of western South Carolina.

At age thirteen, Andrew enlisted with his two brothers in the Continental Army and was captured along with his brother, Robert, by the British at the Battle of Hanging Rock. Already stubborn and unyielding, Andrew was beaten with a sword and nearly killed by an officer for refusing to polish his boots. While prisoners, the two brothers almost starved to death, and both contracted smallpox, resulting in Robert's death and Andrew being physically scarred. His other brother also died while in service, and his mother died within a year, leaving him orphaned and with no family at age fourteen. His experiences led to an intense hatred for the British.

In the late 1780's, he studied law, moved west into what would be Tennessee, and practiced law in the often rough and lawless frontier.

In 1796 Jackson was appointed a delegate to the Tennessee Constitutional convention, and when Tennessee became a state in 1797, he was elected to the U.S. House of Representative and later to the Senate. In 1804 he purchased a plantation near Nashville, built his home, the Hermitage, and became a successful cotton planter.

In 1801, Jackson's road to fame began when he was appointed commander of the Tennessee militia. He soon developed a reputation as a very stern, capable leader, earning the nickname, "Old Hickory." To the Red man, though, he was known as "Sharp Knife," for the saber that he always wore.

When Jackson had heard that the Choctaws had been enlisted to fight the Creeks, he was very pleased. His soldiers were militia, not regulars, and even though some like Davy Crockett and Sam Houston would show themselves to be great military leaders, his men were for the most part back-woods farmers and woodsmen. Jackson knew that vicious fighting would be essential to bring a swift end to the Creek uprising, and the Choctaws, as well as the Cherokees and Chickasaws, were just who he needed.

Also, Jackson's ultimate goal—after defeating the Creeks—was to march on to Pensacola and take the city. With the capture of Mobile the year before, Pensacola was the last stronghold of the Spanish and English on the Gulf coast. Pushmataha and the Choctaws would prove to be of great benefit in that campaign.

"I AM BUT ONE OF THREE CHIEFS of the Choctaw Nation," Pushmataha replied, "but I have been chosen to lead our warriors into battle against the Creeks."

"Very good. Very good," the General said.

The chief invited Jackson to partake of the pipe. The two sat down, and Pushmataha pulled out his pipe, lit it, took a puff, and passed it to Jackson.

Jackson held the pipe up and admired it. "This is a magnificent piece of work. This obviously is not the typical pipe of the Red man."

"It was given to my father many winters ago by a white man who visited my village. It is of great value to me."

"I would say so," the General said as he took a puff. "It would be of great value to a lot of white men back east. I would suspect that someone would pay a nice price for such a prize."

"A high price has already been paid for it," Pushmataha replied.

"It pleases me greatly that your people have chosen to come to the aid of the United States," Jackson said. "For the past several weeks, you have provided a great service in protecting the settlers. Now we look forward to taking the offensive and defeating the Creeks. With your help the Creeks will be no more."

Pushmataha remained stoic, but within he winced. The Creeks were mortal enemies and had been for generations. But there were those of the Creek nation who did not support the uprising. In the area closest to Mobile, along the lower Alabama River, the Creeks had refused to join the more radical, northern faction—the "Red Sticks" as they were called because of the red color applied to their war clubs. Many of the sympathetic Creeks, like the Choctaws, were trying to embrace the white man culture, and intermarriage had become common. In fact, some who had been killed at Fort Mims were sympathetic full-blooded and mixed-race Creeks.

"The Choctaws look forward to being of service to the great General Sharp Knife and to the White Chief in Washington. But does the General know that there are some among the Creeks who do not share the vision of the northern Creeks and wish to remain at peace with the United States."

"Yes, I've done my homework," the General responded. "We will take that into account."

Pushmataha wondered to himself, what does he mean by 'take it into account?'

Jackson continued, "I have heard that the Red Sticks have concentrated their resources on the Alabama River one hundred and sixty miles northeast of here—a place that they are calling their 'Holy Ground.'"

Pushmataha had heard the same. "Holy Ground,"—"Econochaca"—or "Beloved Ground," had been constructed on a high bluff overlooking the Alabama River in the summer of 1813 as a sacred gathering place for the Creeks. It consisted of several hundred lodges and a large store of supplies, surrounded by stakes and fortifications. It was from this encampment that the Red Sticks had come when Fort Mims was attacked.

"I want you and your warriors to join General Claiborne and the Mississippi Militia in destroying that stronghold. It is in such a remote area that I don't think he could find it, much less offer an effective campaign, without your help. If we can accomplish that goal, stab them in the heart and demoralize them, the war is ours."

As they finished their meeting and stood, General Jackson grimaced and held his left shoulder.

"Is Sharp Knife in pain?" asked the chief.

"Oh, it's nothing. Just a bullet wound."

One month earlier, Andrew Jackson, known for his short temper and readiness to fight anyone for any reason, had been wounded in a street fight with the Benton boys in Nashville. His left shoulder had been shattered by a bullet, and he had lost a significant amount of blood. The injury was so great that the physicians involved in his care recommended amputation. Jackson refused. For three weeks he was bed ridden near death, but a week later he was on his way to fight the Creeks. The bullet was finally removed twenty-nine years later by Dr. Thomas Harris, chief of the Navy's Bureau of Medicine, while the President lay on the dining room table of the White House. Under no anesthesia, as none was available at the time, a small incision was made over the bullet, and with a little pressure, it popped out. (Many joked that Jackson had so many pieces of lead in his body from all his duels that he rattled when he walked around.)

AS THE TWO MEN PARTED, the General said, "Push, my friend, if you ever want to get rid of that pipe, I'll be glad to purchase it from you."

"The pipe is not for sale. I will carry it until I die."

IN EARLY NOVEMBER 1813, General Ferdinand L. Claiborne, accompanied by almost a thousand Mississippi Militia and several hundred Choctaw warriors under the leadership of Pushmataha, left Fort St. Stephens traveling northeast. Between Fort St. Stephens and Econochaca there was nothing but a vast forest. There were no military outposts, no supply stations—only wilderness. Winter came early, and travel was slow. Several outposts were established on the way to provide a supply line, Fort Claiborne being the most substantial.

Finally in mid-December, they reached the encampment. The Creeks were well aware of the advancement of the Americans and Choctaws, and ushered their women and children to a safe place. Prophet Francis, the Holy Man, filled the area with his magic, creating a circle around the Holy Ground that would bring death to the enemy if they entered and cause their bullets to fall to the ground. The leader of the Red Sticks, mixed-race William Weatherford, or Red Eagle, prepared his warriors for battle.

WILLIAM WEATHERFORD WAS an unlikely leader of the Creek uprising. The son of a prosperous Scots trader and Princess Sehoy III, daughter of the chief of the Clan of Wind and granddaughter of a Frenchman, Weatherford had appeared to embrace the white man's culture. He had been reared in the ways of the white man on his father's cotton plantation on the Alabama River. He dressed and acted the part of the white man, and with his thick reddish-blond hair, he was for all practical purposes white. When Tecumseh made his plea for the Creeks to join his confederation, Weatherford had spoken against him.

At some point, possibly from the influence of his cousin, Holy Man and mixed-race Prophet Josiah Francis, Weatherford joined the insurrection, leading his nation against the white man. He was the instigator of the Fort Mims Massacre.

"WE WILL ATTACK FROM THREE SIDES with the river behind them to prevent a retreat," General Claiborne said as he squatted down and pointed to a map hastily drawn in the dirt. "As you know, there is no surprise. They would have to be blind and deaf to not know we are here."

It was December 23, 1813. The weather had turned cold, and a freezing drizzle was beginning to fall. The American forces were within a mile of the Holy Ground. Colonel Joseph Carson and the Mississippi Territorial Volunteers were assigned to attack from the right. General Claiborne would command the Third Regiment in the center, and Major Benjamin Smoot with the Mississippi Militia and Pushmataha's warriors would comprise the left. Major Cassel's Calvary Battalion would take up a position along the river to prevent the enemy from escaping there.

"I don't want a single one of those savages to escape," Claiborne continued. "We will all take our positions before the attack, thus preventing any avenue of retreat. No one is to jump the gun."

The General stood up. "Our battle cry will be 'Remember Fort Mims.'"

A mile away in the center of Holy Ground, several hundred Creek warriors stood before their leader and their Holy Man. Excitement and anticipation shown in their painted faces as they held their tomahawks high.

"The Creeks have nothing to fear," Prophet Francis told his people, his hands raised to the heavens. "The Great Spirit will give us victory. Take up your tomahawk and war club. Fight without worry. The white man's weapons will not harm you."

The Creeks were some of the most superstitious of the tribes. Their holy men held great power and position, and their magic was not questioned.

As Carson's men approached their assigned position on the right, they were suddenly met with gunfire followed by a barrage of arrows. A group of Creek warriors had taken up a position outside their fortification, hiding behind a steep embankment. Carson's Militia returned fire and slowly advanced. As they moved forward, a Creek Holy Man leaped to the top of one of the barricades surrounding the Holy Ground, shrieking and dancing, waving a cow's tail in each hand. One of Carson's men took aim and felled him with one shot.

Suddenly shouts of fear came from the fortification. "A Holy Man has fallen! Where is our protection? We shall all die!"

The Creek warriors had been so convinced by Prophet Francis that the weapons of the white man would be rendered useless and that none of them would be harmed, that they were demoralized. Many dropped their weapons and ran in the opposite direction.

By the time Major Smoot and Pushmataha gained their position on the left, hundreds of Creeks had already escaped. William Weatherford—Red Eagle—was left with only thirty Creeks warriors to defend Holy Ground.

Pushmataha and his two hundred warriors breached the barricades and descended on the remnant of warriors, wheeling their tomahawks and war clubs with precision. The Creeks fought bravely, but their efforts were futile. As they fell one by one, William Weatherford found himself alone. The cause was lost. There was no hope of victory. He mounted his horse, Arrow, but there was nowhere to go. Before him were a thousand of his enemy—behind him a twenty-foot drop into the freezing Alabama River.

Pushmataha, with his tomahawk raised high, rushed toward the Creek chief. Weatherford, appearing to fight to the end, spurred his gray steed forward as if he would meet the Choctaw and run him down. But suddenly he turned around, spurred his mount again, and raced toward the edge of the cliff. The horse and his rider leaped off the bluff, plunging into the frigid waters below. With his rifle held high above his head, Weatherford and his horse swam through a hail of gunfire and arrows and emerged on the opposite bank of the river. Red Eagle dismounted, and, being the fine horseman that he was, he checked to make sure Arrow was not injured, remounted, and sped away.

William Weatherford's leap at the Battle of Holy Ground

THIRTY-THREE SCALPS WERE taken that day. Holy Ground was plundered and then burned. Only one soldier was killed—Ensign James Luckett. No Choctaws were lost.

The battle was a great morale boost for the American forces. Other battles of the Creek War—Tallushatchee, Talladega, Autossee, Emuckfau, Entochopco, and Calabee Creek—saw greater loss of life, but none did more to demoralize the Creeks than the Battle of Holy Ground—until the Battle of Horseshoe Bend.

CHAPTER TWENTY

"GENTLEMEN, TOMORROW WE WILL destroy the Red Sticks," General Jackson said to his men. "At the end of the day, they will be no more."

It was March 26, 1814. Six miles from General Jackson's camp over a thousand Creek warriors and three hundred and fifty women and children had gathered on the horseshoe bend of the Tallapoosa River. Winter had been harsh, and many had little food and clothing. Two hundred lodges had been built on the one-hundred-acre crescent, and to protect their village, called Tohopeka, an eight-foot-tall log barricade had been constructed, stretching for four hundred yards across the neck of the horseshoe.

The surrounding water and logs would make for an almost impenetrable barrier to an attack—or a horrific impendence to escape.

At the makeshift American camp, three thousand three hundred had gathered—two thousand infantry consisting of Tennessee Militia and the Thirty-ninth U.S. Infantry under Jackson's command, seven hundred mounted soldiers under General John Coffee, and six hundred Cherokee, Choctaw, and friendly Creek warriors.

The American forces attacked mid-morning on March 27, 1814, and the battle—or rather the slaughter—lasted until late afternoon. At the end of the day, over eight hundred Creek warriors had been killed. Five hundred and fifty-seven lay dead on the peninsula, and another three hundred were floating dead in the Tallapoosa River, shot in the back as they tried to escape. Years later Davy Crockett commented that it was "like shooting dogs." Only two hundred Red Sticks survived. Thirty-two Americans and twenty-three allied Native Americans died in the attack.

THE MASSACRE AT FORT MIMS and the Battle of Horseshoe Bend stand as the two largest massacres in the history of the Americas—Fort Mims: the greatest massacre of the white man by the Red man; Horseshoe Bend: the greatest of the Red man by the white man. No other battle between the white man and the Red man ever came close.

A FEW WEEKS AFTER THE BATTLE of Horseshoe Bend, a man with reddish-blonde hair, dressed in the clothes of a successful planter, rode into Fort Jackson on a gray steed. He inquired of a soldier where he might find General Andrew Jackson.

The soldier, half looking up, pointed to a tent and said, "Over there," and went about his business.

The man dismounted and walked his spirited horse to the tent. As he tied him to a post, the man could be heard saying, "Settle down, Arrow. Easy now."

General Jackson was sitting at a make-shift desk and looked up as the man entered. A look of confusion was on the General's face at this unexpected intrusion, but it was soon replaced by one of familiarity and amusement.

"Well, well, you must be Bill Weatherford. It appears that we have you at last!"

Fearlessly the warrior replied. "If you give me any insolence, I will blow a ball through your cowardly heart."

The amusement on the General's face changed to anger. "How dare you, sir, to ride to my tent, after having murdered the women and children at Fort Mims?"

"General Jackson," Weatherford said firmly, "I am not afraid of you. I fear no man, for I am a Creek warrior. I have nothing to request in behalf of myself; you can kill me, if you desire. But I come to beg you to send for the women and children of the war party, who are now starving in the woods. Their fields and cribs have been destroyed by your people, who have driven them to the woods without an ear of corn. I hope that you will send out parties, who will safely conduct them here, in order that they may be fed. I exerted myself in vain to prevent the massacre of the women and children at Fort Mims. I am now done fighting. The Red Sticks are nearly all killed. If I could fight you any longer, I would most heartily do so. Send for the women and children. They never did you any harm. But kill me, if the white people want it done."[15]

The General's heart softened, and he invited the warrior to share a bottle of brandy with him. For most of the afternoon the two men visited. Jackson learned that Weatherford had indeed instigated the attack at Fort Mims, but his plan was not to harm women and children. In the heat of the battle, his warriors had gone far beyond what he had instructed, and with all the persuasion he could muster, he could not prevent their deprivation. Jackson also learned that starvation among the Creeks was rampant, and that Weatherford's wife had died in a refugee camp shortly after the Battle of Holy Ground. His only wish now was to stop the fighting and to work for the survival of his people.

Jackson was so impressed with the bravery and integrity of the warrior that he let him go. Weatherford participated no more in the war, except to influence the Creeks to surrender.

OVER THE NEXT FOUR MONTHS, the Creek Red Sticks continued to battle, but their war was over. Estimates are that close to three thousand Creek warriors died during the uprising, and an unknown number of women, children, and elderly succumbed to starvation and exposure—both during and after the war.

Finally on August 9, 1814, the Treaty of Fort Jackson was signed ending the conflict.

"Articles of agreement and capitulation made...between Major General Andrew Jackson on behalf of the President of the United States and the Chiefs of the Creek Nation.

"Whereas, an unprovoked, inhuman, and sanguinary war, waged by the hostile Creeks... against the peace, the property, and the lives of citizens of the United States and those of the Creek nation in amity with her, at the mouth of Duck River, Fort Mims, and elsewhere..."[16]

---

[15] Pickett, Albert James. History of Alabama, 1851.

The Creek nation ceded twenty million acres to the United States. The chiefs in attendance were all "friendly" Creeks who had sided with the United States. The Red Stick chiefs were either dead or in hiding.

The chiefs protested the terms of the agreement as being grossly unfair—that the entire nation was being punished for the sins of the renegades—but it made no difference. In Jackson's eyes, they were all the same. The Creeks were also forbidden to have any contact, trade or otherwise, with the British or Spanish. The only concession in favor of the Creeks was article 7: "The Creeks being reduced to extreme want, etc., the United States, from motives of humanity, will continue to furnish the necessities of life until crops of corn can yield the nation a supply, and will establish trading posts."[17]

The terms of the Treaty were very troubling to Pushmataha.

"Where is the reward of loyalty in the eyes of the white man?" he thought. "Yes, the Creeks are the enemy of the Choctaws, but for the past year my warriors have fought side by side with many Creeks who have chosen to side with the Americans. What did they gain? By all appearances, the United States just brushed them aside. For the friendly Creeks, was this civil war totally in vain? Does no one take into account the suffering and deaths that they have experienced at the hands of their brothers in support of the white man?

"And what can the Choctaws expect if we are ever faced with a similar conflict?" he pondered. "Will the white man's justice in dealing with the Choctaws also be blind to loyalty?"

---

[16] Treaty of the Creeks (Fort Jackson), 1814.
[17] Treaty of the Creeks (Fort Jackson), 1814.

Major Sites of the Creek War

AT THE CLOSE OF THE CREEK WAR, Pushmataha was unofficially promoted to Brigadier General by Andrew Jackson. His leadership and daring—as well as the courage of his warriors—had played such a significant role it the success of the campaign, that Jackson wished to honor him. The chief was presented with a uniform, replete with gold epaulettes, a sword, silver spurs, and a hat with an ostrich feather. Rumor was that Jackson had paid close to three hundred dollars for the outfit.

Pushmataha wore the uniform only once, then meticulously folded it up and placed it in safe keeping. Years later, when disillusionment with his friend, General Jackson, was great, the warrior took the uniform from its place of honor, tied a rope around it, and dragged it through the dirt of his village. As the somewhat inebriated chief walked through the village with his unusual train, he stopped at each lodge, shot the nearest chicken with his bow, and stuffed the feathered trophies under his belt. As would be expected, no one had any idea what was unfolding, but knowing their chief, they waited in anticipation to see what would happen. When his belt was full, he enlisted someone to clean his catch and invited everyone to a feast. At the conclusion of the feast, Pushmataha left the once honored gift beside the cooking fire with the bones and entrails.

CHAPTER TWENTY-ONE

"PUSH, MY FRIEND, we are not finished," General Jackson said. "I still need your help. Pensacola needs to be taken."

The war with the Creeks was over, but the war with Britain was not. On August 24, 1814, two weeks after the Treaty of Fort Jackson was signed, the city of Washington was invaded by British troops. Governmental buildings, including the White House, were burned and the Union Jack was hoisted over the city. President James Madison and First Lady Dolly escaped into the countryside, thankfully with Gilbert Stuart's painting of George Washington under her arm. On September 13, Fort McHenry in Baltimore Harbor was successfully defended from British bombardment, inspiring Frances Scott Key to write *The Star-Spangled Banner*.

Also in September, the United States Navy gained a huge victory when it defeated a much larger British force at the Battle of Lake Chaplain, securing her northern borders. But the British were still very active in the waters of the Gulf of Mexico.

"Pensacola is the last stronghold for the British in the southwest," Jackson continued. "Even though their fort is under Spanish control, and even though we are not officially at war with Spain, the British are using it as an arsenal, and they have to be stopped. It's a very tricky diplomatic problem—not drawing the Spanish officially into the war—but I think we should be able to do it."

Pushmataha was hesitant about committing to further battle. Fighting the Creeks had been good for his warriors. They had experienced victory in battle and had brought honor on their nation. But this would be different—getting involved with the white man fighting the white man—it could damage any further dealings with the Spanish.

"I'll be willing to pay your nation for each warrior that enlists," Jackson said. "We'll pay them the same that we would pay our militia."

Pushmataha agreed, not knowing that it would take years and numerous communications with the government before his people would ever see the money.

On November 3, 1814, Jackson and an army of four thousand, including six hundred Choctaw warriors, left Fort Montgomery and arrived at Pensacola three days later. An offer was made to Spanish Governor, Mateo Gonzales Manrique, to surrender. The fort, though Spanish, was primarily manned by British soldiers. If the British would evacuate the fort, Jackson would hold them prisoner until Spanish troops could come and ensure neutrality. Manrique refused.

Pushmataha and his warriors were the first to enter the town. The attack was so brutal and vicious that within twenty minutes, the terrified Governor surrendered.

"PUSH, MY FRIEND, can you help us out one more time?"

After the Battle of Pensacola, Jackson and his troops had hurried to Mobile. There was worry that the British Fleet may attack Mobile. But when he arrived, he found that the worry was not for Mobile, but for New Orleans.

"We have word that the British are gearing up for an attack on New Orleans," the General said. "Our sources tell that they are amassing an army of twenty-five thousand to take the city. I'll be leaving as soon as possible to take command." (The actual number of British was less than ten thousand, but still a formidable force.)

Jackson rubbed his temples and shook his head. "As you are well aware, many of my men are militia. They have farms and families and have fulfilled their obligation. I'm afraid that most of them will be leaving soon, heading back to Tennessee and Mississippi. The Louisiana Militia has been called up, and we should be able to count on the citizens of New Orleans, but I need as many seasoned fighters as I can get. I would appreciate it if you could come."

IN EARLY DECEMBER, Jackson arrived in New Orleans and declared martial law. By the time he faced off with the British at Chalmette Plantation on January 8, 1815, Jacksons forces had swelled to almost four thousand. His was a very diverse group of men—U.S. Regulars, New Orleans Militia, Kentucky and Tennessee Volunteers, Jean Lafitte's band of outlaws, former Haitian slaves, New Orleans gentry, and Choctaw warriors.

This motley band performed admirably against an overwhelming enemy. When the smoke cleared, two thousand of the almost eight thousand British soldiers lay dead or wounded on the field. Jackson's losses were seventy-one, with only 13 dead.

The Creek Wars and the Battle of New Orleans did more than anything to catapult Andrew Jackson to the forefront of American politics and ultimately to the White House fourteen years later. His faithful friend, Pushmataha, could not know that the man that he helped make a national hero would, as President of the United States, be one of the biggest proponents of removal and/or extermination of the Red man that the United States would ever see.

"PUSH, MY FRIEND, come join me," the General said through the ever-present interpreter, John Pitchlynn. Jackson placed his arm around the chief's shoulder and ushered him down Chartres Street. "It's time to celebrate! There's a little tavern down here, Pierre Maspero's place. We'll share us a bottle."

The battle was over. Citizens and soldiers were celebrating up and down the streets of the Crescent City, and Jackson wasn't about to be left out of the revelry.

As they walked along, Jackson chuckled, "I wouldn't be surprised if we ran into that cutthroat—but useful—Jean Lafitte and his brother, already downing a bottle or two of Maspero's best brandy."

Before the battle at Chalmette Plantation, *La Bourse de Maspero*, or Maspero's Exchange as it was called by the Americans, had become the primary gathering place of Jackson and the leaders of New Orleans as they planned for the coming fight. Here Jackson had convinced the Lafitte brothers, Jean and Pierre, to join in the defense of New

Orleans—in exchange for pardons for piracy and other crimes against the United States.

JACKSON LOOKED AROUND the crowded tavern. There were no Lafitte brothers, but the place was packed with men in different stages of inebriation, cursing and laughing and bragging about how they had picked off the Redcoats like pigeons on a fence.

The three found a table in a corner and sat down. The General ordered two bottles of brandy and three glasses.

"The Choctaws are my kind of fighters," Jackson said as he downed a glass. "I've always said that if you are going to fight someone, you fight them. You don't mess around. Use every resource you have to defeat them. If you hesitate, you'll lose.

"I've had my share of fighting," he continued between swigs, "and you always go for the throat—for the kill. Do it right with the first blow and then it is all over. Plus, you make sure you are at the advantage."

Jackson, known for his many street duels, would often wear thick, loose-fitting clothing at the scheduled events, hiding his thin frame and making a deadly shot seem falsely easy. He would allow his foe the first volley, and then take his time for a carefully placed, deadly return.

"The British fight like fools," Pushmataha said as he joined in the drink. "To stand in formation with no cover—they ask for death."

"I must agree with you," Jackson said. "That style of fighting works if you don't mind losing a lot of men. When there were no guns and battles were fought with swords and spears, it worked, but not anymore."

"The gun has changed war," the chief said as he pulled out his pipe. "In the past, warriors saw death as it came—the tomahawk, the sword, the knife. The two were face to face—the intoxication of triumph or death written on their faces and seen in their eyes. Now death comes from far away. There is no warning. The dying warrior can no longer look into the face of his foe and congratulate him on being a better warrior."

Jackson shook his head. "Push, I'm not sure I would go that far—congratulating someone for sticking a knife in my belly, but I see what you say. There does seem to be more honor in that type of killing and death than a slug in your heart from someone fifty yards away."

The General lifted his glass as a toast. "But no more talk of war and death. Only intoxication. Here's to a night neither one of us will remember!"

PUSHMATAHA SLOWLY LIFTED his head off the table.

"Where am I?"

His thoughts and sight were not focusing well. He heard laughter and singing. He squinted as he looked around.

"Ah, the tavern," he thought to himself. "How long have I been asleep?"

It was dark, and lanterns had been lit, casting shadows against the walls as men moved about. Across the table General Jackson sat with his chin on his chest, asleep and snoring softly. Pitchlynn was also sleeping, his head resting on the table. A half-gone candle sat in the middle of the table, the wax puddling at its base.

He looked down at his glass and contemplated whether to pick it up again.

"No," he thought as he rubbed his temples. "That's enough. I'll just have a smoke instead."

He reached into his pocket for his pipe... The pocket was empty.

"The pipe!"

He looked down at the table. There were nearly empty bottles and glasses, but no pipe.

Panic gripped him. "Where is my pipe?"

He stood up and felt in his pockets again—nothing. Suddenly he was wide awake. He grabbed the candle and held it high. He lowered it under the table, but there was nothing there. He lifted Pitchlynn's head hoping he was resting on it. Nothing was there. He looked around at the crowd. Everyone was engaged in conversation, or singing, or asleep. No one seemed to be minding him at all.

The chief slumped back into his chair, trying to decide what to do.

"The General had admired the pipe and wanted to buy it," he thought. "Could he have taken it?"

Pushmataha reached over and felt the General's coat pocket. Nothing at all.

"Hey, what are you doing?" the bartender shouted from behind the counter. "Going through a white man's pocket will get a savage like you strung up.

"Get out of here before I shoot you myself."

Rage filled the chief.

"Someone in here must have it," he thought. He reached for his tomahawk and began to rise.

"I'll go through this crowd like I have done with the Creeks. I will find it. Not a man will be standing."

Pushmataha paused, sat back, and took a deep breath. Reason again took control.

"No. This will accomplish nothing except to get me and a lot of other people killed."

He dropped his head. Forty years he had kept the pipe. At no time had it been outside his grasp. It had been his tie with the past—of better times when life was good; of childhood when there were no worries—except whether to spend the day playing ball or fishing or hunting.

It was a reminder of a father who showed his love by sacrificing himself so that his son would live. The pipe spoke of a lost adolescence—of perseverance and commitment, and of determination and purpose, of hunger and loneliness, and of learning to live depending on no one and surviving and succeeding against insurmountable odds. It spoke of battle and savagery, and of triumph over enemy and death.

The pipe spoke of a time when the Choctaws were a powerful nation and depended on no one or nothing, except the land that they hunted and the air that they breathed. There were no fences or boundaries to tell the Choctaws where to live and where to go. The land belonged to no one.

It was a time when the white man did not rule the Choctaws. A time before the Choctaws learned that the white man was a thief—of his land and of his pipe.

After a moment he stood and left the tavern. He left the city of New Orleans traveling northeast.

CHAPTER TWENTY-TWO

FOR MOST OF ITS FIRST one hundred years of existence, the United States was plagued by a problem that each President had to face—dealing with conflicts with the Native Americans over land. President Washington in the 1790's was the first to formulate and implement a plan, and that plan, with little modification, was passed from President to President. Parts of the policy were written down; some of it was understood.

Washington and his Secretary of War, Henry Knox, knew that as the United States grew, the land had to be made available. But obtaining the land from its original owners, by whatever means, was resulting in hostilities and conflict. To lessen the conflict, the United States had three options on how to deal with the Red man: assimilation, removal, or extermination. Each President used one, two, or all three options. Washington and the first four or five presidents focused primarily on assimilation. For them, extermination seemed too shameful, and until the Louisiana Purchase, removal was not an option, for there was no place to send them.

Presidents during the forty years before the Civil War, focused primarily on removal. It was a temporary solution, but served to make land available to the masses of whites who were flooding into the new South. After the Civil war, the policy, especially west of the Mississippi, was extermination.

Henry Knox's reasoning for assimilation was that if the Red man could be taught to live like the white man—become "civilized"—obtaining his land would be easier. Create a market society in which the arrow and gun of the hunter-gatherer were replaced with the plow and pencil, and the Red man would be tied to a small area of land. Farmers and merchants had no need for vast amounts of land and would be more willing to part with their land. Plus, the "savagery" of the Red man's lifestyle could not exist in or near the world of the "civilized" white man.

The deerskin trade played well into the governmental policy of the time. The Red man had become accustomed to the things of the white man, things that he purchased with what appeared to be an endless supply of skins. Soon his very existence depended on the white man's things. Without them, he couldn't hunt or cultivate his land or cook his food. The tools he used and the clothes he wore were no longer made but bought. The skills of self-sufficiency, which the Choctaws had practiced from the beginning of time, were lost surprisingly fast.

And with the disappearance of the deer, the Choctaw suddenly found himself with nothing to bargain, except his land. For him to survive, he must "manufacture" something—produce something of worth to barter or to sell.

The United States government, primarily through the agents, stepped in and helped the Choctaws become productive members of this era—helped them learn to produce goods of value in the white man's economy. The agent introduced farming skills and husbandry skill. Black smithy was taught, and women learned the art of spinning and weaving cloth from cotton. The Choctaws welcomed the teaching and understood that their existence and future depended on it. Chief Homastubby, at a meeting with commissioners in Natchez, said, "Send women to the Choctaw to go among our people and teach them to spin thread and weave cloth, and the thing will extend itself. One will teach another."[18] In 1817, two thousand spinning wheels and several hundred looms were delivered to the Choctaw Nation for their use.

The Choctaws had always been a nation of farmers, primarily subsistence farmers for personal use, but by the mid 1810's they were venturing into large scale planting and cultivating. Many of the Choctaws, especially the chiefs and sub chiefs, rivaled the white settlers in their acreage of cultivation of cash crops, such as cotton, and

---

[18] Carson, James Taylor. *Searching for the Bright Path-The Mississippi Choctaw from Prehistory to Removal*, 1999, p. 68.

owned sizable herds of cattle, hogs, and horses. Many, like Mushulatubbee who in 1816 succeeded Homastubby as chief of the Okla Tannap, owned black slaves.

Fanchimastabe's vision of thirty years earlier had finally come true: no more were the Choctaws in the forests hunting the bear and the deer. The warriors were in meadows surrounded by fences, feeding cattle and hogs.

ALONG THE NATCHEZ TRACE, places of business, or "stands," were an opportunity for the Red man to enter the business world as merchants and innkeepers. Even though most of the stands were opened by white men, such as Louis Lefleur, Josiah Doak, and Noah Wall, many were owned and operated by Choctaw entrepreneurs like David Folsom and Greenwood LeFlore. (Greenwood, the son of Louis, Americanized his last name by changing the spelling.)

New settlers in the Mississippi Territory were surprised, and pleased, to find the Red man more than willing to sell them food and clothing and cattle and horses until they could get their small farms established and productive.

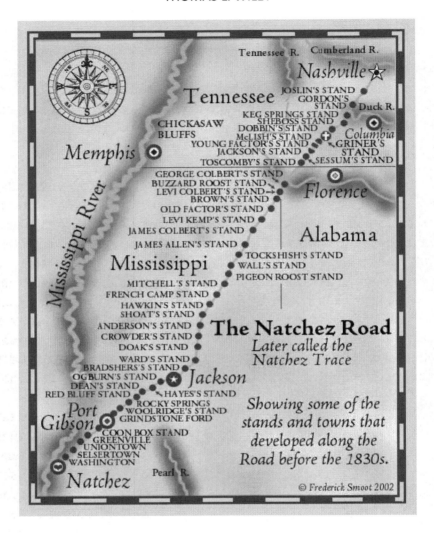

Natchez Trace

EDUCATION AND THE LEARNING of the white man's writing and numbers became an important goal of both the Choctaws and the American government. In the eyes of the agents, this would make assimilation easier; in the eyes of the Choctaws, it was for survival. Pushmataha was one of the major proponents for educating the new generation. Even though he never learned to speak English—much less read or write it—the chief understood that without education, the Choctaws would be doomed to a lifestyle of subservience and poverty.

Schools would need to be established to educate the Choctaw children in the ways of the white man. This undertaking, however, would not be free for the Choctaws. As in all dealings with the white man, there was a price. And again, it was land.

IN OCTOBER 1816, Chiefs Mushulatubbee, Apuckshanubbee, and Pushmataha met with Commissioners John Coffee, John Rhea, and John McKee at Fort St. Stephens for the purpose of establishing an annuity for the continued education of the Choctaw children. When the council met, the white man's pipe that Pushmataha had passed at almost every council for the past several decades was noticeably absent.

Following introductions and formalities, John Coffee was the first to speak, his words translated by longtime interpreter, John Pitchlynn.

"The President of our great nation, James Madison, sends greetings to his friends and brothers, the Choctaw Nation. He wishes for me to again express his appreciation for the support given by your people during the wars with the British and the Creeks. He is convinced that without your help, the course of the conflict would have been disastrous for both of our nations.

"Today we meet to discuss and formulate a plan for the education of your people. Before I present our plan, I wish to tell the wise chiefs how proud I am that your nation sees and understands how important it is to learn the ways of the white man. Education will be your key to the future. Without it, you are doomed.

"Schools, places where the children can gather and learn, are necessary, and our President—with your aid—wishes to build them throughout your land. Here the children will not only learn the language of the white man, but how to live and provide for themselves in the world of the future.

"Our proposal is to provide six thousand dollars to the Choctaw Nation annually for the next twenty years for the establishment and provision of schools. Also, we will initially provide ten thousand dollars for goods for trade schools and other supplies as deemed necessary. To offset the cost—which you see is substantial—we propose that the Choctaws 'cede to the United States all their title and claim to lands lying east of the following boundary, beginning at the mouth of Oktibbuha, the Chickasaw boundary, and running from thence down the Tombigby River, until it intersects the northern boundary of a cession made to the United States by the Chactaws, at Mound Dexter, on the 16th November, 1805.'"[19]

OVER THREE MILLION ACRES of land was ceded—all of the remaining Choctaw land east of the Tombigbee. Only ten thousand acres were in present day Mississippi, the rest in Alabama. It was prime farm land—rich and fertile—for the ever-growing fields of cotton. The town of Columbus, Mississippi, would become the major port on the Tombigbee for this area.

The chiefs readily agreed, placing their hopes of the future on the education of their children. Within a few years the American Board of Missions, under the leadership of Cyrus Kingsbury, established schools in all three districts of the Choctaws.

The initial plan by the missionaries was to teach in English only, with the hopes that over time all communication, both within the Choctaw communities and with the world at large, would be English. The Choctaw language would surely die, and the Choctaw culture with it. As with so many misguided attempts to replace "bad" with "good," conflicts resulted.

"The Choctaw mission," the Reverend Kingsbury wrote, "was commenced with a mistaken idea that the great object should be to

---

[19] Treaty of Fort St. Stephens, 1816.

instruct the children in the English language. The adults and their native language, it was supposed, would soon pass away and leave a generation educated and regenerated by the transforming influence of Christian schools. This would supersede the labor and expense of translation—the plan was inviting in theory, but in the practical working out of it there was perplexity and disappointment."[20]

With the prodding and foresight of the Choctaw leaders, instructions were soon given in both Choctaw and English. A written language of the Choctaws was created, with dictionaries, Bibles, and other material being translated for their use, saving the ancient tongue of the sons and daughters of Chahtah from extinction.

ALTHOUGH ASSIMILATION into the white man's culture was the aim of American policy of the time, legal protection and justice through the court was often lacking. The Choctaws were forbidden by law from filing complaints or suits in the court system. If one felt wronged, he presented his case to the agent who would file the complaint—if he thought there was just cause. The agents were less than excited about prosecuting their white brothers and rarely would take up the cause of the Red man. Theft, especially of cattle and horses, became a wide spread problem when the white man realized there was no recourse.

Altercations between the white man and the Choctaws occurred but were surprisingly rare. In cases of a white man being killed by a Red man, the scales of justice and public opinion weighed heavily against the latter.

GIDEON LINCECUM SAT UP in his bed.

"Was that a gun shot?" he asked his wife, Sarah.

"That's what it sounded like," Sarah answered, pulling the covers up to her chin.

---

[20] Lewis, Anna. *Chief Pushmataha-American Patriot*, Exposition Press, 1959, p. 112.

"It sounded like it came from down by the ferry house." Gideon pulled his boots on and grabbed his gun. "I'll go check and be right back."

The Lincecums, with their two children, his parents, and several slaves, had settled in Possum Town on the east bank of the Tombigbee River shortly after the land was made available with the Treaty of Fort St. Stephens. The rich soil of the nearby black prairie was drawing settlers to this small community, later renamed Columbus.

Along with farming cotton in the fertile black dirt, Gideon had established several businesses, including a ferry service across the Tombigbee.

Gideon hired a man named, Louie, to run the ferry and do other jobs as needed around the plantation. Although Louie was not the most reliable employee, he was available and functioned fairly well, as long as he was sober.

Louie had a knack for learning languages and within a few months had mastered enough Choctaw to communicate and become friends with the locals. Most nights a group of them would gather at the ferry house to share a jug with Louie. The gatherings sometimes ran late into the night, but Gideon didn't complain as long as things didn't get rowdy enough to disturb his sleep.

AS GIDEON APPROACHED the ferry house, he could make out at least a dozen figures scattering through the woods into the dark. He cautiously looked into the single room ferry house. Lying on the floor was Louie, dead with a gunshot wound to his neck. Sitting in the far corner was an old Choctaw woman with her hands folded, looking at the corpse.

"Louie and Atoba, they were drunk," the woman said. "Louie wanted to sell a gun to Atoba. Atoba didn't want the gun. Atoba tried give the gun back. The gun went off; killed Louie. Accident."

"If it was an accident, why did everyone run away?" Gideon asked.

"Not good for a Choctaw to kill a white man. Bad."

Atoba was the brother of Mushulatubbee, chief of the Okla Tannap, or northeast district. At one time he had been a mighty warrior, but time and alcohol had taken their toll. He spent most of his time either trying to find someone to share a bottle with, or trying to recover from a night when he was successful.

But Atoba still had his honor.

The next morning two Choctaw men showed up at Gideon's home, requesting some powder and lead for Atoba.

"What does he need this for?" Gideon asked.

"Atoba did wrong. He killed a white man. Atoba wants to die from same gun at noon today."

"But I understand it was an accident," Gideon said.

"No matter. A life for a life. That is the law."

"Well, you can tell him he'll get no help from me," Gideon said. "I'll be no part of a man killing himself over some crazy accident."

"No matter," one of the men said. "We will find powder and ball from someone else. Atoba not afraid to die. He is a Choctaw and warrior."

Gideon sighed and shook his head. "This is foolishness. Tell me where he's planning on doing this, and I'll get there as soon as I can. And if you get there before me, tell him not to do a thing until I can speak to him. Maybe I can talk some sense into that old fool."

When Gideon arrived at the appointed spot, Atoba was sitting on a stump with the gun in his hand; six of his friends were standing near. As Gideon approached, Atoba stood and addressed the white man.

"In my drunkenness last night, I killed your man, Louie. It is right for me to die. His shilup, his spirit, will not rest until he is avenged. I am not afraid to die. I am still alive now only because you wished me to wait. But now you are here."

He raised the gun and handed it butt first to Gideon. "Louie was your man. I give you permission to be the avenger. Take the pistol. I am ready to die."

"Listen to me, Atoba," Gideon said. "I'm not about to shoot you. Everyone says it was an accident. And if it was an accident, there's no reason on earth for you to die. It would be a horrible injustice, not justice."

The white man put his arm around the shoulders of the Red man, and the two sat down on the stump.

"Let me tell you what we'll do," he said. "We'll take this to the proper authorities and have it reviewed—have a trial. If the white man's jury acquits you, I want you to drop this whole idea. If the jury finds you guilty, well, that's another thing. How about it?"

Atoba thought for a moment, nodded his head, and spoke. "I will agree to your plan only if I have word that if I am condemned, I will be shot and not weighed like a dog."

The Choctaws called hanging "weighing," To be weighed was considered a most humiliating way to die.

GIDEON FILLED OUT the proper papers with the justice of the peace, and a trial date was set for a month later.

Word rapidly spread through the area about this drunken savage who had killed a poor, defenseless white man, and by the time of the trial, a large crowd of low-life white men had gathered in Possum Town to witness the event. Rumors circulated that if the jury didn't come to the right verdict, they may have to take the law into their own hands. The rowdies were also upset that the presumed guilty Red man had been allowed to go about his business during the waiting period and wasn't locked up for this savage deed that he had done.

Gideon Lincecum shook his head in disgust when word got to him about the unrest. Did these men not realize that there were probably fewer than three hundred white men within a thirty-mile radius of Possum Town, and in the blink of an eye, the Choctaws could have a thousand warriors on their heads? Keep your mouths shut. Let the law take care of it, and abide by the verdict.

The place of the trial was to be at an oak grove just outside of Possum Town, and on the appointed day fifty white men in different stages of inebriation gathered to make sure justice was served. The appointed time was noon, and at 11:30, no Red man was in sight. The accused was nowhere to be found. The crowd was becoming restless and indignant that this murderer had been let loose. How could the court be so foolish as to think this renegade would come to trial on his own accord? It wouldn't surprise them a bit if he had fled the area and was now in hiding out west of the Mississippi River.

At one minute before the noon hour, three hundred Choctaw warriors rode into the grove, all of them well armed. Leading the group were the three chiefs, Apuckshanubbee, Mushulatubbee, and Pushmataha—followed by the accused, Atoba, with his head held low, shame written on his face.

The white crowd became quiet. The warriors dismounted, hitched their horses to the nearest bushes, and leaned their weapons against the trees. Silently they approached the center of the grove. Many of the white men appeared to be trembling, frightened at what was about to happen. Their "pale faces" looked unusually pale.

Suddenly the visitors broke ranks, dispersed through the crowd, smiling, shaking hands, greeting the surprised men in broken English and Choctaw. The white men cautiously began to respond, smiling and nodding their heads in relief.

The Honorable William Cocke called the court into session.

William Cocke, originally from Virginia, had been a colonel in the Revolutionary War serving in what would become Tennessee, fighting the Native Americans. After the War he practiced law for a few years in Virginia and North Carolina before returning west and joining Daniel Boone in exploring Kentucky and Tennessee. He settled in Tennessee, and along with Andrew Jackson was a delegate to the state constitutional convention. In 1796 he was elected the first Senator from Tennessee and was succeeded a year later by Andrew Jackson. While serving on the state's circuit court in 1812, he became the first Tennessee judge to be impeached, tried, and removed from office for using his office for personal gain.

His political carrier bounced back quickly, and he served as a colonel under Jackson during the Creek Wars. In 1814 he was appointed by President Madison federal agent to the Chickasaw nation. While in that capacity, he also served as judge and magistrate for the region. He died in Columbus in 1828 and is buried in Friendship Cemetery.

A TABLE AND CHAIRS HAD been set up under the oak trees, and five justices of the peace assembled, with the honorable Mr. Cocke presiding. Cocke, well versed in the etiquette and respect of the Red man, invited the three chiefs to sit at the table with the justices. Atoba took his seat before the court.

Almost twenty-five witnesses, mostly Choctaw women, were called to the stand. It seemed that the fairer sex enjoyed the company of Louie and his jug as much as, if not more than, the aging warriors did. The testimonies were translated by the ever-present John Pitchlynn, and each story was the same. From all accounts it was obviously an accident. Many told that the two, Atoba and Louie, were the best of friends, and neither would have willfully harmed the other. It was an unfortunate drunken mishap. Even Gideon Lincecum took the stand and gave his version of the story.

It soon became clear to the crowd that the court would find poor Atoba innocent, and rumblings began among the incensed rowdies. During a break in the proceedings, one of the Choctaws who could understand English heard them plotting mischief and told Pushmataha. Pushmataha promptly walked to the table, lifted a book, and slammed it on the table, startling everyone.

"It is to you, my white brothers, that I wish to address myself this fair day. I had kept my seat among the wise and good men who were conducting the investigation of my friend, Atoba's case until I satisfied myself that the trial is a fair one; and I had, as there was no further use for my presence, gone off a little way, and was seated in a pleasant place, amusing myself with the contemplation of the magnitude of the government and wonderful greatness of the American people, when one of my own countrymen came and informed me that a number of white men, now present, who have no families or anything else that is valuable in the country to detain them when they are guilty of an outrage, are counseling among one another; and their aim is to break up the peace and friendly intercourse that has always obtained between the Chahtas and the American white people. It must be prevented. It will be put to a stop to—"[21]

Cocke interrupted the chief at this point—a grievous insult to the Choctaws who would never interrupt another while he was speaking, no matter how long the discourse lasted or how much he disagreed with his words.

"Brother Push," the Judge said. "You speak too bold and plain; it might occasion the spilling of blood."

Pushmataha did not even look toward the Judge, but continued with his discourse.

"I would have you, my white brothers, to understand that I have visited the big white house where our father, the President, resides and locking my five fingers with his five fingers we made a treaty of peace, in the presence of that Being under the shadow of whose far spreading wings we all exist, whose strong arm extends through all orders of the animal creation and down into the lowest grass and herbs in the forest. It was in the presence of this shiombish—spirit—that we made our peace, swept our paths clean, made them white and on my part, and I speak for the entire Chahta people, there has been no track made in them. If, after investigation, this unfortunate man, Atoba, shall be found guilty, we will give him up, cheerfully submit him to his destiny. We came here determined to do that. But on the other hand, if he is not found guilty, we shall sustain him like men, and we will do it at all hazards.

---

[21] Publications of the Mississippi Historical Society, Volume 9, 1906, p. 433.

"I here frankly confess that I feel no misgivings in relation to the wise and very respectable gentlemen who are managing the trial. I know them all personally; I am satisfied with them, and shall yield to their decision in the case.

"But it is to the reckless, loose crowd of irresponsible men to whom I have made allusion; men who are here today and there tomorrow; men who care no more for the white man than he does for the red man, and who would be willing to sacrifice both for a frolic with a big jug of whiskey. These are the kind of men I speak of. They are here close by; they hear my voice now; and when they have matured their plot and make the attempt to put it into action, if the officers of this well conducted council desire that it shall be suppressed, and are not in sufficient force to accomplish it, let them call on me and I will instantly bring to their aid at a single whoop all the Chahtas who are on the ground. If the court does not see fit to call the red people to its assistance, and suffers a riot to occur here today, I shall take it upon myself to assume the responsibility in suppressing any outrage that may be attempted in the Chahta grove of red oaks, either while the council holds its session or after they have adjourned."[22]

He then turned to Judge Cocke and said,

"Speak not to me of blood. I was raised in blood."[23]

When the chief had finished, not a person spoke. The mouths of the fifty half-drunken white men in attendance were fixed in a half open position. When they finally looked around, they noticed that the arms of the warriors were no longer resting against trees. They were in

---

[22] Publications of the Mississippi Historical Society, Volume 9, 1906, p. 433.
[23] Publications of the Mississippi Historical Society, Volume 9, 1906, p. 433.

the hands of the warriors. The rowdies had been so spellbound and shocked by the words of the chief that they had failed to notice the movement among the Choctaws to retrieve their weapons.

After a few more moments of silence, several of the men commented that it was getting late in the day and that it was time for them to be moving on. They politely bid everyone good-bye and within minutes were gone.

The proceedings continued, a few more witnesses spoke their piece, and Atoba was found innocent of murder—the death ruled an accident.

Sadly, the one-time great warrior, Atoba, was not pleased with the verdict, for he continued in a melancholy state and within a month was found drowned in the Tombigbee River.

THOMAS L. WILEY

CHAPTER TWENTY-THREE

DURING THE CREEK WARS, migration into the Mississippi Territory came to an abrupt halt, but once the Treaty of Fort Jackson was signed, the flood gates again opened. In 1816, one traveler counted four thousand immigrants coming into the Territory during his nine-day journey.

Whereas, in the earlier migration most settled in the Natchez area and the lower Tombigbee, this new migration saw settlement throughout the Territory. The largest numbers were settling in what would be the state of Alabama—the former Creek Nation—because of its close proximity to the original thirteen states. From 1810 to 1820, the Mississippi part of the Territory more than doubled from 31,306 to 75,448; the Alabama section increased sixteen-fold, from 9,046 to 146,863.

Men were making it rich. New strains of cotton were being developed that were ideal for the Mississippi Delta soil and climate, and refinements of the ginning process were making yields per acre unimaginable. Slaves were brought in by the thousands to provide the workforce: from 1798 to 1817 their numbers increased from 4,000 to 70,000.

Cotton was literally king, and prices paid in Europe and along the east coast were at an all-time high. Mississippi, in a few years, would become one of the wealthiest states in the Union. At one point, there were more millionaires per capita in Natchez than any other city in the world.

Along with wealth came influence. These former backwoodsmen were rapidly making themselves known in Washington, clamoring for recognition in the governing process. Mississippians were no longer living in the frontier—the frontier had moved west of the Mississippi River. It was time to become part of the Union.

On December 10, 1817, they got their wish. Mississippi became the twentieth state.

"WHY, LOOK WHO'S HERE," the Frenchman said as he gave his friend a big bear hug. "Where have you been? I haven't seen you in years."

"I have been busy with war."

"That's what I hear," Lefleur said. He grabbed a jug, and the two sat down at a table in the common room of the inn. It was early January 1818: a little too cool to enjoy the outside.

"I hear you followed Old Hickory all over the territory fighting his battles. Made a pretty good name for yourself—as if you didn't already have an impressive reputation before."

The white man took a swig from the jug.

"What brings you way up here, my friend?" he asked. "You're a long way from home."

"I wanted to see what was happening along the trail—what the white man calls the Natchez Trace."

Lefleur pointed around the room at the eight or nine men who were enjoying a drink. "As you can see, there are more white folk than you can shake a stick at. And more coming every day. It's so unlike it was thirty-five years ago when you first showed up at my trading post on the Pearl River. At that time, I was about the only white man in the region."

The white man began to laugh. "My friend, it strikes me as funny—I used to make a living trading with the Red man. Now all my trading is with the white man—coming through on their way to the Promised Land. And I have to be honest with you; I'm making a lot more money here with my little inn, my French Camp, than I ever did with those deer skins."

Pushmataha pulled out his pipe. It was a traditional stone pipe with a wooden stem.

"My friend, where is your fancy pipe with the deer? Don't tell me you have retired that old thing."

"Stolen," the chief replied as he broke up a leaf of tobacco with his fingers and pressed it into the bowl. "The white man shows thanks for my help by stealing my pipe."

"Sorry to hear it. That was a fine piece. It'd be hard to find one as nice as that."

Pushmataha lit the pipe, took a few puffs, and passed it to his friend. He then took a swallow from the jug and rested back in his chair.

"I hear that the land which has been called the Mississippi Territory is now a state, like Tennessee and Kentucky."

"Yes, it happened last month," he answered. "I'm not sure if it's a good thing or not, but statehood was approved by the Congress in Washington. For better or worse, we are now bonified members of the United States of America."

"They divided the territory in half," the white man continued. "The western half is the new State of Mississippi. The eastern half has been named the Alabama Territory after your cousin tribe, the Alabamas. Word is that in a year or two the new territory will also become a state and be called 'Alabama.'"

Pushmataha, deep in thought, puffed on his pipe. After a moment he spoke.

"If the great leaders of the United States are so kind as to name our future sister state after a small, obscure tribe like the Alabamas, it seems to me that the proper name of the new state in which we now reside should be 'Choctaw'—especially since we own over half of the land."

The chief shrugged his shoulders. "Or if they don't like 'Choctaw,' maybe they could call it 'Chickasaw,' or 'Yazoo,' or 'Pascagoula,' or 'Tunica.' Why call it by the name of a muddy, silt-filled old river?"

Lefleur took another drink and laughed. "Push, my friend, you're sounding like a seasoned politician. Next thing you'll be recommending is for the Congress to change the name of the state to 'Pushmataha.'"

"'Pushmataha,'" the chief nodded as he repeated his name. "'The Great State of Pushmataha.' Sounds pretty good to me."

The white man burst out laughing. "Well, I'll see what I can do the next time I run into Governor Holmes. But don't get your hopes up too high."

He took another swig, chuckled, and winked at his red friend. "If the Governor won't budge, maybe we can get your name and the names of your sister tribes on a county or a town. We've already done it for the Natchez and Biloxi. How would that be?"

"Well, if that's all you can do..." the chief snorted and then laughed. "But hopefully, unlike the Natchez, we will still be around to enjoy the honors."

Within a few years, Choctaw, Chickasaw, Yazoo, Pascagoula, and Tunica did become names of counties and towns in Mississippi. But before the honor was bestowed, the nations of the Red man were banished to the west of the Mississippi River—no longer welcomed in the places that would bear their names.

The two friends continued to laugh and visit and enjoy the jug and pipe.

"Why did they divide the land?" Pushmataha asked. "A larger state would have more power."

"I asked the same question," Lefleur answered. "It seems that the division had been in discussion from the first day the Territory was formed twenty years ago in 1798. Politics was what it was all about, with the eastern part of the territory pitted against the western. And, you won't believe it, but the two sides changed their minds—did an about face—right in the middle of the debate.

"Initially the leaders in Natchez wanted it to be one big state, stretching from Georgia to the Mississippi—the bigger the better— with them in control. The leaders in the east—Fort St. Stephens and the settlements along the Tombigbee—wanted to be separate. They were worried that they would essentially be ruled by Natchez and have little input in the governing process.

"Well, all of a sudden, settlers started pouring into the old Creek Nation and before long the population density shifted. The Tombigbee group realized that they were getting the upper hand. With their majority vote, they could run the state. They could even move the capital from Natchez to Fort St. Stephens, and there wasn't a thing Natchez could do." (Fort St. Stephens did become the first capital of the State of Alabama two years later.)

Lefleur took a drink and laughed. "It seemed that overnight the two groups switched sides. The Natchez faction suddenly wanted to split and keep their own little kingdom. The east wanted one big state. Black became white, and vice versa, with no grey in the middle.

"They continued to argue, and finally, a year ago, leaders of both sides met at the home of John Ford at Lott's Bluff to fight it out. They called the meeting the Pearl River Convention."

(Lott's Bluff was located on the Pearl River ninety miles south of Lefleur's Bluff. In 1819 Lott's Bluff was renamed Columbia, Mississippi, and served as the capital of the state in 1821. The next year the capital was moved permanently to a more central location— Lefleur's' old home place, Lefleur's Bluff—and the name was changed to Jackson.)

"The easterners at the meeting outnumbered the westerners, and the vote went to join the Union as one state.

"Here's where the backroom politics came into play." Lefleur rubbed his hands together as he continued. "William Lattimore was the Mississippi territorial delegate to Congress and was already in Washington working toward statehood when the Pearl River Convention met. Lattimore, a medical doctor in Natchez, was very much a proponent of division. When word got to him that the vote was for a single state, he ignored it and went right on with his original plan. His 'argument' when it was all over was that the entire area would be served better with four senators instead of two.

"Within a few weeks, President Monroe signed Lattimore's resolution to make Mississippi a state and Alabama a territory. That was it. Thanks to one man and his backroom 'medicine,' the one became two."

Lefleur paused and scratched his chin. "Hopefully he made the right decision."

Pushmataha continued to smoke his stone pipe as he intently listened to his friend. At times he would nod his head in understanding; at others he would shake it in disbelief. He was surprised and appalled at this breach of the will of the people. This was not the way that he perceived the government of the United States to function.

After a few moments, the chief softly said, "So much for the democratic process."

Lefleur sat his jug on the table, leaned toward his friend, and smiled. "You're getting a firsthand look at democracy. It seems to work the best when things go in one's favor. If it doesn't, then everybody wants to be a dictator. But like it or not, it's the best there is."

In a more serious tone, the white man continued. "Push, my friend, one thing you said a few minutes ago worries me—the statement that in this new state of ours the Choctaws own over half the land. And another fourth is claimed by the Chickasaws. You know as well as I do that the white man won't sit back and let anyone control that much land. He's going to come 'asking' for it. Mark my word; it's just a matter of time."

Before the ink on the 1817 Mississippi Constitution was dry, the white man again came "asking" for more land.

Mississippi/Alabama Split 1817

CHAPTER TWENTY-FOUR

"GRANDFATHER, THE FISH took my bait."

Pushmataha reached for the lines and skewered a cricket on each hook for the umpteenth time. The two boys dropped the lines back into the Noxubee River. A moment later a slight wind rippled the waters, making it look as if the bobs were going under. Both boys jerked their lines out of the water, sending the hooks high into the air.

"Be patient," Pushmataha said. "Not only watch the float, but feel the tension on the line. A good fisherman can fish with his eyes closed. If you pull the line too fast, the nani (the fish) will let go. Wait for the tug of the fish, then gently and smoothly pull, setting the hook."

The boys lowered their lines back into the water and waited.

The cool of winter was gone, and the sky was clear, a perfect day for the "imafo" (grandfather) and his two "ippok naknito" (grandsons) to enjoy each other. As they sat quietly, the chief smiled and thought of the past. Fifty years ago—had it really been that long? —he sat in this very spot and listened as his own grandfather taught him the art of fishing and patience. But more than fishing, it was a time when they talked. The wise old man would tell him of the past—of his ancestors and the spirit world, and of the animals and plants of the forest. Those were good times.

As they impatiently waited, one of the boys said, "Grandfather, tell us about the black squirrel eating the sun."

"And then tell us about the man hunting for the sun," the other boy chirped in. "That is one of my favorites."

Pushmataha laughed to himself. If he had told these stories once, he had told them a thousand times. His grandsons could surely recite those tales as well as he could. If fact, if he varied the narration—left something out or changed the flow—one of them would usually correct him. But they loved to hear him tell the tales—as he loved to hear his grandfather of old tell them over and over. This was how history was passed. Repeat the stories until they are a part of the child's being, and they will not be forgotten.

"LONG AGO," THE GRANDFATHER began, "there lived a squirrel who was different from all of the others in the forest. His coat was as dark as the night, as black as coal. There was none like him, none as beautiful, for his black fur glistened in the sun. One would think that the black squirrel would be proud of his beautiful coat and would show it off to all of his grey brothers, but that was not so. During the day he stayed hidden in the shadows. Only in the darkness did he feel safe, for his coat gave him no protection, no camouflage. Unlike his grey brothers who would become almost invisible against the trunks and branches of the oaks and hickories, the black squirrel was as obvious as a blot of ink on white parchment. And when the sun was the highest and the day the brightest, he was the most obvious. In the shadows he stayed; in the darkness he felt safe.

"During the day as his brothers played, he only watched.

"'Come and play with us,' his brothers said as they scampered from tree to tree. 'The heat of the sun gives us pleasure, and his rays warm our hearts. It will do the same for you.'

"'No,' he replied. 'The hawk and the owl will surely see me and feed me to their young. I will stay hidden until the sun sleeps in the west, and the shadows become long. Then I will come and play with you.'

"But when darkness fell and the black squirrel finally came out to join his brothers, they were tired, ready to return to their nests for the night. Day after day he watched alone, and night after night he played alone. Soon he began to hate the sun.

"One day the black squirrel was resting quietly, observing the world from his place of darkness. The sun was exceptionally bright and warm that day. There was not a cloud in the sky, and the sun shone high for all to see. The black squirrel looked up and in anger said, 'I will destroy the sun. I will climb to the tallest tree. I will take the sun and eat it. Its rays will no longer fall to earth. All will be dark, giving me freedom and protection.'

"The black squirrel climbed to the top of the tallest tree in the forest. He ventured out on its highest branch and began to nibble at the sun. Slowly the light of midday began to fade, and darkness began to sweep across the land.

"Below, in the villages where the children of Chahtah and Chickasah lived, our fathers and mothers became frightened, for it was becoming dark in the middle of the day. They shielded their eyes to the rapidly fading sun and looked up. What they saw was beyond belief! There, outstretched on the highest branch of the tree was the black squirrel, nibbling away at the sun!

"In unison, they shouted, 'Funi lusa hushi umpa!' 'The black squirrel is eating the sun!'

"'What shall we do? We cannot let him continue! The sun will soon be gone!'

"'We must frighten the black squirrel away! Everyone make noise—the loudest ever heard in all the land, and hopefully the black squirrel will stop his feast and run away!'

"The women of the villages began to shout and call out. They grabbed their pans and beat them together. The children took their tin cups and hit them with sticks. Warriors raised their guns to the air and shot at the sun, hoping that one of their bullets would hit the black squirrel and stop his mischief. Even the dogs joined in and howled at the fading sun. The birds were so frightened and confused that they sought to find shelter in the trees and roosted as if it were nighttime.

"After an hour or two of noise and clamor, there was a glimmer of hope. The squirrel had enough of the shouting and noise. He stopped eating and scampered away. The sun slowly regained its strength and shone again in all its radiance.

"Happily, and with great relief, the people jumped and shouted. 'Funi lusa osh mahlatah!' 'The black squirrel is frightened!' 'We have saved the sun!'

"My sons," the grandfather said as he finished, "remember the story of the black squirrel, for on occasion he still gets angry, or hungry, and tries to devour the sun. When that happens—when the midday sun dims even though there is no cloud in the sky—we must frighten the black squirrel away. Like our fathers and mothers before us, we must make noise as much as we can."

With a twinkle in his eye, he added, "Now, the white man will tell you that it is not the black squirrel that causes the sun to dim, but it is the moon casting its shadow over the land—an eclipse—but we know better. It is the angry little black squirrel that nibbles at the sun."

"GRANDFATHER! A NANI! A fish! Look! A fish! I feel a fish!" the boy shouted as he lifted the line.

Dangling from the hook was a small bream about four inches in length. Pushmataha grabbed the fish with one hand and tried to work the hook out with the other.

"The white man's hook," he said to himself, "are so difficult to remove. The old Choctaw bone hook had no barb. It would slide right out. This hook is like working an arrow out of the tough hide of a buffalo. But then, unlike the old hooks, rarely does a fish flop its way to safety."

Finally, the hook was loose. He held the fish up. Even though it was not worth the trouble to clean, he exclaimed, "My, what a catch!"

It was his grandson's first catch and would be in the frying pan that night. He placed it in the basket and baited the hook again.

IN THE DAYS TO COME, negotiations with the United States would make Pushmataha feel as if he were the tiny fish, the nani, and that the white man was the fisherman, the nanabi. The initial cast of the line, which would occur in only a few months, would be by a novice in negotiations. It would be too harsh, too fast, and too obvious. The Choctaw would spit the hook out. The second cast, however, would be more gentle, yet firm—thrown by an expert in negotiation. The barbs could not be as easily dislodged, and the Red would again be at the mercy of the white man.

"THAT WAS FUN," the boy exclaimed as he dropped the line back into the water. "Grandfather, while we wait for another bite, tell us about the man hunting for the sun."

Pushmataha leaned back and softly spoke.

"Long ago in the time of our ancestors, a great council was called for celebration. Hash Haponi, the month of cooking, had passed, and the first frost had fallen. Winter was soon to come with her cold and rain, but the people were happy, for the corn had been plentiful, and the hunt successful. The baskets in the storehouse were overflowing with bounty. There would be no hunger when the nights were long and the days were cold. Now was the time to show appreciation to the Great Spirit for the abundance he had bestowed.

"The warriors and women danced and sang and feasted for several days. They raised their arms to the sky and thanked the Great Spirit for sending the rain and the sun, and for blessing them in the harvest.

On the last day of the celebration, the great chief spoke late into the night of the beauty and wonder of Nature and the richness of the earth. He spoke of the birds that soared through the air and the animals that inhabited the forests. He marveled at the sun and its life-giving warmth, and the moon and stars and their soft glow in the night.

"'The sun remains a mystery to me, even in my old age,' the chief spoke 'I wake early in the morning to watch him rise in the east and give light to the land. Through the day, I look up to see him travel across the sky and bestow warmth and life. I shade my eyes and watch him disappear in the west before the night.

"With my own eyes, I have seen where the sun awakens. As a youth, I traveled many moons to the east and came to a great body of water. There I witnessed the awakening of the sun from his sleep. In a shining magnificence, he lifts himself from the waves of this endless sea and begins his journey through the blue sky.

"'But I have never seen where he sleeps,' the chief lamented. 'This troubles me. I have often wondered where the sun goes when he passes behind the hills to the west. Where does he rest when the day is over?

"'Many times, I have desired to journey west to solve the mystery, but responsibilities have prevented me. Now I am old and crippled. I cannot go myself. Is there one who will go for me? Is there a warrior who will venture to the west and find out what becomes of the giver of light and life?'

"The people loved their chief and all wanted his wish to be fulfilled. But who would go?

"At once a young warrior named Oklanowah, 'Walking People,' stood and said, 'I will go. I will venture to the west to find where the sun sleeps.'

"The village was proud of this young warrior and bade him well as he embarked on his journey. But there was one who cried—a beautiful young maiden who loved Oklanowah.

"'Please do not go!' she begged. 'The journey will be long, wrought with adversity and danger. You may never return!'

"'But I must go,' the warrior said. 'My chief wishes it. I will return one day with great honor. Then I will claim you as my bride. I will leave my wampum with you to remember me. Someday I will return.'

"Many years later the warrior returned. He was now an old man. His adventure had taken him far, and he had experienced many hardships, but he now returned to claim his bride. When he entered the village, he was a stranger, for no one remembered Oklanowah.

"For many days he wandered through the village until he found an aged and cripple woman who remembered the story of Hattak Owa Hushi Osh, 'The Man Hunting for the Sun,' for she was the young maiden he had left long ago. She still counted his wampum every day and waited for his return.

"The aged warrior told her that he was Oklanowah, now returned from his journey.

"She did not believe him.

"'No,' she said, 'the warrior I wait for is young and handsome. He is swift on his feet and stands tall. I do not wait for an old man.'

"He tried to convince her and told her of the days in the past when they would visit and of their love for each other, but she still would not believe. She withdrew to her lodge and continued to count his wampum and waited.

"Deeply sadden, the old warrior spent his last days telling the villagers of his adventure. He told of the deserts he crossed and the mountains that he had climbed and the strange people and animals that he encountered. And yes, he did find the resting place of the sun. Like his birth in the east, the sun rests at night in a great, blue water.

"Day after day he told of his journey, but he soon grew weary and tired.

"Before the moon for planting corn had come, the aged warrior died and was buried at the sacred mound Nanih Waiya. Soon the old woman also died and was buried next to her unrecognized, yet faithful, Oklanowah."

"A FISH! LOOK! Now I have one!" the other grandson shouted. "Look! Look!"

He gently pulled up a fish not much bigger than the earlier catch.

"You have done well," the grandfather said. "Both of you have mastered the art of fishing. Remember, if you pull too fast and hard, you will lose the fish. A gentle touch is what you desire. A feel for the tug and a firm setting of the hook make for a good fisherman."

For several more hours, the grandfather sat with his grandsons, baited hooks, and told stories that hopefully would be passed to their grandchildren in another fifty years. But the chief was worried that it would not happen. The world was changing, and the art of storytelling was disappearing. Grandfathers no longer spend time with their children's children on the banks of rivers as they did in the past telling stories of long ago. Children were too busy with school and learning the white man's ways. For them the old ways were old and were not worth saving. And among the elderly, there was a loss of pride as they saw their once great nation being whittled away. There was poverty and despair—and then, there was the bane of civilization, whiskey. Too many old men forgot their hopelessness—and their past—with the numbing effects of the jug. In a drunken stupor, there was little desire to pass on the tales of their forefathers.

Late in the afternoon the sky began to darken, and streaks of lightening shot across the sky. Low rumble of thunder told the fishermen that the storm was getting close.

"The great birds, Heloha and Melantha, are in the heavens again," the chief exclaimed. "Listen! Heloha (thunder) has laid another egg among the clouds! Hear it rumble as it rolls among the puffs of white and grey! And look! Her mate, Melantha (lightening), he streaks across the sky! You cannot see him, for he is very fast. But you can see the trail of sparks he leaves."

As the rain began to fall, Pushmataha reluctantly gathered their things together. "It is time for us to go," he said. "We must go back to the village. Your mother and father will be waiting."

"Let's come back tomorrow," one of the boys said. "Tell us about the great battles of the Choctaws in the past."

"Yes," the warrior thought, "even those need to be remembered."

CHAPTER TWENTY-FIVE

MR. CALHOUN TAPPED HIS FOOT as he waited outside the President's office.

"Why in the world do I have to deal with these land disputes?" he thought. "Don't they know that I have much more important things to worry about?"

Two years earlier in 1817, thirty-five-year-old John C. Calhoun had been appointed Secretary of War by President James Monroe. One of his many responsibilities was overseeing the Indian Affairs Office which coordinated all federal contact with the Red man, whether it be battling them in war or feeding them during relief efforts. Not until 1849 would the Department of the Interior be created and the Indian Affairs Office be placed under its jurisdiction and be renamed the Bureau of Indian Affairs.

As Mr. Calhoun waited, he reviewed the letter he had recently received from Mississippi Governor David Holmes. This must have been at least the fifth or sixth letter he had received complaining, begging, demanding that something be done about the Choctaws.

Governor Holmes was in a quandary. Settlers were coming into his newly formed state by the droves, and they needed land. The Choctaws and Chickasaws, by treaty, owned almost three fourths of the land in the state—an absurd amount of land to be controlled by no more than twenty thousand Choctaws and even less Chickasaws.

Mississippi was unable to do anything about it. By law, all land claimed by the Red man was under federal control, and the states had no say-so in the matter. Settling on Choctaw land was a federal offense—though this little fact was summarily ignored—but of more importance, the settlers could not be deeded the land as long as it belonged to the Red man. Technically, they were squatters with no rights.

The door opened, and Mr. Calhoun was ushered in.

"John, good to see you," President Monroe said as he rose to shake hands. "To what do I owe this visit—pleasure or business?"

"Mr. President, thank you for seeing me on such short notice. I'm afraid it's business." Calhoun presented the letter to the President. "A message from Holmes in Mississippi again. He wants us to do something about the Choctaws."

"He is definitely persistent," the President said as he skimmed the paper. "I still can't believe they need more land. Hasn't it only been a year or two since they got three million acres through the treaty at Fort St. Stephens? Have they run out of land already?"

"Sir, it's been three years. And most of that land is in the Alabama Territory."

The President shook his head as he handed the paper back to Calhoun. "What do you recommend?"

Monroe then half-jokingly added, "It's a shame we can't just shoot them like we did the Creeks."

"No, Sir," Calhoun answered with no emotion. "Unlike the Creeks, the Choctaws have been a staunch ally of the United States. It would be hard to justify."

Monroe cleared his throat and eyed the Secretary of War as if to say, "You know I was not being serious."

Calhoun continued, "I've met with Senators Walter Leake and Thomas Williams from Mississippi, and they have come up with a plan that should work. As you would expect, both of them are anxious to get this thing settled as quickly as possible.

"Their plan is to use a provision in the Treaty of Hopewell of 1786.

"For generations—long before the white man was in the picture—the Choctaws have regularly crossed the Mississippi River and hunted in the west—in the land of the Caddos, Osages, and Quapaws. In Choctaw these hunts are called "owa chita," the "big hunts." That's where the Ouachita River in the Arkansas Territory derived its name.

Well, these hunts are a part of their tradition and culture, and the Choctaws see it as their right to hunt those lands, which, as you would expect, has caused quite a bit of conflict in the past. And now that the game is scarce in Mississippi, they are depending more and more on these forays to provide meat. In fact, there are reports that a few of the Choctaws have taken up permanent residency in these lands because of the better hunting."

"Don't we own most of the Quapaw land?" the President interrupted.

"Yes, Sir," Calhoun answered. "Thirty million acres according to the Quapaw Purchase last year."

THE QUAPAW, OR ARKANSAS, tribe— "the People of the South Wind"—had at one time been a powerful Nation, numbering in the thousands and inhabiting the eastern half of present-day Arkansas and part of lower Oklahoma. Following contact with French explorers in 1689, a smallpox epidemic decimated their population. The tribe never recovered, and at the time of the Louisiana Purchase in 1803, they numbered less than six hundred. In 1818, the United States purchased most of their land, thirty million acres, for four thousand dollars in goods and an annual payment of one thousand dollars.[24]

"SIR, ACCORDING TO THE TREATY of Hopewell, the Choctaws are restricted from hunting in any land that is not theirs. The Mississippi Senators recommend that this breach of the law be brought to the Choctaws' attention, and that the United States Government offer to allow them to continue hunting in the West only if they will cede land. And if they don't agree, those who live west of the Mississippi will be forced to return to Mississippi."

The President nodded his head. "Send a letter to Mr. Holmes letting him know that this is our plan. Hopefully that will settle him down for a while."

---

[24]Key, Joseph. Arkansas State University. *"Quapaw,"* The Encyclopedia of Arkansas History and Culture.

IN AUGUST 1819, a general council of the Choctaws was called to meet with representatives of the United States to discuss this grave matter. The hope was that General Jackson, a shrewd and effective negotiator, would head the commission, but he had vowed to have no more dealings with treaties with the Red man. Instead, the commission was headed by Thomas Hinds.

Major Thomas Hinds had made a name for himself as the leader of the Mississippi Dragoons during the Creek War and the Battle of New Orleans. Following the war, he entered the political arena. He ran unsuccessfully for Governor in 1820 but then served in the Congress for several terms. His most long-lasting achievement was being a member of a commission, along with Lieutenant Governor James Patton and Dr. William Lattimore, which was appointed by the State Legislature in 1821 to find a suitable place for the seat of state government. The new capital was named Jackson, in honor of General Jackson, and the county was named Hinds.

Major Hinds' skill as a negotiator fell short. Before the commission had arrived, the purpose of the meeting had already leaked to the Choctaws. They were not happy. The sentiment among the leaders was, "How can the United States ask us for more land? Do they think that we can be frightened with these idle threats? The owa chita, the 'big hunt' to the west, will continue as it has since the days of our grandfathers. We will not be intimidated."

But the words spoken by Pushmataha at the council were much more subdued.

"This day we have made up our minds deliberately to answer our great father's talk. Children, even after they have grown to be men, ought to regard the advice of their fathers, as when they were small. I am sorry I cannot comply with the request...

"We have already considered your proposition to purchase some of our lands. We have decided that we have none to spare. If a man should give one-half his garment, the remainder would be of no use. When we had land to spare, we gave it, with very little talk, to the commissioners you sent to us at Tombigbee, as children ought to do to a father. We hope our father will not be displeased. He has made us happy from our infancy. We hope the same protection will be found in the arm as formerly...

"[And concerning] those of our people who are over the Mississippi, [they] did not go there with the consent of the Nation: They are like wolves; it is the wish of the council that the President would direct his agents to the West to order these stragglers home, and if they will not come, to direct them where he pleases."[25]

"WHAT DO YOU MEAN, it didn't work?" the President said as he threw his hands up and then started to pace behind his desk.

"It was a complete failure," Mr. Calhoun said. "The commission walked away with absolutely nothing. The leader of the Choctaws, Pushmataha, wouldn't budge, and unless he buys into it, it will never happen."

President Monroe continued to pace. "This cannot be allowed to happen. Do you know how much influence Mississippi has already achieved in the few years since it became a state?"

"Yes, Sir," Calhoun said.

The Secretary of War understood that the words "influence" could easily be replaced with the word "money."

"The Mississippi delegation will be breathing down my neck in no time," the President continued. "I'm sure they have already been apprised of the failure."

"Yes, Sir. I'm sure they have."

"I want another meeting scheduled with the Choctaws as soon as possible," the President said. "And I don't want a repeat of this last

---

[25] Lewis, Anna. *Chief Pushmataha-American Patriot*, Exposition Press, 1959, p. 127.

one. Do whatever it takes to get that land. Offer them a trade. Give them the Quapaw land."

"How much of it, Sir?"

"All of it, if that's what it takes. And get Andrew Jackson. I want him to head this commission."

"But, Sir, he has vowed to never participate in..."

"I know what he said," the President interrupted. "Send him a letter. Tell him that it's a personal request from me. The Choctaws know him and trust him. If anyone can make this happen, he can. He's a shrewd negotiator, and he will get them to agree.

"And get the agents in Mississippi—the ones we are paying to look out for those savages—get them to start earning their pay," Monroe continued. "They have a lot of influence with the natives and need to be using it. They need to make the Choctaws understand how important it is for them to negotiate—that they don't have a choice."

"Anything else, Sir?" Calhoun asked.

"Yes, I will have Congress approve twenty thousand dollars to be used to make the negotiations work smoothly. I want the commission to use it as they see fit—bribe the chiefs, give them presents, throw a big party, get them drunk—whatever it takes to get that land."

ANDREW JACKSON RELUCTANTLY agreed to chair the commission. In response to John Calhoun's letter, he wrote, "I had determined never to have anything to do again with Indian treaties... [But] I never can withhold my services when requested by Mr. Monroe, and I owe a debt of gratitude to the people of Mississippi and their late governor for their support in our late struggle with Great Britain—I feel it is a duty therefore to endeavor to serve them when they, by their representatives, believe it in my power."[26]

Jackson owed a debt of gratitude to the people of Mississippi, but time would make it apparent that the General felt no debt was owed to the Choctaws who had so faithfully supported him in that same war.

---

[26] Lewis, Anna. *Chief Pushmataha-American Patriot*, Exposition Press, 1959, p. 131.

"PUSH, MY FRIEND, I don't think there is a thing you can do about it," Lefleur said as he wiped his brow. He leaned forward—his sweat-soaked shirt stuck to his back and chest. "You were able to hold them off last year, but I'm afraid that the cession is inevitable."

It was August 1820. Relief from the heat and humidity was at least a month away, when the cool winds of fall would finally make Mississippi livable again. The meeting at Doak's Stand was set to take place in two months, the first week in October. According to General Jackson, negotiations always went better when the weather was cool. No need in having the hot weather a distraction and everyone sweaty and unhappy.

"There are too many white men pouring into the area along the Huch-chalusachitoh and the Yazoo River," Lefleur said. "The State of Mississippi is not going to stop pushing until that land is made available for sale."

The watershed of the Huch-chalusachitoh (the "Big Black River") and the Yazoo River with its tributaries—the Sunflower, the Yalobusha, and the Tallahatchie Rivers—covered a large flat, fertile area in west central and north Mississippi which would later be known as "The Delta."

Lefleur continued. "I'm sure you have heard that General Jackson is to be the chairman of this commission."

"Yes," Pushmataha replied. "Sharp Knife is a friend of mine and of the Choctaws. He understands what the land means to our people. His recommendations will be good and fair."

Lefleur shook his head in exasperation. He then let out a sigh and placed his hand on the Red man's shoulder.

"My friend, I hate to be negative, but Jackson does not have the best interest of the Choctaws in mind. He is representing the United States, and they want that land. They failed with Major Hinds, and they are confident that Jackson's ability to deal will get the job done this time.

"The entire state of Mississippi is jubilant that Jackson has agreed to the task. In fact, the *Natchez Gazette* reported that the city's Fourth of July festivities last month centered on Jackson's upcoming appearance. At a banquet, toasts were made to his health and his success. One of the toasts was that the distinguished General's visit would result in 'a speedy and just extermination of the Indian claims.'"

Lefleur walked over to a table, rummaged through some papers, and returned to his friend.

"And here's an article from the *Natchez Republican* that lets you know the sentiment of the white man."

He began to read and translate. "'The purchase of this tract of country has long been a desideratum with our citizens but the prospect of acquiring it has never been so flattering as at the present. And we look forward with pleasure to the period, and we deem it not far distant, when the rich and extensive prairies shall whiten with their luxuriant products and the din and bustle of active husbandry supersede the whoop of Indians, and the howling of the beast of the forest; when the comfortable farm house shall rise upon the ruins of the wigwam, and all that is now a dreary waste, present a scene of comfort, civilization, and wealth.'"[27]

Pushmataha's stomach tightened. "The ruins of the wigwam? A dreary waste?" he thought. "Are the Choctaws waging a losing battle with the United States? Is there any hope for the Red man? Is there no one to champion the cause of the Red man but the Red man himself?"

"Push, my friend, as I've told you in the past you are not going to win. You will lose that land, either peacefully or otherwise. My recommendation is to sign the treaty but to come away from the negotiations with as much as you possibly can."

ON SEPTEMBER 14, GENERAL JACKSON left Nashville traveling the Natchez Trace. Two weeks later he arrived at Doak's Stand, located on the Trace half way between Lefleur's Bluff and Frenchman's Camp. The General's charge by the President was to make this cession happen. Use whatever means—reason, flattery, coercion, threat of trade restrictions, threat of war, even bribery and

---

[27] *Natchez Republican* Aug 29, 1820.

blackmail—to get the Choctaws to sign. In the course of negotiation, the General would resort to all of these means.

Two days after his arrival, Major Hinds and John McKee, the other members of the commission, joined him. A small company of soldiers also arrived with provisions for the meeting—an abundance of food and whiskey.

The Choctaws slowly began to arrive in small groups. Their response to the gathering was quite varied from friendly to hostile. For many it was just another social gathering, a time for big talk and stickball.

The three district chiefs, Pushmataha, Mushulatubbee, and Apuckshanubbee arrived with their sub chiefs, mingos, and ball players. Within a few days several hundred had gathered for the event.

Pushmataha and Mushulatubbee had resigned themselves to the inevitable and were ready to proceed. Apuckshanubbee had not.

Apuckshanubbee was now close to eighty years old and still believed that the Choctaws could hold out against the encroachment of the white man. He made it very plain that he would cast his vote against cession.

"The Choctaws must not abandon the old ways," he held. "We must hold on to what we have. Do not be fooled by these promises and gifts. We cannot allow anymore of the land of our fathers and grandfathers to be taken away."

Not wanting to be indebted to the white man in any way, he and his men refused to partake in the food. They had brought their own provisions. And concerning the whiskey—the missionaries had warned him that the plan of the commission was to get the Choctaws drunk so that they would be more agreeable. He and his men refused to take the white man's oka humi. When Jackson heard this, he had the missionaries removed from the area.

"GENERAL, THE WORD IS that he has no intention of signing." Major Hinds said. "At the last meeting, it was Pushmataha who was the hold out. This time it's Apuckshanubbee."

"I wouldn't be quite so sure of that," Jackson replied. "Tell the chief that I want to have a private meeting with him. I have some information I wish to share with him."

James Pitchlynn, mixed-race son of longtime interpreter, John Pitchlynn, was a strong proponent of the treaty and had informed the General of a "situation" concerning the chief's family that might affect his vote.

THE GENERAL AND THE OLD CHIEF sat down to meet. After pleasantries had been passed through the interpreter, Jackson grinned and said, "Puckinub, I hear that one of your granddaughters has recently married."

Jackson fondly called the old chief "Puckinub."

The chief smiled back. "Yes, she is my favorite child. She has stolen the heart of her grandfather, and now she steals the heart of another."

"Well, give her my congratulations."

Jackson leaned back in his chair. "Now, I understand he's a white man. Welch is his name—am I right?"

The chief's eyebrows lifted slightly. "Yes, you are."

Jackson sat quietly with his elbows resting on the arms of the chair and his index fingers rubbing his lower lip. He began to nod smugly. Apuckshanubbee glanced up at the interpreter, and a hint of apprehension appeared in his stoic eyes.

The General finally spoke. "And the information I have is that Mr. Welch is a deserter from the United States Army—am I right? And am I also right in my information that he has been hiding out in your village for the past year?"

The smile on the old chief's face suddenly disappeared.

"My dear Puckinub, don't look so gloomy. Why, I have some good news for you. Mr. Welch just arrived here at this gathering. He is my 'invited guest' for the occasion. At this very moment he is 'visiting' with several soldiers a short distance from here."

Jackson leaned forward. His jaw began to tighten and his eyes narrowed. "Puckinub, do you know what we do with deserters?"

Apuckshanubbee did not respond.

The General stood up. "I have a lot of power, and so do you," he said. "With one word that boy's name can disappear forever from the rolls of the military. It will be as if he had never been a soldier at all. No one will ever come hunting for him. That's my power. Now, your power is in helping me make it happen."

The old chief's chin dropped to his chest. After a moment, he lifted his head, stood, and without a word left the tent.

"I think we are ready to meet," the General whispered to himself.

THOMAS L. WILEY

CHAPTER TWENTY-SIX

SHORTLY AFTER PUSHMATAHA arrived, he made a visit to his old friend, Sharp Knife.

"Push, my friend, how have you been?" The two men shook hands vigorously. "You're looking good—for an old man. Put on a little weight I can see, but you still have that boyish look about your face."

"The white man's ways have made me lazy," the chief said. "Too much sitting and not enough hunting."

"Yes, it's easy for that to happen." The General laughed. "But I tend to have the opposite problem. I can't seem to keep these bones of mine covered with any meat at all. My friends tell me that if I want to get into politics, I need to fatten up. Governors, Senators, and Presidents don't need to look poorly."

Jackson put his arm around Push's shoulder and ushered him to a couple of chairs in the corner of the one room building.

"Josiah," the General shouted to one of the two Doak brothers, Josiah and William, owners of the establishment. "Bring us a bottle of brandy and a couple of glasses."

He then laughed. "Push, my friend, the last time I saw you we were doing this very same thing—enjoying a bottle together. How long has it been? Five years? We had just whipped the British at Chalmette Plantation and were celebrating in New Orleans."

He put his hands up to his temples as if he had a headache.

"I don't remember much about that night, but I do remember waking up, and you were gone. What happened to you?"

"I had some business that needed taking care of," the chief said.

"I see," the General nodded. He had a look on his face that said, "I know more than I'm letting on."

"One of my men said he saw you leaving town, and you looked like you had lost your best friend."

Pushmataha didn't say anything as he thought about that night and the missing pipe.

"Push," Jackson said as he reached into his vest pocket, "you mind if I smoke?"

With that, he pulled out the white man's pipe and began to press a bit of tobacco into the bowl. He looked up and matter-of-factly said, "You been missing this?"

Pushmataha's eyes lit up. "Where did you get that?" he exclaimed.

"From a scoundrel."

Jackson lit the pipe, took a couple of puffs, and handed it to the chief.

"A few days after you left, we started on the long trip back home to Tennessee. We must have been on the road for only a few days when one night I was sitting at a fire with several soldiers. One of them pulled out a pipe and began to smoke. My friend, there are not very many pipes that look like this one, and I asked him where he got it. He said he took it from a drunken Choctaw in a tavern in New Orleans."

The General threw his hands up and hooted. "Can you believe it? That fellow stole the pipe from right under our noses! He apparently had no idea who you were or that it was I who was sitting right across from you at the time.

"Well, as you would expect I was livid. This low-life had stolen the pipe from one of the greatest warriors I have had the pleasure to fight beside. And right in front of my eyes to boot!

"I pulled out my pistol—I was so mad I was ready to kill him. If the guy next to me hadn't stopped me, I would have. Instead, he got a lashing that he will never forget. I bet he didn't sleep on his back for a month."

Pushmataha held the pipe up to eye level. He couldn't believe that this touch with the past had returned. Surely, he had thought, his father's pipe was lost forever. He turned it in his hands. It looked and felt as good as it did the last time he held it. Nothing had changed. The deer on the bowl continued to look to the heavens as the smoke swirled upwards.

"I didn't use it," the General said. "I didn't want to take a chance of damaging it."

"Sharp Knife," the chief said, "I wish to thank you for…"

"Don't mention it," Jackson said as he waved him off with his hand.

Josiah Doak approached the table and placed the bottle and glasses on the table. The General filled the glasses and lifted his for a toast.

"To friendship," he said. "May ours last forever. May nothing tarnish the bond that exists between our hearts."

Over the next several days the friendship between these two great men would not only become tarnished, but would be strained to the point of breaking.

AS TIME APPROACHED for the meeting to begin, the area around Doak's establishment took on the air of a large campground gathering. There were the Choctaws and Commissioners present to treaty, the military to feed and keep order, and the crowd of onlookers who showed up to watch. Even newspaper reporters were present. The treaty was big news—not only for the State of Mississippi but for the entire nation.

During the pre-meeting lull, one of the reporters requested an interview with Chief Pushmataha. The life of the great chief was what legends were made of, and soon the young reporter was spellbound by the tales, translated by an interpreter, that flowed so freely from this Red man's mouth.

During a brief pause, the reporter said, "I understand you have never divulged your origin. No one knows where you come from. A great man such as you should not withhold this information from his people or from the world."

Pushmataha stood and with a slight smile and a twinkle in his eye said, "So be it."

He then began to speak.

"IT WAS A LONG TIME AGO; at the season when the glorious sun was pouring down his brightest, balmiest and greatest life-giving influence; when the gay flowers, bedecked in their most gorgeous habiliments, were sweetest, brightest and most numerous; when the joyous birds in full chorus were chanting their gleeful songs of life and love, full of inspiration; when all nature seemed to quiver in rapturous emotion. 'Twas noon. The day was calm and fair and very pleasant.

"There was a beautiful wide spreading plain, with but few trees on it. One there was of giant size and venerable age. It was a red oak, and its dark waving branches, overshadowing an immense area of the beautiful green plain, had bid defiance and braved unscathed the storms of many winters. There it stood, vast in it proportions, calm in its strength, majestic in its attitude. It had witnessed the rise and fall of many generations of animal life. But everything must have its time, fulfill its destiny.

"That magnificent red oak, the prominent feature on that far reaching landscape, and had been for centuries, had not accomplished the object for which the Great Spirit had planted it. There it was in full foliage, casting its dark, widely spreading shadow upon the sunlit plain. All nature was clad in smiles of joy on that bright day.

"Anon a cloud was rising in the west; a black, angry threatening cloud, looming upwards and rapidly widening its scowling front. Harshly grumbling as it whirled its black folds onward, nearer and nearer, very soon it overspread the whole heavens, veiling the landscape in utter darkness and appalling uproar. It was a sweeping tornado, fringed with forked lightning, thunders rolling and bellowing; the winds fiercely howled and the solid earth trembled. In the height of this confusion and war of elements a burning flash of fire gleamed through the black obscurity. A shattering crash, followed by a burst of terrific thunder that, heavily rumbling through the surging storm, seemed to shake down the humid contents of the fast-rolling cloud in irresistible torrents. Awful sounds assailed the startled senses in all directions as the frightful tornado swiftly swept by in its devastating course.

"Soon it passed and was all calm again. The sun poured down his beaming rays in his wonted brilliancy; but the vast, time-honored sylvan king, the red oak, had been slivered into fragments, its odd-shapen splinters lay widely scattered on the rain-beaten plain. Not a vestige remained to mark the spot where once stood that towering tree. Not even a snag of the stump remained. The object of its creation was accomplished, and in its place, there was a new thing under the sun! Shall I name it? Equipped and ready for battle, holding in his right hand a ponderous club, standing erect on the place of the demolished red oak, was your dauntless chief, Apushimataha."[28]

With that, the chief sat down.

The young reporter could not speak. It was as if the Creation Story in Genesis had just been spoken to him by God. There was no doubting the chief's story. He knew that the truth could not have been any more real than the tale he had just heard.

WITH APUCKSHANUBBEE'S change of heart, the atmosphere of the meeting was almost one of revelry and excitement. On October 9, the day before the council was to meet, the different districts engaged in a stickball tournament with the chiefs and commissioners looking on.[29]

---

[28] Lincecum, Gideon. *The Life of Apushimataha*, 1861, Republished as *Pushmataha- A Choctaw Leader and His People*. Introduction by Greg O'Brien. The University of Alabama Press. 2004. p. 88.
[29] Stickball players were paid $8.00 a day to play at the gathering—a hefty sum in that day. Professional athletes were well paid long before there was football or

That night a great celebration was held with dancing and singing around a great bonfire. The Hopi called on Shilup Chitoh Osh, the Great Spirit, to guide the council that was to open on the morrow.

Whiskey flowed freely, but Pushmataha drank little. It was not that he didn't enjoy the oka humi. Through the years he had acquired a not-so-healthy taste for the "bitter water." But tonight, he must remain sober. His mind must remain clear for deliberations. There was too much at stake for the Choctaws.

On October 10, the council was called. The commissioners, General Andrew Jackson and Major Thomas Hinds, and the three chiefs, Apuckshanubbee, Mushulatubbee, and Pushmataha, formed the inner circle, and the lesser chiefs and observers circled outward—as had been the custom since the days of Chahtah and Chickasah. Among the interpreters was John Pitchlynn, who had witnessed every council since the meeting at Hopewell Plantation thirty-four years earlier.

The pipe was passed. Many recognized the long-lost white man's pipe of Pushmataha. Several nodded and commented favorably at seeing this emblem which had been absent for the past several years.

General Jackson was the first to speak.

"Esteemed members of the great nation of the Choctaws. The great chief in Washington, the President of the United States, sends his greetings. He wishes that he could join us for this great occasion, but the responsibilities of governing such a large country prevent him from doing so. I am his messenger, along with Major Hinds, and we will do our best to convey his desire to his Red children.

"It is stated to your father the President that a large proportion of his Choctaw children are in distressed condition, and require his friendly assistance. They live upon poor land, and are not willing to cultivate it. The game is destroyed, and many of them are often reduced to almost starvation. A few are to be found in Alabama, Louisiana, and Mississippi. A number are scattered over the country form Tennessee to New Orleans. Many have become beggars and

---

baseball.

drunkards, and are dying in wretchedness and want. Humanity requires that something be done for them.

"And it is not necessary for me to tell the Choctaw Nation that the State of Mississippi is in need of land. Settlers continue to come, desiring to live and farm in her fertile lands. With this influx, the land allotted for the white man seems to grow small. It is no longer adequate. Even as we speak, settlements spread beyond the confines of the cities and villages and are encroaching on the boundaries of the Choctaw Nation. In some areas, they have, against the will of the President, built their houses and barns on land that is rightfully claimed by the Choctaws.

"The desire of the President is to solve this problem by making a trade. He sees this as beneficial for both the white man and the Choctaw. With this arrangement, the white man will gain the land he needs, and the Choctaw will actually receive more land than he gives.

"The land that the great chief wishes to trade with the Choctaws is west of the Mississippi. It lies between the Red River and the Arkansas River. It is a large area with tall trees, fertile lands, and many rivers. The buffalo, antelope, deer, beaver, turkey, and bear are plentiful and have not been decimated in that land like they have been in the land that the Choctaws now own. Honey and fruit trees abound.

"In exchange for this land, the President wishes a small strip of land called the Huch-chalusachitoh, or the Big Black River Country."

The General continued to describe both lands, giving the boundaries of each in terms and landmarks that the Choctaws could relate to. When he finished, he sat and waited for the Choctaws' response.

The Choctaws did not answer immediately. Realizing the importance of this council and the gravity of their decision, the council passed the pipe again. They could not respond without first performing this sacred ceremony. When it was done, Pushmataha rose and spoke, addressing his own people first.

"This is General Jackson, the great warrior," he said motioning toward the General. "Many of you have heard of him. Some of you have seen him before; others of you have served under him in many successful battles. For all this, and because of his position as a representative of the President of the United States and his great character as a man and a warrior, the Choctaw people owe him respectful replies concerning his propositions." [30]

The chief then addressed the commission. "I recommend that the council adjourn until tomorrow in order that the Choctaws might have time to discuss among themselves the propositions outlined by the General." At that the council was adjourned.

As they left the area, Hinds whispered to Jackson. "All of this ridiculous ceremony and drama frustrates me to no end. We need to stop this procrastination and get on with the business at hand."

"Mr. Hinds," Jackson replied, "this is the way the Choctaws do things, and it would serve you well to take note. I have learned that the key to good negotiation, no matter the parties involved, is letting your opponent lead for a while. Make sure the pace is comfortable for him. It's like riding a horse. Let him have a little control. Neither hold the reins too tightly to slow him nor beat him with a stick to speed him, and he will perform better. We will follow the lead of the Choctaws."

THAT NIGHT THE LEADERS of the Choctaws met to discuss the proposition. There were concerns. They knew that the land that they would receive was not as wonderful as the General had said and that the land they would give up was not "a small strip of land." But overall, they felt that it was a good trade and would sign the treaty. They would be giving up approximately five million acres of homeland for thirteen million acres of Quapaw land, and still have ten million acres left in Mississippi. Also, they knew that they really didn't have a choice. If they did not agree, the land would surely be taken from them by force.

"But we will not sign immediately," Pushmataha said, "we must negotiate. Ask for much and hope for little."

---

[30]Cushman, H. B., *History of the Choctaw, Chickasaw, and Natchez Indians*, 1899, Edited by Angie Debo, 1962, p. 60.

The next day at noon the council reconvened. After the usual formalities, Pushmataha rose to speak.

"I, PUSHMATAHA, have been appointed to reply to the proposition of the commissioners. Appreciating the magnitude of the negotiations and being in contact with two such great men who represent the great chief in Washington, I am overcome with a feeling of incompetence. But then, it should make little difference in the capacities of the two parties when business is intended to be transacted in a fair and honest way. Whether one party is represented by as great a man as General Jackson and the other a fool, the results should be the same. It is the responsibility of the wise man to protect the interests of the fool, keeping him on safe footing.

"From what I have already discovered, this great transaction, now about to take place between two friendly nations who dwell almost in mixed society together, is not to be conducted on those equitable principles, and it is not safe for me, the fool that I am, to rely upon such expectations.

"The object and benefits to be derived by the United States are great and very desirable. If this were not so, the President would not have sent two of his greatest warrior generals to conduct the treaty in his behalf. I am friendly towards the United States and particularly so to these two distinguished agents, for I have served under and side by side with them in the hour of peril and deathly strife. I have aided them in the acquisition of Florida and a considerable portion of the Creek country.

"Under these conditions, I had intended to strike the bargain. I had thought that it was to be one of those kinds of swaps that could be fairly made and would accommodate both parties. I will do my best, and hope to succeed, in presenting our side of the negotiation in such a manner as to convince the commissioners that further misrepresentation will not be necessary."[31]

When he finished, he sat down without glancing to either his fellow Red men or the commissioners seated next to him.

General Jackson rose. He walked forward and turned around. A look of concern and confusion was on his face. He stood silently for a moment, rubbing his chin as if to collect his thoughts.

"Brother Push, you have uttered some hard words. You have openly accused me of misrepresentation and indirectly of the desire to defraud the red people in behalf of my government. These are heavy charges, charges of a very serious character. You must explain yourself in a manner that will clear them up or I shall quit you."[32]

Again, Pushmataha stood to speak. In his eyes was the fire of a great warrior and a great orator.

"AS MEN GROW OLDER, especially great men, enthralling themselves with much business on the field of growing fame, they become impatient and irritable. They dare not stop on the path of their rushing and varying necessities to parley with the ignorant. They must make short work with all such obstructions. There is no honor in permitting the feeble or the foolish he may meet in his precipitate course to pass. No allowance is to be made or forgiveness offered for him. He must yield to the mere say so of the warily moving seeker of fame or be crushed. I have been making observations on that cast of character a long time, and find but little difference in their public

[31] Lincecum, Gideon. *Life of Apushimataha*, Publication of the Mississippi Historical Society, Volume 8-9, 1906. p. 469.
[32] Lincecum, Gideon. *Life of Apushimataha*, Publication of the Mississippi Historical Society, Volume 8-9, 1906. p. 469.

action. In their private intercourse the whole thing is changed.

"My great friend, General Jackson, who familiarly calls me brother, whom my inner soul loveth, and in whose presence I always felt myself a mere boy, has become excited at some of my remarks, and has hastily called on me to explain them, and that explanation must be satisfactory or he will 'quit us,' the meaning of which, as I suppose, is that should I fail to make the 'amende honorable' he returns to his government and informs them that the insulting obstinacy of the Chahta people is such that an honorable treaty cannot be negotiated with them. Then comes the horrors of war against us. All I have to say about it is that I hope they will have the good sense and the justice to put it upon those only who have raised the fuss to do the fighting. It would indeed be a great error in the justice of any government to involve the innocent inhabitants of two nations in the ruinous consequences of war on account of a misunderstanding betwixt two of their ministers...

"I shall take much pleasure in my explanation to render a plain and irrefutable interpretation of what I have said, and I will present in a very clear light the misrepresentations in relation to the quality of the country west of the Mississippi and the size of the country on this side of the great river...

"In the first place he speaks of the country he wishes to obtain in the swap as 'a little slip of land at the lower part of the present Chahta nation,' whereas it is a very considerable tract of country. He has designated the boundaries of it himself, and I am very familiar with the entire tract of land it will cut off from us. In the second place, he represented the country he wishes to exchange for the 'little slip' as being a very extensive country 'of tall trees, many water courses, rich lands and high grass, abounding in game of all kinds—buffalo, bear, elk, deer, antelope, beaver, turkeys, honey and fruits of many kinds.'

"I am also well acquainted with that country. I have hunted there often, have chased the Comanche and the Osage over those endless plains, and they have sometimes chased me there. I know the country well. It is indeed a very extensive land, but a vast amount of it is exceedingly poor and sterile, traceless, sandy deserts, nude of vegetation of any kind. As to tall trees, there is no timber anywhere except on the bottom lands... [He is right that] the buffalo in the western portion are very numerous and easily taken; antelope, too, are there and deer almost everywhere except in the dry, grassless desert... Turkeys are plentiful on all the water courses. There are, however, but few beavers, and the honey and fruit are rare things... The river bottoms are generally good soil but liable to inundation during the spring season, and in the summers the rivers and creeks dry up or become so salty that the water is awful for use... and will purge a man like medicine.

"This account differs widely from the description given by my friend yesterday and constitutes what is my reply to him I styled a misrepresentation. He has proved to me by that misrepresentation and one egregious error that he is entirely ignorant of the geography of the country he is offering to swap, and therefore I shall acquit him of an intention at fraud. The testimony that he bears against himself in regard to his deficiency of a knowledge of the geography of that far off country manifests itself in the fact that he has offered to swap to me an undefined portion of Mexican territory. He offers to run the line up the Canadian River to its source and thence due south to the Red River. Now I know that a line running due south from the source of the Canadian would never touch any portion of the Red River, but would go into the Mexican possessions beyond the limits of even my geographical knowledge."[33]

General Jackson interrupted him: "See here, Brother Push, you must be mistaken. Look at this map; it will prove to you at once that you are laboring under a great geographical error yourself."[34] He then spread out the map.

Pushmataha examined it closely and then said, "The paper is not true," and he began to trace out the actual courses of the rivers and the land involved in the swap.

Jackson shook his head. "You must be mistaken. At any rate I am willing to make good the proposition I have named."

"Very well," replied Pushmataha, "and you must not be surprised nor think hard of me if I point your attention to another subject within the limits of the country you have designated west of the Mississippi which you do not seem to be apprised of. The lower portion of the land you propose to swap is a pretty good country. It is true that as high up the Arkansas River as Fort Smith the lands are good and timber and water plenty; but there is an objectionable difficulty lying in the way... What I ask to know is whether the American settlers [who live in this land] are to be considered Indians or white people?"

"General Jackson whispered to one of his aids and then replied. "As for the white people on the land ... there are perhaps a few hunters scattered over the country, and we will have them ordered off."

"I beg your pardon," replied Pushmataha. "There are a great many of them, many of them substantial, well-to-do settlers, with good houses and productive farms, and they will not be ordered off [so easily]."[35]

---

[33] Lincecum, Gideon. *Life of Apushimataha*, Publication of the Mississippi Historical Society, Volume 8-9, 1906. p. 471.

[34] Lincecum, Gideon. *Life of Apushimataha*, Publication of the Mississippi Historical Society, Volume 8-9, 1906. P. 471.

[35] Lincecum, Gideon. *Life of Apushimataha*, Publication of the Mississippi Historical Society, Volume 8-9, 1906. p. 472.

The General was beginning to appear irritated, either at his lack of knowledge or at the profound knowledge of his opponent.

"I will send my warriors, and by the eternal I'll drive them into the Mississippi or make them leave it."

"Very well," replied the chief. "The matter is settled as far as the land west of the great river is concerned. We will next consider the boundary and country the Chahtas are to give you for it, and if we can agree upon that, the trade will be completed. You have defined its boundaries, and they include a very valuable tract of country, of considerable extent, capable of producing corn, cotton, wheat and all the crops the white man cultivates. Now, if we do agree to terms and run this line, it must, as a part of this contract, be very clearly understood, and put on paper in a form that will not die nor wear out, that no other alterations shall be made in the boundaries of that portion of our territory that will remain until the Chahta people are sufficiently progressed in the arts of civilization to become citizens of the State, owning land and homes of their own, on an equal footing with the white people. Then it may be surveyed and the surplus sold for the benefit of the Chahta people."

"That," said General Jackson, "is a magnificent arrangement and we consent to it readily." [36]

Pushmataha and the other chiefs understood that the days of the hunter—the days when the Redman could venture where he wanted, hunt where he wanted, and place his lodge where he wanted—especially east of the Mississippi, were rapidly coming to a close. The Choctaw had to learn the ways of the white man and become "civilized" or move. He had no other choice—except to disappear from existence. If he stayed in Mississippi, he had to learn to lay claim to parcels of land and manage the land as the white man did. And when that happened, the stipulations that Pushmataha demanded would ensure that the remaining land—land that was not "owned" by

---

[36] Lincecum, Gideon. *Life of Apushimataha*, Publication of the Mississippi Historical Society, Volume 8-9, 1906. p. 472.

an individual Choctaw—would not be ceded but would be sold by the Choctaws for a profit.

Pushmataha also knew that there were many Choctaws who were not ready for the white man's ways and wanted to continue the lifestyle of their forefathers for as long as they could. The Quapaw land would allow them a place to migrate and continue a nomadic existence. To benefit those who wished to migrate, Pushmataha made another demand, that "those who choose to go west [will be furnished] with a good rifle gun, bullet molds, a camp kettle, one blanket, and ammunition to last one year, corn to support them on the journey and for one year after getting there."[37]

He also demanded that "out of the lands we are about to [give up], fifty-four sections of a mile square each shall be surveyed and sold to the best bidder by the United States, for the purpose of raising a fund to support the Chahta schools in the western country of the Chahtas, the whole to be placed in the hands of the President of the United States to be dealt out by him for school purposes only in the Chahta Nation...

"One more specification and I am done. There are a good many warriors who have not been compensated for their services during the campaign to Pensacola. Pay them, and settle with those who have good houses and are living on the ceded territory, and if you, the commissioners, agree to what I have proposed, it is a bargain."[38]

On October 18, 1820, the Treaty of Doak's Stand was signed. Five million acres of prime farmland in Mississippi were traded for thirteen million acres of land in the future states of Arkansas and Oklahoma. Choctaw individuals were not required to leave the ceded area. If they wished to stay, each would be deeded one square mile to include his improvements. For those who desired to move, their homes would be appraised and reimbursements made, and provisions as stipulated by Pushmataha would be made to assist in their migration to

---

[37] Lincecum, Gideon. *Life of Apushimataha*, Publication of the Mississippi Historical Society, Volume 8-9, 1906. p. 473.

[38] Lincecum, Gideon. *Life of Apushimataha*, Publication of the Mississippi Historical Society, Volume 8-9, 1906. p. 473.

the land in the west. The warriors who participated in the war in Florida were finally compensated after waiting over five years. Land would be sold to further the education of the Choctaw children.

Pushmataha truly felt that the Treaty of Doak's Stand would help in the assimilation of the Choctaws into the white culture. His vision was that one day the Red man would live and work alongside the white man. In his closing remarks at the council on that cool October day, the great chief said,

> "I HERE VENTURE the prediction that the day will come, and there are many children and some grown men here today who will live to see it, when the highly improved Chahta shall hold office in the councils of the great nation of white people and in their wars with the nations of the earth. Mixed up in the armies of the white man, the fierce war whoop of the Chahta warrior shall strike terror and melt the hearts of an invading foe. Mind that, Pushmataha has this day declared it, and his words of prophecy are not uttered foolishly or trivially. I believe it thoroughly, and the contemplation of the great and so happy a change in condition of my people is cheering to this old heart."[39]

Some would say that his prediction has yet to come to fruition.

---

[39] Lincecum, Gideon. *Life of Apushimataha*, Publication of the Mississippi Historical Society, Volume 8-9. 1906. p. 475.

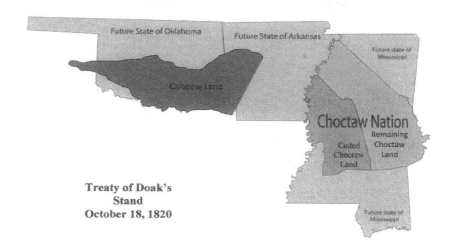

Treaty of Doak's Stand 1820

CHAPTER TWENTY-SEVEN

"MR. PRESIDENT, I SEE no alternative but to delay the migration of the Choctaws from Mississippi."

President Monroe rubbed his temples in frustration as John Calhoun continued to speak.

"The settlers in the Arkansas Territory are all up in arms. They say that Jackson had no right to trade their land to the Choctaws. They are demanding that the treaty be renegotiated."

Two years had passed since the Treaty of Doak's Stand had been signed, and things initially progressed smoothly. Preparations were well underway to help relocate those who wished to migrate to the Quapaw Land, and surprisingly a large number of Choctaws wished to move. The agents in Mississippi had done a fairly good job in convincing the Choctaws that their freedom in the west was better than a square mile of land in Mississippi. Congress appropriated $65,000 to aid in the relocation, and agents were hired for the new land to help the move run smoothly.

But a problem surfaced that brought everything to a halt. A year after the treaty was signed, Calhoun sent Henry B. Downs to survey the land west of the Mississippi that the Choctaws now owned. He found that the maps used in the treaty were inaccurate—as the uneducated Choctaw chief had warned—and getting things straightened out was more of a problem than anyone anticipated.

Downs found that not only were the renderings of the Canadian and Red Rivers wrong, but the eastern boundary that had been agreed upon gave the Choctaws a considerable amount of land in the newly formed Arkansas Territory. Quite a few whites had already settled in this area along the Arkansas, Red, and Ouachita Rivers—again as the

Choctaw chief had warned—and more were coming in every day. According to the Treaty these settlers were now squatters in Choctaw territory and should be removed. In Jackson's words "by eternal I'll make them leave it or drive them into the Mississippi."

The relocation suddenly became one big headache for the President and the Secretary of War.

Calhoun continued. "Jackson was so eager to get the treaty signed that he set the eastern boundaries too far east. That is Jackson's failing; he acts before he thinks."[40]

"It's hard to imagine," Calhoun smirked, "but that guy wants to be President."

Monroe laughed. "Yes, he does—with a passion—and I have no doubt that he will make it. Now we do have to give him some credit with the boundaries. He was using maps that were erroneous. I understand that they were based on old French and Spanish drawings."

"Yes, sir, that's true," Calhoun admitted. "But he tends to make up his own rules as he goes, and the country is now paying for it."

The Secretary of War placed his satchel on the President's desk. "Now getting back to the settlers in the Arkansas Territory. They're not going to budge. Many of them have put a lot of work in building their homesteads and have too much at stake to pick up and leave. They say that they will not be intimidated by the government. And their numbers are growing. Settlers are heading across the Mississippi River by the droves."

Calhoun reached into his satchel and pulled out a stack of papers. "Here are dozens of letters from the Arkansas Territorial Legislature and private citizens voicing their protest. They not only object to the boundary claims, but they insist that there are too many savages in Arkansas as it is, and they can't handle anymore. They are extremely upset at how their government is handling this situation. Here's an editorial from the Arkansas *Gazette* voicing their sentiments. '… The government cares less for her citizens who helped fight the American Revolution and England than she does for a few ruthless savages.'"

---

[40] Lewis, Anna. *Chief Pushmataha-American Patriot*, Exposition Press, 1959, p. 165.

The President began to pace with his face turned to the floor. "What a mess! On the east side of the Mississippi the citizens are breathing down my neck to get the natives moved, and on the west, they're demanding that it not happen. It is a no-win situation, and those savages are caught in the middle."

He paused, looked up, and chuckled. "Are you sure we can't just shoot the poor savages and get it over with? That would, by far, be the simplest solution."

"Don't think that I haven't considered it," the Secretary of War answered.

"Send a letter to the Mississippi Governor—what's his name?" Monroe asked.

"Walter Leake," Calhoun replied. "Remember, he was here in Washington as one of their Senators before becoming Governor.

"That's right. Walter Leake—and the Arkansas Territorial Governor..." Monroe scratched his head.

"James Miller," Calhoun again replied, perturbed at the President's lack of knowledge of the southwest leadership.

"Yes. Mr. Miller. Send them a post that we are halting the relocation until the matter of the boundaries is settled. And tell Leake that I want a meeting called as soon as possible with the Choctaws to discuss renegotiating the treaty. He's not going to be happy with the delay, but smooth his feathers. Tell him we will get the savages moved—it's just going to take a little longer than we anticipated."

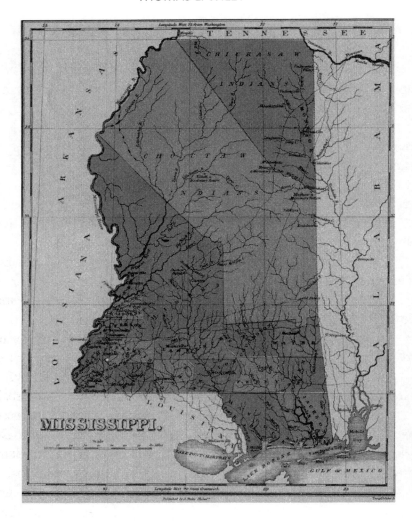

Mississippi, 1822.
Denoting Remaining Choctaw and Chickasaw Land
Following the Treaty of Doak's Stand.

"WELL, LOOK AT THAT!" the Frenchman exclaimed.

He and his Red friend had just sat down at the table and had poured themselves a drink when the chief pulled out his pipe and began to fill the bowl with tobacco. Pushmataha took a few puffs and passed it to his friend.

"I thought this thing was stolen!" Lefleur said as he turned the pipe in his hands, surprised to see this magnificent piece of art again. "How in the world…"

"It *was* stolen," the Red man interrupted. "It was taken by one scoundrel and thief and returned by another."

Pushmataha related the story of the pipe's return.

"Well, my friend, I'm glad you have it back. And it looks as good as it did the last time I saw it."

The two talked about old times and family as they shared the pipe and the bottle.

"My children are about grown," Lefleur said. "One of my middle sons, Greenwood, is trying to get involved with the politics of the Choctaw Nation. I think he has his eye on being chief someday."

Pushmataha was well aware of Greenwood Lefleur/Leflore. Three years earlier, at age twenty, the young Leflore had been present at Doak's Stand as part of the Okla Falaya, or Western, District contingency under the leadership of Apuckshanubbee. He had even signed the treaty as one of the hundred lesser chiefs and mingos.

But Pushmataha was wary of Leflore and several other up-and-coming mixed-race Choctaws, including David Folsom of the Okla Tannap District and Robert Cole of the Okla Falaya. These less-than-pure Choctaws were very aggressive in their desire to lead, and Pushmataha worried that their primary interest may not be what was best for the Choctaw people. Pushmataha had made it known on several occasions that no mixed-race should ever be made a primary chief. He did not voice this sentiment to his friend on this day as the two visited.

During a lull in the conversation, Lefleur eyed the Red man with curiosity. "My friend, to what do I owe this visit from the chief of the

Okla Hannali. I know you didn't come all this way to show me your pipe and talk about family."

Pushmataha puffed on his pipe for a minute before answering. "William Ward, the United States agent to the Choctaws, tells us that the President wants to renegotiate the last treaty. He says that the white man feels that the boundaries of the treaty were in error and wishes to redraw them. He wants a council called as soon as possible."

Lefleur placed his glass on the table and leaned back. "Yes, my friend, I've also heard this. The white settlers in the Arkansas Territory have raised quite a ruckus. Some of the land that was given to the Choctaws in the treaty is claimed by them, and they're not happy about it."

Pushmataha spoke. "When the council at Doak's Stand was finished, all was settled. We made a treaty—a trade—in good faith. The terms were written on paper and signed by Sharp Knife and Hinds and the chiefs of the Choctaws. The treaty was to be 'renewed, continued, and declared perpetual.'[41] It was to be a testament of everlasting friendship between our two peoples—to last as long as the sun continues to rise in the east. All involved—white man and Red man—were pleased.

"But now the President wishes to destroy the paper and write it anew. He says there were errors in the treaty."

Pushmataha spat on the ground. "Sharp Knife was told that the rivers were not drawn correctly, and he was told that there were settlers in the area of the Arkansas. I spoke these words to him myself. He gave his word that the discrepancies would be corrected and that he would make things right if we signed. He said that he would personally remove the white men if necessary. He gave his word. Has he become a liar? Is his word no good?"

"My friend," Lefleur said, "it's not as simple as Jackson breaking his word. It's quite complicated. The view is that the government gave away land that was not rightfully theirs to give. That land had already been settled. The President says that it would not be right to forcefully

---

[41] Treaty of Doak's Stand 1820.

remove the settlers from the land that they had worked and claimed—land that was rightfully theirs."

Pushmataha's jaw tightened and he clinched his fist.

"'Not right to forcefully remove them from land that was rightfully theirs.' My white friend, do you not see the irony of the words that you just spoke? Do the words not catch in your throat and choke you? Do you not know that for as long as the white man has been in contact with the Red man, he has taken? He kills and steals and lies and makes false promises to take from the Red man what is rightfully his. He does it without remorse. He sees no shame in his deeds. It is as if he views the Red man as less than human, below his concern, and treats him as an animal, as a dog, to be trampled upon."

Lefleur did not respond. There was no response that would be satisfactory.

Pushmataha continued. "Even now the State of Mississippi demands that our people leave the land of our forefathers, but the President tells us that those who wish to migrate cannot until the treaty is rewritten. What recourse does the Choctaw have? What is he to do? It is as if he is being backed into a corner with nowhere to go, and a wolf is closing in. If he does not fight back with all he has, he will surely die."

A look of concern came over Lefleur's face. This talk of fighting did not sound good. "What do you propose to do?" the white man asked.

The chief leaned forward and with fire in his dark eyes he said, "We will fight."

He then leaned back and his face softened.

"But do not worry. The fight will not be with the gun or the bow, for the Choctaws would surely lose. We are not fools. To bear arms against the United States would lead to the extinction of our race. No, instead we will fight back with words and papers.

"Major Hinds is calling for another council and wishes to meet immediately. I have spoken with the other chiefs, Apuckshanubbee and Mushulatubbee, and we will not meet. We are tired of meeting. Nothing is to be accomplished by a council with him. All he will desire to do is take. He will not meet with the desire to give. No, we will not council."

"But, my friend," Lefleur said, "You know as well as I do that he won't take 'no' for an answer. If you don't meet, he'll force his plans on your people without you having any say in the matter. And how can you fight with words and paper if you don't meet?"

"We have decided that the only way for the Choctaws to be heard is to council with the White Chief personally and appeal directly to him. We will request an audience with the President."

CHAPTER TWENTY-EIGHT

IN SEPTEMBER 1824, PUSHMATAHA made a visit to his old friend George S. Gaines at Fort St. Stephens. Five years earlier in 1819, Alabama had been admitted to the Union, and Fort St. Stephens, the territorial capital, had become the first state capital. Within months, however, the capital was moved to Cahawba, a more central area of the state, signaling the doom of this once thriving town on the Tombigbee River. At its height, St. Stephens boasted several thousand citizens—the largest town west of Georgia and east of Natchez. In the 1820's the population began to decline, and a yellow fever epidemic sealed her fate. Within two decades the once bustling metropolis was a ghost town.

The two men shared a drink and a smoke as they visited.

"The town's drying up," Gaines said. "Governor Bibb is to blame: he recommended the capital be moved. Most of the 'important people' have already gone. Also, boats aren't stopping here like they used to. They are traveling further north, to Possum Town—or Columbus as they now call it. When they return, their hulls are almost scraping the bottom of the river with all the cotton they have loaded. That Black Prairie must really be fertile land."

Gaines sighed deeply. "Hopefully we'll survive."

"The white man will survive," Pushmataha said. "His town may die, but he will live. The Choctaw is different. I worry that his continued existence is in jeopardy. Ironically, without the help of the white man—who is the cause of his decline—the Choctaw will surely die."

Pushmataha paused as he puffed on his pipe.

"In two weeks I leave for Washington. I will appeal to the white chief for help. Our lands to the west are in danger of being lost."

Gaines nodded in agreement. "I understand your concern. I worry about the direction this country is taking in dealing not only with the Choctaws but with all the nations of the Red man. There seems to be no compassion. They can't see beyond their own white faces. And as far as that land dispute, it's going to be an uphill battle for your people to keep it. It's hard to deal with the government when they have their minds set."

"My nephew, Nittuckachee, will go with us to Washington," the chief said. "He is wise and will one day become a chief of the Choctaws."

Pushmataha drew on his pipe and stared straight ahead.

"If I do not return, furnish him with a keg of powder. I wish there to be a great celebration from my people for my life that is gone."

Gaines sat still for a moment, not really knowing how to respond to such a request for a celebration. Did the chief really think he would not return? Gaines knew that the Red man often had premonitions that came to pass.

"My friend," he finally said, "I'll be glad to."

TWO WEEKS LATER the Choctaw delegation began their long journey to Washington. In addition to the three district chiefs, Pushmataha, Apuckshanubbee, and Mushulatubbee, the group included Nittuckachee, Red Fort, Talking Warrior, and mixed-race Choctaws David Folsom and Robert Cole. Interpreters accompanying the group were I. L. McDonald and the ever-present John Pitchlynn.

Unknown to the group, Washington was in the midst of political turmoil—experiencing a change in leadership and policies that occurs every four years due to the election process. Monroe was finishing his second term, and a new white father, John Quincy Adams, had been elected and would be inaugurated the next spring. His Vice President would be John C. Calhoun.

Neither Monroe nor Calhoun was willing to take on the cause of a group of savages when one of them was on the rise and the other was on the way out. And another factor that played against the Choctaws— the defeated candidate for President was none other than Andrew

Jackson. Like him or not, there was little chance of getting help from him, and the "bad blood" that so often flows in the campaign and election process would color the new President's desire to help anyone who was considered a friend to his recent opponent.

The group traveled northeast by land along the Natchez Trace to Nashville. From there they traveled through Kentucky, crossing the Ohio River at Maysville, Kentucky. At Chillicothe, Ohio, the party travelled east on the newly constructed National Highway to Baltimore and finally arrived at the nation's capital.

Travel was slow. The eighty-plus year old Apuckshanubbee had insisted on going even though his health was declining. He still remained one of the most outspoken of the group on not yielding to the white man's demands. Blackmail had caused him to falter at Doak's Stand, but in Washington his voice would be heard.

"WE WILL STOP HERE for the night and ferry across the Ohio River in the morning," the governmental escort announced. "I'll find a place for us to take supper and stay for the night."

It was late on the evening of October 10 when the delegation arrived in Maysville. The October weather was cool, and a light drizzle chilled the air even more.

The three chiefs slowly climbed out of the stagecoach. Apuckshanubbee could hardly move. His tall frame had been cramped in the cold, damp coach for hours, and his rheumatism had him "stove up." For several minutes, until his legs allowed him to move on his own, he held onto David Folsom's arm.

Soon the escort returned. "We'll be staying at the tavern of Captain John Langhorne. It should do satisfactorily, and he will have a meal ready for us shortly."

"So, you're from Mississippi," Langhorne commented as he placed several bottles of brandy on the table. The government was picking up the tab for the journey. There was no need for restraint.

"Yes," interpreter John Pitchlynn answered, "We are a delegation from the Choctaw Nation traveling to Washington to meet with the President."

"I have ties to Mississippi," the innkeeper replied as he served the group a steamy venison stew. "I was born there forty-five years ago in 1779. I don't remember much about it, though. Pa died from the pox when I was four, and my Ma moved us to Kentucky shortly after that to be with family. It was a real frontier back then—savages everywhere—but I understand it's pretty tame now."

As the last word left his mouth, he suddenly gasped and looked around at the "savages" sitting at his table.

"Don't be concerned," Pitchlynn said as he blew on a spoon of stew to cool it. "Most of them don't speak a word of English, and those that do didn't bring their scalping knives."

Pitchlynn and the few who did understand English burst out laughing.

BRANDY FLOWED FREELY, and the men sat and drank and laughed. After a while, the aged Apuckshanubbee stood up unsteadily.

"Whiskey soothes my bones like bear grease on an old wagon wheel," he said as he stumbled to the door. "I will walk the streets. I need to move around tonight, for tomorrow my knees will again be touching my chin as we travel. I must prepare myself."

The group continued to visit and drink. After about an hour, Pushmataha became concerned that the old chief hadn't returned.

During a lull in the conversation, Pushmataha looked toward the door. "Apuckshanubbee hasn't returned. Someone should check on him."

"I will go," David Folsom said and began to laugh. "It wouldn't be right for a chief of the Choctaw Nation to be sleeping on the streets when there's a warm bed inside."

I'll join you," interpreter McDonald said. "You need someone who speaks good English. Yours is so bad that if you get lost, no one will know that you're asking for directions."

The two laughed as they headed out the door. The rest of the party continued to visit and drink.

Thirty minutes later the door burst open. Folsom and McDonald rushed in carrying a limp Apuckshanubbee. The long grey hair on the back of his head was matted with dried blood.

"Quickly," Folsom said, "get him to a bed! He's badly hurt!"

Apuckshanubbee was taken to the nearest bed. Captain Langhorne sent one of his servants for the doctor.

Out of breath, Folsom began to relate the story.

"Shortly after we left, we came upon a crowd overlooking a steep ravine. One of those standing there said that he thought he saw someone fall over the edge, but it was dark and he was not positive. McDonald and I, expecting the worst, climbed down the steep embankment and found Apuckshanubbee at the bottom—unconscious and in bad shape. With the help of some of the crowd, we retrieved him from the ravine and brought him here without delay."

The doctor arrived within minutes and examined the old man thoroughly. "He appears to have a severe concussion and may even have a fractured skull. His shoulder is definitely fractured. It does not look good."

Two days later the old chief died, never having regained consciousness.

THE PRESENCE OF THE CHOCTAW delegation in their little community and now the death of one of their chiefs was the talk of the town. Not since Daniel Boone had settled there for a short time thirty years ago and opened a tavern had there been this much excitement in Maysville. Almost five hundred townspeople attended the funeral as the ancient warrior was laid to rest in Old Maysville Cemetery. Even the Methodist Minister, Reverend Corwine, spoke a few words of comfort and hope at the graveside.

The death of his old friend concerned Pushmataha greatly. Even though the two had not seen eye to eye on many matters, Apuckshanubbee's heart was good, and he always did what he thought was right for the Choctaw people. Some saw the old chief's ancient ways as a hindrance to the treaty process, but Pushmataha felt that his voice would have been good in council with the President, ensuring that the white chief understood the heart and soul of the Choctaw Nation.

Robert Cole was in line to become chief of the Okla Falaya. Pushmataha had his doubts about how well this young mixed-race Choctaw could lead and whether his decisions would be colored by the white blood that flowed in his veins. Could he be depended on to lead his Red brothers with their best interest in mind?

And even though he was certain that Apuckshanubbee's death was an accident, it concerned him that the governmental escort, as well as the mixed-races in the delegation, seemed relieved and almost glad that he was gone.

AFTER THE BURIAL, the delegation continued their journey through Ohio and Virginia and arrived in Washington on October 27, 1824. They took up lodging at the Tenneson Hotel where all delegations of the Red man resided while on official business in the capital. The staff, used to dealing with the natives, was more than eager to follow the instructions of the government—entertain and feed their guests at the expense of the government. According to the national leaders, the best way to get the savages ready to treaty was to fill them with food and liquor. Over the next few months, the government did just that. They reimbursed the hotel $2,149.50 for liquor, $2,028 for food, and $1,134.75 for clothing to keep the Choctaw delegation entertained.[42]

"WE ARE READY TO MEET with the President."

The partying had gone on long enough. The delegation had enjoyed themselves at the expense of the United States for almost two weeks, and the inactivity was becoming tiresome. It was time to get down to the business at hand. Also, the November weather in Washington had turned cold and wet, and these southern natives were ready to get back to where "cold" was fifty degrees.

The delegation had yet to have any contact with the President or the Secretary of War, except for a note delivered by a Presidential aide

---

[42] Lewis, Anna, *Pushmataha-American Patriot*, Exposition Press, 1959, p. 171.

welcoming them to Washington and telling them to have a good time. Every few days the aide returned to the Tenneson to check on them and make sure everything was satisfactory.

"President Monroe and Mr. Calhoun have been very busy of late," the aide replied to Pushmataha's desire to meet. "It should only be a few more days until a meeting can be arranged."

After another week of waiting and continued vagueness from the aide on a meeting time, Pushmataha decided to submit a report to Mr. Calhoun in the form of a letter.

"Sir:

"At the period about two years subsequent to the treaty which was made with our nation in the autumn of the year 1820, some of the chiefs were notified by Colonel William Ward, the United States agent, that it was a desire of the Government to procure a modification of the treaty, and that for that purpose commissioners had been or would be appointed to meet the Choctaws in council. We were surprised at the proposition, especially when we learned that the contemplated treaty was with a view of repurchasing some of the lands which had been given to the Choctaws beyond the Mississippi by the Treaty of 1820. We knew that white settlers were on the land proposed to be ceded. General Jackson was informed of the fact. He stated that the arm of the government was strong and that the settlers should be removed. They have not, however, been removed, nor have we learned that any efforts have been made to effect their removal.

"We told the United States agent that we were not, at that time, willing to meet the commissioners. We wished to visit the President and hold a talk with him. We have often met commissioners. We have stated to them at different times some of the many grievances, and we have asked for redress. They had uniformly stated in reply that they were unable to grant them, that their power was limited.

"We, therefore, on this occasion wished to visit the President, the fountainhead of all power, and have a full understanding with him on all points of difference between our white brothers and ourselves. We have accordingly arrived—twenty years since our last visit.

Pushmataha, Chairman, Mushulatubbee, David Folsom, Robert Cole, Talking Warrior, Nittuckachee, Red Fort. Interpreters, John Pitchlynn, I.L. McDonald."[43]

THE PRESIDENT LOOKED UP at Mr. Calhoun as he finished reading the letter.

"John, they do understand that this is not negotiable? The land in Arkansas *is* going to be ceded back to the United States."

"No, Sir," the Vice President-elect answered. "The Choctaws still think that they have bargaining power."

The President placed the paper on his desk. "They need to realize that the question is not will it happen, but how it will be done with the least uproar among the citizens in Mississippi and the settlers in Arkansas.

"And that land in the eastern section of Mississippi," he continued, "are they aware that it is to be given up also?"

There was an area of prime farmland along the Tombigbee River which Mississippi was demanding to be ceded from the ever-shrinking Choctaw holdings.

"They have not been informed of that yet, Sir."

Calhoun tried not to show his frustration. He was soon to be the Vice President of the United States and felt that he had more important things to deal with than working out the details of an agreement with a bunch of savages. They just needed to be told that was the way it was going to be and get on with it. Calhoun was also strongly considering running for Presidency in another four years, and he knew that the Red

---

[43] Lewis, Anna, *Pushmataha-American Patriot*, Exposition Press, 1959, p. 173

man could not vote. Appeasing the voters in Mississippi and Arkansas was much more important than satisfying a few savages that had no input into the democratic process.

"Inform them about that land," the President said. "But otherwise, keep them waiting. The longer they are kept sitting and stewing, the easier negotiations will be. And while they are waiting, get Charles King to draw their pictures."

CHARLES BIRD KING, one of the most noted portrait painters of the time, was the son of Revolutionary War Captain Zebulon King. Following the War, the family moved from the comfort of Rhode Island to the wilds of Ohio, where, in 1789, Zebulon was killed and scalped by the Shawnee. Charles was only four years old at the time, and he and his mother moved back east to be with her family. Under the encouragement of his artist grandfather, the young King became an accomplished portraitist and opened a studio in Washington. Among his patrons were John Quincy Adams, John C. Calhoun, Henry Clay, James Monroe, and Daniel Webster.

In 1822, King was enlisted by Thomas McKenney, United States Superintendent of Indian Affairs, to paint portraits of Native American dignitaries who were visiting Washington on official business. McKenney was very sensitive to the plight of the Red man and was well aware of their potential extinction in the coming years. Native Americans were in Washington frequently, and McKenney conceived the idea of at least preserving their images on canvas. Over the next twenty years King painted one hundred and forty-three portraits. He charged the government twenty dollars for a bust and twenty-seven dollars for a full portrait.

"HOLD STILL," KING SAID through interpreter John Pitchlynn as Pushmataha fidgeted.

The Choctaw delegation had been in Washington for almost a month, and they had yet to lay eyes on Calhoun or Monroe. Finally, a little diversion had surfaced. This man wanted to paint the portrait of the great chief, Pushmataha.

"And please, try not to cough."

In the recent few days, the chief had developed a cough. Initially it was nothing to worry about but it was gradually worsening.

"I usually paint the natives in their ceremonial garb," King said to Pitchlynn. "But if he wants to be painted in a general's uniform, so be it. The epaulets do give him a more distinguished look."

King stepped back from the canvas, looked at the chief, and shook his head.

"Are you sure this is the legendary Pushmataha that we've heard so much about—who's made such a name for himself as a warrior and a negotiator? Why, he looks like a potbellied old man—except for that boyish face of his."

Pitchlynn began to laugh.

"Oh, yes," he said. "Don't let his looks fool you. He's a pretty vicious fellow when you get him riled up. And he has the mind and tongue of Socrates and Shakespeare."

"Well, then. I'll try to keep him happy and get this painting finished."

"What did the painter say," Pushmataha asked with a perplexed look on his face.

"He says that he has never painted such a distinguished and mighty looking chief as the great Pushmataha." Pitchlynn covered his mouth and began to snicker. "He says that your strong, majestic face reveals a leader beyond compare. Your picture will one day hang in a place of honor, and young men will stand in awe as they gaze upon it."

Pushmataha straightened up and held his head high. He then let out a deep cough.

"And tell him," King added, "a little whiskey will help with that cough."

Pitchlynn thought to himself, "A little whiskey? With the amount the chief has been consuming, he should either be healed or pickled by now!"

The government had allotted three dollars a day for liquor for each member of the Choctaw delegation, but Pushmataha and his fellow delegates were averaging eight dollars and twenty-one cents a day.

Pushmataha by Charles Bird King, 1824.[44]

---

[44] Two other portraits of Pushmataha were also done by King in 1824. Both were destroyed by the Smithsonian fire of 1856. The portrait used on the cover of this book was done by John William Gear in 1837, as a copy of one of the originals.

CHAPTER TWENTY-NINE

"WHAT MORE DO THEY WANT?" Pushmataha said when he was told that not only did the United States want to redraw the Quapaw land but wanted more land in Mississippi.

"And no one will speak with us. Every sliver of information comes to us through aides. Will we ever meet face to face?"

Attitudes toward the Choctaws had changed significantly since the last time they had visited Washington. At that time the United States needed the Choctaws' help in dealing with the Spanish and in battling the English. The leaders had bent over backwards to please their Red friends. Pushmataha had been ushered in to see the great Thomas Jefferson within a day or two of arriving in the capital.

Things were so different now. There was peace in the southwest, and the leaders in Washington saw no use or benefit in the Choctaws' friendship. There was no reason to give them favors. In fact, the Red man was a hindrance. He was in the way, preventing progress and development of the ever-expanding nation. Previous loyalty and friendship seemed to have no bearing at all.

With no direct communication with Monroe or Calhoun, Pushmataha sent another correspondence to Mr. Calhoun, outlining the Choctaws' response to this new information.

"We have come to the conclusion that we cannot sell any more of our land bordering on the Tombigbee..." In a conciliatory tone he continued. "The government must be satisfied of our friendly disposition toward our white brothers. In war we have given them our assistance, and in peace we have endeavored to show our hospitality. Our determination, therefore, cannot be supposed to result from any unfriendly feeling. It is the result of a thorough conviction in our own minds that we act in uniformity with the wishes of our countrymen."[45]

There was no response, and the delegation continued to wait. Boredom led to more drink, and Pushmataha's cough worsened.

ANOTHER DIVERSION SURFACED while the delegation waited. The Marquis de La Fayette arrived in town as a guest of the nation. Almost fifty years had passed since he had served under General Washington in the War for Independence, and he was being celebrated as a national hero. Accompanied by his son, George Washington La Fayette, the General toured the nation and visited all twenty-four states during his eighteen months stay.

At one of the official parties in Washington, government officials decided to invite the Choctaw delegation to the festivities to add a little color. An appearance and address by the famed Pushmataha were always welcomed and entertaining. The Choctaw delegation was elated to meet the great French warrior—and to get out of the hotel.

Both Mushulatubbee and Pushmataha were given the privilege to speak.

"You are one of our fathers," Mushulatubbee began, "that fought the war with General Washington. We take you by the hand as a friend and father. We have always walked in the white paths of peace; and in these paths we have traveled to visit you. We offer you our hands which have never been stained with the blood of Americans. We live in the South, where the sun shines hot upon us. We have been neighbors of the French, neighbors to the Spanish, and neighbors to the English; but now our only neighbors are the Americans, in the midst of whom we live as friends and brothers."[46]

[45] Lewis, Anna, *Pushmataha-American Patriot*, Exposition Press, 1959, p. 174
[46] Lewis, Anna, *Pushmataha-American Patriot*, Exposition Press, 1959, p. 179

Pushmataha followed. His elocution, delivered in his usual profound sincerity and dignity, captivated the General and the audience. His sickness and cough had not diminished his fervor.

"About fifty years ago you drew your sword, the companion of General Washington; with him you traveled and warred against the enemies of America. In spilling the blood of our foes, you generously shed your own, thereby consecrating your devotion to the cause on which you were engaged. After the termination of war, you returned to your own country, and now you revisit this land, blessed by the benediction and honored with the grateful attention of a numerous and powerful people. You see everywhere around you, crowding to your presence, and clasping your hands with filial affection, the children of those with whom you fought in defense of this country. We had heard of these things even in our remote land, and our ears were filled with desire and anxiety to see you. We have come. We have taken you by the hand and are satisfied. It is the first and last time. We shall meet no more. We part on earth forever. This is all I have to say."[47]

The two great warriors of the Revolution, neither citizens of the nation that they fought for, in that short visit developed a bond and friendship that transcended language and nationality. They visited the rest of the evening, and the next day the chief accompanied the General on his journey to Baltimore.

La Fayette continued his travels through the nation as a hero. Pushmataha returned to Washington to wait in anticipation and dread of having more of his people's land ripped from his hands.

---

[47] Lewis, Anna, *Pushmataha-American Patriot*, Exposition Press, 1959, p. 179

OCCASIONALLY, THERE WERE other diversions and parties that the Choctaw delegations were invited to attend. Pushmataha not only delighted in speaking at these gatherings, but he also enjoyed playing a joke or two on his hosts and their guests.

At one such occasion, he noticed a group of young ladies who were quietly visiting with each other. With interpreter John Pitchlynn beside him and a twinkle in his eye, the chief approached the young maidens, bowed politely, and said, "My friend the interpreter has often read in my presence from a Big Book which has many strange things. Among the best of the very strange stories there was one about angels. The book said they looked exactly like people and yet they were so delicate in their formation that the inhabitants of this world could not feel them when they tried to handle them. Now I have been observing these six bright and most elegantly beautiful beings all evening, and I have come to the conclusion that if there are any such being as angels, a thing I have never before credited, these must be some of them. To satisfy my curiosity on the subject, I solicited my friend to come and talk for me and to ask for me the privilege to touch the pretty creatures to see if I could feel them."[48]

The young ladies began to giggle, flattered at the old chief's words. They consented to his wish, and in a most delicate and tender manner, he touched each of their arms and squeezed them gently.

"They are people," he exclaimed. "I would never have believed it. It is sure enough somebody, and I must say a mighty nice somebody, but perhaps if they are not angels now, they will turn out to be later."[49]

TIME MOVED SLOWLY. Soon the occasional parties were tiresome, and there seemed to be nothing of substance to occupy their time. The cold confines of the city were becoming difficult for these warm weather forest dwellers.

---

[48] Lincecum, Gideon, *Life of Apushmataha*, Publications of the Mississippi Historical Society, Vol. IX.
[49] Lincecum, Gideon, *Life of Apushmataha*, Publications of the Mississippi Historical Society, Vol. IX.

Finally, a correspondence wanting to negotiate was sent from Mr. Calhoun. Still there was no face-to-face encounter. The message stated that the United States wished to purchase from the Choctaws five million acres of the thirteen million acres of Quapaw land that had been ceded. But the price offered was woefully low. Pushmataha, whether due to his illness or due to the obviously insulting proposition of Calhoun, became bolder in his speech.

> "We shall speak with some freedom, but not without respect. We esteem you, our friend and brother, as the organ of our Great Father, the President of the United States, who has shown himself always to be the friend of the Red man. We approved you, therefore, with respect, but at the same time it is not inconsistent with that respect to speak frankly and openly on the subject of our business. The price which you offer us for the land is altogether inadequate....
>
> "We do not wish to embarrass our Father, the President... We do not mean to assume anything like a threatening tone. When the arm of the government is lifted, we are weak; we are powerless. We rely on your justice, and for that we patiently wait."[50]

In response to his letter, Pushmataha got silence.

"I'LL HAVE A PHYSICIAN see him, if he will allow it," the proprietor of the hotel, Joseph Tenneson, said to John Pitchlynn.

It was mid-December. The two men were standing at the door to the parlor where the delegation was sitting and enjoying a drink. Pushmataha was with them, smoking his white man's pipe. Every few minutes he would let out a deep, wet coughing episode that made one wonder if his innards would burst.

---

[50] Lewis, Anna, *Pushmataha-American Patriot*, Exposition Press, 1959, p. 178

"A physician would be good," Pitchlynn said, "and I don't think he will object. He's getting sicker each day, and the alcohol and tobacco aren't helping. He's beginning to lose his strength."

Later that afternoon the physician arrived. Pushmataha had never been evaluated by a white medicine man before. And unlike the Choctaw healers, this man had no chants or songs. Instead, he wanted to put his hands all over his body.

The doctor felt the chief's wrist. He examined his fingernail beds and held up a candle to get a good look in his mouth. He pulled down the chief's lower eyelids and examined the whites of his eyes which had recently turned a dingy yellow. He felt his neck and armpits. He thumped on his thick chest with his fingers and then pressed his ear to his back.

The physician leaned back, eyed the chief with concern, and finally nodded knowingly. "He's got the croup," he said. "May even be developing consumption. I usually recommend a stiff shot of whiskey for this, but with the way he smells, he's already tried that.

"The treatment I would recommend now is phlebotomy. He needs to be bled."

With that, he reached into his bag and pulled out a jar filled with what looked like slimy black worms. "Leeches are the most effective way to do it."

Nothing had been translated to the chief to this point. He looked at the jar, looked up at Pitchlynn, and with a bit of apprehension is his voice asked, "What is this!? Yasinti—leeches?"

Pitchlynn remained silent with his mouth open.

"The key to good health is the blood and arteries," the doctor said. "When the blood gets too thick, the body doesn't work properly. The capillaries and vessels become overloaded, and the humors are no longer in balance. Infection can then set in, as it has in his case. Bleeding him will thin the blood—allowing the blood to flow more freely from the internal organs outwards. He will then be able to rid himself of plethora.

"Also," he continued, "as the mass of blood is reduced, the heart is stimulated and beats faster and with greater force.

"And finally, when a swoon is experienced by the patient, there is great relaxation of the body systems which allows the humors—the blood, the phlegm, the black bile, and the yellow bile—to find their balance."

Pushmataha remained silent while the physician spoke—his eyes fixed on the jar. When he had finished, the chief asked, "What did the healer say?"

Pitchlynn scratched his head. As best he could, he related what the physician had said. "And he wants to place about forty of the leeches on your body to suck out the blood."

Pushmataha let out a cough that watered his eyes and made him gag. When he had recovered, he said, "I have listened to the medicine man of the Choctaws chant and sing. I have seen him shake his magic dust over the sick. I have even seen him kill a fowl and drip the blood to elicit a cure. Often in my objective thinking I have questioned whether this did anything but to appease the poor sick soul until the Great Spirit healed, or refused to heal. But the white man's medicine—this is beyond belief! Does he think me a fool to allow him to bleed me to death to heal a cough? No. I will continue with my own medicine—brandy."

PUSHMATAHA CONTINUED to get sicker and weaker.

Negotiations were at a standstill. He began to worry that his mission would never be accomplished. He wondered if the deliberations would remain in this state of limbo forever. But Pushmataha did not have forever. Time was his enemy, and out of a sense of urgency and foreboding, he decided to appeal directly to the President. This message was truly one of a sick and disappointed old man.

"Father, I have been here many days, but have not talked with you and have been sick... You have no doubt heard of me; I am Pushmataha. When in my country, I often looked toward this Council House and desired to see it; I have come, but I am troubled and would tell my sorrows for I feel as a little child reclining in the bend of its father's arms, looking up into his face in childish confidence to tell of its troubles. I would now recline in the bend of your arm, and trustingly look in your face; therefore, hear my words...

"As a nation of peoples, we have always been friendly, and ever listened to the talks of the American people. We have held the hands of the United States so long that our nails are long as birds' claws and there is no danger of their slipping out. We have given our country to them until it is very small... I came here when I was a young man to see my father Jefferson. He told me if ever we got into trouble we should come and tell him and he would help us. We are in trouble and have come. This is a friendly talk. It is like a man who meets another and says, how do you do."[51]

The President never responded. The demands of the nation were too great. The loud voices of the white man were drowning out the pleas of the Choctaws. Progress would stop for no one.

---

[51] Lewis, Anna, *Pushmataha-American Patriot*, Exposition Press, 1959, p. 183

CHAPTER THIRTY

ON DECEMBER 23, 1824, Pushmataha and the delegation were doing what they had been doing for the past two months—sitting and drinking.

The coughing spells were worsening, and the chief had begun running fever. When he coughed, a pain shot through his chest, and the phlegm he was now producing was blood tinged. He was having difficulty taking a deep breath, and walking made him winded.

"I will go outside," he said as he stood and walked slowly to the door. "The fresh air will aid me and combat the fever."

As he left the Tenneson, he walked slowly, watching his unsteady step. After a short distance, he felt a little better. The cool air seemed to be refreshing him and he was breathing a little easier. He walked on. He passed several groups of people and nodded politely. They smiled back.

Two blocks from the hotel he started feeling weak. His head began to feel strange. It was as if the world were spinning out of control. The buildings before him became dark and blurry. He felt himself start to fall. Pushmataha collapsed on the street.

THE PHYSICIAN STOOD up and gathered his things.

"He's a very sick man. I doubt he'll last a day. There's nothing I can do. Even the leeches would be of no benefit now."

There was no need for an interpreter. Pushmataha knew his life was almost over. He asked his Choctaw brothers to gather around him.

"I am dying and will never return to our native and loved land," he said with labored breath. "But you will go back, and as you journey along you will see the forest and hear the birds sing in the woods, but Pushmataha will see them no more... When you return home, you will be asked, 'Pushmataha katimaha? Where is Pushmataha?' And you

271

will answer, 'He is dead.'" The chief sighed deeply. "I have always felt that I should die in the land of strangers."[52]

Pushmataha motioned to the group to come close. He then reached into his pocket and pulled out his pipe. He examined it closely, as he had done so many times in the past, knowing that it would be the last. His mind raced back to his youth when his father would smoke, and he would watch as the smoke disappeared in the air. He would imagine that the buck and two does were gazing upward to the clouds in the heavens.

He asked Nittuckachee to fill the bowl and light it. Nittuckachee did as he was asked and handed it back to his uncle.

"You have seen this pipe many times," he spoke softly. "We have shared it as we sat before the fires of friendship on many occasions. We shall share it once more."

Pushmataha took several puffs and passed it to his fellow countrymen.

"In the past, before many of you were born, this pipe was shared with great leaders of our Nation who are no more—Tuskona Hopia, Fanchimastabe, Mingo Poos Coos, Taboca, Yockonahoma, Pooshemastubie, Homastubby, and Apuckshanubbee. The smoke from its bowl has opened many great councils of the Choctaws and has sealed important deliberations and treaties with the white man.

"I have kept the origins of the pipe to myself since the days of my youth. But now, as I lie here never to rise again, I wish not for its story to die with me. When you return to the land of our ancestors, take not only the pipe, but its history."

Pushmataha coughed, gathered his breath, and began. "The pipe was given to my father a half of a century ago."

He continued to speak, telling of his youth and of Bernard Romans' visit and his gift of friendship. He told of the journey to the banks of the great Misha Sipokni with his father and of the anguish and anger he experienced that day. He spoke of his lost youth and the quest for his father's pipe and his father's killer, of his travels to the

---

[52] Lewis, Anna, *Pushmataha-American Patriot*, Exposition Press, 1959, p. 185

west into the lands of the Osages and Comanches where he honed his skills of survival and battle, and of the avenging of his father's death. He told of the pipe's disappearance following the Battle of New Orleans and its return by the great Sharp Knife.

In great detail he spoke of the treaties that the pipe had been a part of and of the fear he was experiencing for the future of his people. He warned that the insatiable hunger for land by the white man could not be stopped, and that the only way for the Choctaws to survive was to learn to live beside them in friendship. To battle the white man was to ask for extinction. Diplomacy was now the only weapon of choice. He charged those who were gathered around him with the task of leading their Nation through the difficult times that lay ahead. The survival of their people was now in their hands.

He motioned to Nittuckachee to come closer. "Take the pipe," he said. "I entrust it to you."

Pushmataha placed the pipe in his nephew's hand, leaned back, and sighed.

"Now, before I die, I wish to see Sharp Knife."

GENERAL JACKSON HAD BEEN in town for several days—busy contesting the Presidential election. When he heard the request, he dropped everything and came immediately. As the General entered the room, the chief began a round of coughing that seemed to drain his sick body of all the energy it had left. When the spell ended, he could hardly breathe.

"Push, my friend," the General said as he pulled a chair to the bed.

Pushmataha reached out his hand, and Jackson took it firmly. A minute passed. The chief finally gained enough strength to speak.

"Sharp Knife, we have been allies on the battlefield and adversaries in council. We both have strived to serve our nations and our countrymen, though the paths have diverged greatly. Still, I have respected you as a father and loved you as a brother.

"I fear for my nation. We are becoming orphans with no one to look out for us and no one to speak for us. And as orphans with no one to care for us, I fear that we will be no more—that ours will be the fate of the Mohicans and the Iroquois, never to walk the paths of this earth again.

"I beg you, my friend," he continued, "with the honor that you hold among your people and with the pity that you must have in your soul for me and my people, save us from extinction. Care for us as you would your own child. Draw us to your bosom, for we are as helpless babes. Do not let us be cast aside as ones who are unwanted. Save us."

Jackson squeezed the old chief's hand. "Rest easy, my dear friend. I will care for my friends, the Choctaws. Do not worry for them. They will not only survive; I will see to it that they excel. Mark my word."

Pushmataha rested back on his pillow. He was satisfied with his friend's promise.

But he had no way of knowing that it was a hollow promise—that it would be dashed to the ground with no thought of pity or honor. Four years later, the first order of business of President Andrew Jackson would be to banish all Red men from land east of the Mississippi. And his "friends," the Choctaws, would be the first to experience the humiliating "Trail of Tears and Death" to the west.

"Also promise me," Pushmataha said, "that I will be buried in a place of honor. And have them fire the big guns over me."

This promise he did fulfill.

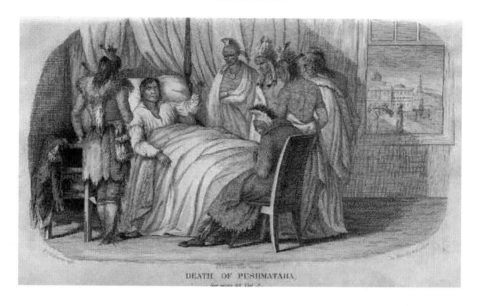

Death of Pushmataha by F.O.C. Darley, 1846.

ON CHRISTMAS EVE, 1824, the Washington *Gazette*'s front page read:

> *"This morning, a few minutes after 12 o'clock, Pushmataha, the principal chief of a district of the Choctaw Nation of Indians, died. He departed this life at the hotel of Mr. Joseph Tenneson in the city where he had been residing with other Choctaw delegates, during their late pending negotiations with the Government for the disposal of a portion of the lands of the Nation.*
>
> *"This chief was remarkable for his personal courage and skill in war, having engaged in twenty-four battles, several of which were fought under General Jackson. He was emphatically the friend of white men, never having raised his arm in hostility against them.*
>
> *"Pushmataha was also a man of great eloquence. He possessed a rich and fertile imagination with a sound*

275

understanding, and was classed by his Choctaw countrymen among the first of their warriors, and was considered the greatest of their orators.

"He fell victim of the distressing malady of croup... He bore his affliction with great firmness, was conscious of his approaching end, and predicted with unusual sagacity the hour at which he would die. This prediction was literally fulfilled.

"We had a personal opportunity of witnessing the last moments of this chief and are satisfied that death had few or no terrors for him. He gave with great composure directions to his friends and associates for the disposition of his property, recommended his family to the fatherly care of the Nation, and breathed his last amid the tears and regrets of his companions and acquaintances. Whilst living he had conciliated the friendship of all who knew him."[53]

AT TWO O'CLOCK ON CHRISTMAS DAY the great Chief of the Choctaws was buried in the Old Congressional Cemetery with pomp and circumstance fit for a national hero. Two thousand lined the streets as the Marine Band played and the big guns were fired.

Andrew Jackson himself led the processional. Even though four years later the future President would betray his promise to the dying Choctaw, that day he honored the Chief as a friend and as one of the greatest Native Americans he had ever known.

And the American nation likewise honored this man who they knew had literally saved their country. If thirteen years earlier Pushmataha had not succeeded in steering the Choctaw Nation away from Tecumseh and his Native American confederation, the outcome of the war with the British in 1812 could have been different. The combined forces of the Red man and the British could very well have resulted in a blistering American defeat and the loss of her new and

---

[53] Washington *Gazette*, December 24, 1824.

hard-fought independence. The least the American public could do was honor him on this snowy Christmas Day with their presence.

Senator John Randolph of Virginia eulogized the great warrior before the Senate Chamber as "one of nature's nobility; a man who would have adorned any society." He further stated that he was "a warrior of great distinction; he was wise in counsel, eloquent in an extraordinary degree, and, on all occasions and under all circumstances, the white man's friend." These words would later be inscribed on his tombstone.

"He was laid in his grave," David Folsom wrote. "The minister prayed for us. When it was over, he was covered with cold clay, and we left him in the midst of several hundred people. I assure you, my dear friend, that I was thankful there was so much honor paid to our departed chief."

The delegation returned to the Tenneson Hotel to wait in sadness.

ONE WEEK LATER, on December 31, Secretary of War, John Calhoun, sent a message to the delegation that he was ready to resume negotiations. The disheartened Choctaw delegation was worn out and ready to go home. Mushulatubbee had been chosen as leader and sent a message to Calhoun to draw up the agreement and tell what the Government was willing to pay. The new leader was in no mood to negotiate.

On January 14, 1825, the treaty was signed, redrawing the eastern boundary of the Quapaw land and giving up the majority of the land that the Territory of Arkansas had demanded. In return, all debts that the Choctaw Nation owed to the United States and any trading houses were forgiven, and the Choctaw Nation would be paid six thousand dollars a year forever.

The delegation departed for home, disheartened over the loss of two of its greatest leaders and worried about the fate of their Nation. But as they traveled, they did not allow their sadness to turn into despair. For the last words of their great leader, Pushmataha, would not let them. For he had said:

"Chaeta sia hoke!"— "I am a Choctaw!"

THOMAS L. WILEY

Gravestone of Pushmataha, Old Congressional Cemetery,
Washington D. C.

CHAPTER THIRTY-ONE

THE NEXT SEVERAL YEARS were transition years for the leadership of the Choctaws. Of the three chiefs who had led for the past several decades, only Mushulatubbee remained. A new generation of leaders was making its voice heard. Many of them, like David Folsom, Robert Cole, James Pitchlynn, John Nail, and the Lefleur/LeFlore brothers, were of mixed races.

The autonomy of the three districts was being called into question. Many in the Nation felt that the three chief system was no longer functional and that a single leader was needed to deal with the United States and the State of Mississippi. Greenwood LeFlore was chosen as the first principal chief.

In 1828 Andrew Jackson was elected President and took office the following spring. His Vice President was John C. Calhoun, serving his second term in the nation's second highest office. Calhoun's aspirations of serving in the highest office had subsided.

One of Jackson's first acts as President was the removal of the Red man from east of the Mississippi. The first on his list were the Choctaws, and he wasted no time. On September 27, 1830, on the bank of the Dancing Rabbit Creek in present-day Noxubee County, Mississippi—after days of threats, cajoling, and bribery—Secretary of War John H. Eaton and General John Coffee signed a treaty with the Choctaw Nation. Eleven million acres of land—all of the remaining Choctaw land in Mississippi and Alabama—was ceded to the Unites States. It was one of the largest non-wartime transfers of Native land in the history of the United States.

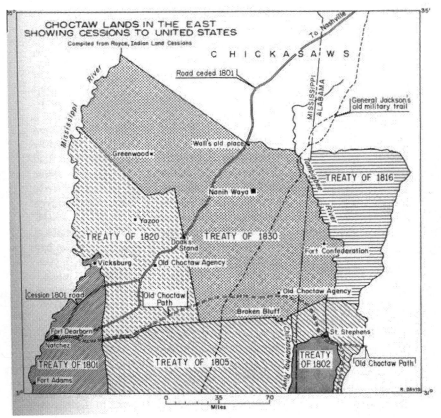

Choctaw Lands and Cessions.

For his part in the treaty, Greenwood LeFlore received a thousand acres of prime farmland in present day Carroll County, Mississippi. He chose not to migrate with his fellow countrymen, but instead remained and became a very wealthy planter and Mississippi politician. He served in both the State Legislature and Senate, and at his death in 1865, had amassed over fifteen thousand acres of Delta farmland. Many of his fellow Choctaws felt that he had let them down—his land and his future a bribe.

Greenwood Leflore, First Chief of United Choctaw Nation.

The Choctaw Nation was "encouraged" to move west. Those who stayed in Mississippi had to register as citizens of the State of Mississippi and of the United States, subject to all of the laws and regulations with all special "rights, privileges, immunities and franchises of the Indians" repealed. Autonomy east of the Mississippi was no longer an option. It would be almost impossible for them to function as a separate society in Mississippi. For this reason alone, many decided to leave their homelands and travel the six hundred miles to the land they had been given ten years earlier.

Twenty-two-year-old mixed-race George W. Harkins, who would later become chief in the new Nation, wrote a letter to the American people while he waited for removal, revealing the heart of the Choctaw Nation.

"It is with considerable diffidence that I attempt to address the American people... But having determined to emigrate west of the Mississippi river this fall, I have thought proper in bidding you farewell... Believing that our all is at stake and knowing that you readily sympathize with the distressed of every country, I confidently throw myself upon your indulgence and ask you to listen patiently. I do not arrogate to myself the prerogative of deciding upon the expediency of the late treaty, yet I feel bound as a Choctaw, to give a distinct expression of my feelings on that ... important subject.

"We were hedged in by two evils, and we chose that which we thought the least. Yet we could not recognize the right that the state of Mississippi had assumed, to legislate for us. —Although the legislature of the state was qualified to make laws for their own citizens, that did not qualify them to become law makers to a people that were so dissimilar in manners and customs as the Choctaws are to the Mississippians... We as Choctaws rather chose to suffer and be free, than live under the degrading influence of laws, which our voice could not be heard in their formation.

"Much as the state of Mississippi has wronged us, I cannot find in my heart any other sentiment than an ardent wish for her prosperity and happiness.

"I could cheerfully hope, that those of another age and generation may not feel the effects of those oppressive measures that have been so illiberally dealt out to us; and that peace and happiness may be their reward. Amid the gloom and horrors of the present separation, we are cheered with a hope that ere long we shall reach our destined land, and that nothing short of the basest acts of treachery will ever be able to wrest it from us, and that we may live free...

"Yet it is said that our present movements are our own voluntary acts—such is not the case. We found ourselves like a benighted stranger, following false guides, until he was surrounded on every side, with fire and water. The fire was certain destruction, and a feeble hope was left him of escaping by water. A distant view of the opposite shore encourages the hope; to remain would be inevitable annihilation. Who would hesitate, or who would say that his plunging into the water was his own voluntary act?

"Painful in the extreme is the mandate of our expulsion. We regret that it should proceed from the mouth of our professed friend [President Jackson], for whom our blood was co-mingled with that of his bravest warriors, on the field of danger and death.

"But such is the instability of professions. The man who said that he would plant a stake and draw a line around us, that never should be passed, was the first to say he could not guard the lines, and drew up the stake and wiped out all traces of the line...

"I ask you in the name of justice, for repose for myself and for my injured people. Let us alone—we will not harm you, we want rest. We hope, in the name of justice, that another outrage may never be committed against us, and that we may for the future be cared for as children, and not driven about as beasts, which are benefited by a change of pasture...

"Friends, my attachment to my native land was strong—that cord is now broken; and we must go forth as wanderers in a strange land! I must go—Let me entreat you to regard us with feelings of kindness, and when the hand of oppression is stretched against us, let me hope that a warning voice may be heard from every part of the United States, filling the mountains and valleys will echo, and say stop, you have no power, we are the sovereign people, and our friends shall no more be disturbed...

"We go forth sorrowful, knowing that wrong has been done... [I] cannot stay, my people [are] dear to me, with them I must go. Could I stay and forget them and leave them to struggle alone, unaided, unfriended, and forgotten, by our great father? I should then be unworthy the name of a Choctaw, and be a disgrace to my blood. I must go with them; my destiny is cast among the Choctaw people. If they suffer, so will I; if they prosper, then will I rejoice. Let me again ask you to regard us with feelings of kindness.

Yours, with respect, GEORGE W. HARKINS."[54]

George Washington Harkins, Chief of Choctaws at Time of Removal.

---

[54] Niles' Register, February 25, 1832, 41:480

BEGINNING IN 1831 and continuing over the next two years, sixteen thousand Choctaws made the journey west to the Indian Territory—"Red People"—"Okla Humma"—Oklahoma as the future state would be called.

From the start, the removal, under the supervision of the War Department, was fraught with difficulties. Secretary John Eaton resigned in April 1831 and was replaced by Lewis Cass of Michigan, who had little knowledge or experience with the Choctaws or in the removal process. Transportation to the new land, which was to be by riverboat and then wagon, was haphazard and was often completed on foot. Supplies for the journey and to sustain the Choctaws after they reached their new land were not adequate.

And then, there was the weather. The winter of 1831-1832 was one of the worst in memory. Snow blanketed Mississippi, Arkansas, and Oklahoma, and temperatures reached zero degrees.

Almost twenty-five hundred Choctaws died on this, the first of the "Trail of Tears and Death"—the Chickasaws, Seminoles, Creeks, and Cherokees would follow later. The journey and first few years were especially hard on the young and elderly. The last of the great chiefs, Mushulatubbee, died of smallpox soon after arrival in his new land. Nittuckachee, Pushmataha's nephew who had been entrusted with the white man's pipe, died in 1845.

Mushulatubbee, Painted by George Catlin.

DESPITE THE DIFFICULT BEGINNINGS, the Choctaws in their new land soon flourished and prospered. By the late 1830's they had transformed this wilderness into productive plantations and farms growing cotton, corn, pecans, and livestock. A unified government was formed which retained the three districts organization but was governed by a Principal Chief and General Council.

For the six thousand Choctaws who chose to remain in Mississippi, the path led in a different direction. Living in small communities within the land of the white man, they were subjected to discrimination and neglect. Except for a notable few, such as Greenwood LeFlore and Jackson McCurtain who led the First Choctaw Battalion during the Civil War, the Choctaws in their native land dropped into obscurity, living primarily as sharecroppers and subsistence farmers. They were considered neither white nor black and were essentially ignored in their poverty. By the late 1800's, their population had dwindled to less than two thousand.

After almost eighty years, the United States finally addressed the needs of the dwindling tribe of Choctaws in Mississippi. In 1918 the Choctaw Agency was established by the U. S. Bureau of Indian Affairs to address the poor living conditions of the Mississippi Choctaws. Based in Philadelphia, Mississippi, the Agency erected schools and medical facilities, but it was not until Franklin D. Roosevelt's Indian Reorganization Act of 1934 that there was real change. The Act encouraged Indian societies to reorganize, and reinvestment of Indians with land was started. In 1945 the Mississippi Band of Choctaw Indians was organized and a Constitution and By-Laws was approved by the Secretary of the Interior. Thirty-five thousand acres of land scattered in several counties in east-central Mississippi were designated the Choctaw Indian Reservation.

Thus ushered in a new day for the Choctaws. As stated on the Mississippi Band of Choctaw website, the future of their Nation looks bright.

"Through effective Tribal governmental leadership, good economic planning and diversification, and increasing self-reliance, the picture is much brighter for the Choctaw people. Because of the revitalization of our communities, made possible by the Tribe's creation of jobs, educational opportunities, improved housing and healthcare, and an overall elevation of the Choctaw standard of living, the renaissance of Choctaw cultural arts has been assured. Our native culture and mother language, once standing on the threshold of extinction, has not only been rescued from loss, but has been reinvigorated and energized through our own successful efforts that we hope will continue well into the future. Today we see Choctaw Self-Determination in its finest hour, and we are able to celebrate once again not just our perseverance, but our triumph."

THOMAS L. WILEY

EPILOGUE

"DO YOU HAVE ANY MORE?" the old gentleman asked as he picked up each old pipe, examined it closely, and placed it back on the counter.

The antique dealer scratched his head. He had already looked in every nook and cranny of his store and had gathered every one he could find. On the counter before the old gentleman were at least two dozen of the vintage smoking devices.

"Let me take another quick look," he answered. "There may be another one or two I missed."

"Granddaddy, how much longer?" the boy asked as he looked up and tugged on the old man's coat sleeve. "I wanna go home."

"Just one more minute, son." He picked up another pipe, examined it closely "When the man comes back, we'll go."

The store owner returned caring a small leather-bound case. "This is the last one."

Not wanting to do any more damage to the already crumbling leather, he softly blew the dust off, opened the case with care, and gently lifted the pipe out.

"This one has been here for years," he said.

He then chuckled. "An old Indian brought it in—must have been at least twenty years ago—he said it belonged to an Indian chief."

He handed it to the old gentleman. "I had forgotten I had it. It was stuck behind some old books."

"This isn't Indian," the gentleman said as he lifted it up to eye level. "This is meerschaum. It's probably Italian."

He pulled out a jeweler's eye piece and examined it closely. "But it is old. It's good workmanship, and it's in excellent shape."

He turned it in his hand. "And he said it belonged to an Indian chief?"

"Yea," the dealer replied. "I think he said Pushmataha, if I remember correctly. It's been a while. The old man looked like he needed the money. I think I gave him ten bucks for it."

"The little boy's eyes got big. "Wow! An Indian pipe!" he exclaimed. "Is it a peace pipe? Did a chief really smoke it? Can I hold it?"

The grandfather smiled and handed it to the boy.

"Wow! This is neat!" he exclaimed. "Look at the deer! I bet when the pipe is lit, the deer look like they're looking up at clouds!"

"That's very observant of you," his grandfather chuckled. "Now be careful with it. We don't want to break it."

He looked at the store owner. "Will you take thirty dollars for it?"

The store owner shrugged his shoulders. "Yea, that'll be fine."

"Wow!" the boy said. "My very own Indian pipe. Smoked by a real chief!

"Granddaddy, who was Pushmataha?"

(Author's note: I have the pipe.)

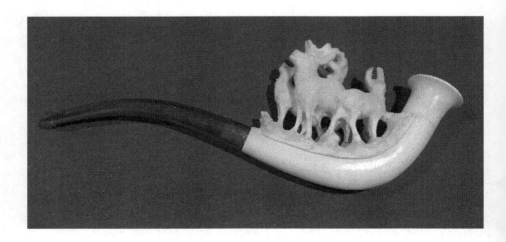

Pushmataha.

SELECTED BIBLIOGRAPHY

- *Alabama Indian Tribe History.* <accessgenealogy.com>.
- *American History Timelines-War of 1812.* <http://americanhistory.about.com/library/timelines/bltimelin ewar1812.htm>.
- *Appleton's' Journal: a Magazine of General Literature.* D. Appleton and Company. Volume 4, Issue 71. 1870
- Arkansas *Gazette.* 1822.
- Arthur, Stanley Clisby. *Old New Orleans: A History of the Vieux Carre, Its Ancient and Historical Buildings.* 1936.
- Birchfield, D. L. From "*How the People Found a Home,*" The Encyclopedia of North American Indians, 1977.
- Braund, Kathryn E. Holland. Auburn University. *Battle of Holy Ground.* Encyclopedia of Alabama. October 8, 2008. <http://www.encyclopediaofalabama.org/>.
- Braund, Kathryn E. Holland. Auburn University. *Bernard Romans.* Encyclopedia of Alabama. March 6, 2007. <http://www.encyclopediaofalabama.org/>.
- Braund, Kathryn E. Holland. Auburn University. *Creek War of 1813-14.* Encyclopedia of Alabama. October 28, 2008. <http://www.encyclopediaofalabama.org/>.
- Bryan, William Jennings. *The World's Famous Orations, Vol. VIII America-I, 1761-1837*, Funk & Wagnall's Company, New York, 1906.
- Bunn, J. Michael and Williams, Clay. *Mississippi's Territorial Years: A Momentous and Contentious Affair (1798-1817)* Mississippi History Now. Nov 2008.

- Carson, James Taylor. *Searching for the Bright Path-The Mississippi Choctaw from Prehistory to Removal*. University of Nebraska Press. 1999.
- *Choctaw Chronology*, Mississippi Band of Choctaw Indians. <http://www.choctaw.org/>.
- *Choctaw Clans*. <http://jennferhsrn2.homestead.com/clan.html>.
- *Choctaw Government in the Nineteenth Century*. Bishinik Newspaper. February 1979.
- Cushman, H. B., *A History of the Choctaw, Chickasaw, and Natchez Indians*. 1899. Edited by Angie Debo. University of Oklahoma Press. 1962.
- Delta Farm Press. Feb 1, 2002.
- Denson, Miko Beasley. *Welcome from Miko Beasley Denson*. Mississippi Band of Choctaw Indians. <http://www.choctaw.org/>.
- DeRosier, Arthur H., Jr. *The Removal of the Choctaw Indians*. The University of Tennessee Press. 1970.
- *Descendants of John Langhorne, 1640*. <http://www.livelyroots.com/langhorne/d5.htm>.
- *Descendants of Shomaka or Shumaka, Choctaw Nation*. <http://jenniferhsrn2.homestead.com/shomaka.html>.
- English, Ginny. *War with Creeks, 1813-14, Mississippi Territory*. <http://www.natchezbelle.org/sw/creek.htm>.
- *Ft. Mims Massacre, Baldwin County, Alabama, August 30, 1813*. <http://canerossi.us/ftmims/massacre.htm>.
- *Fort Tombigbee*. National Park Service. March 2005 <http://www.cr.nps.gov/history/online_books/explorers-settlers/sitee1.htm>.
- Fuller, Myron. *New Madrid Earthquake*. 1912.
- Gardner, Chief David. *A Brief Talk on Choctaw History*. Hello Choctaw. December 1, 1976.
- Green, Len. How to Lose a Nation in Seven Not-So-Easy Treaties. Bishinik Newspaper. October, 1978. Page 6-8.

- Halbert, H. S. *Bernard Roman's Mississippi Map of 1772*. Mississippi Genealogical and Historical Research. From Publications of the Mississippi Historical Society, Vol. VI. 1902
- *History of Old St. Stephens*. The St. Stephens Historical Commission. 2007. <http://www.oldststephens.com/history>.
- *History of Wild Swine in the United States*. Illinois Federation for Outdoor Resources.
- *Horseshoe Bend National Military Park. History and Culture*. <http://www.nps.gov/hobe/historyculture/index.htm>.
- Hudson, Peter James, *A Story of Choctaw Chiefs*, Chronicles of Oklahoma, Vol. 17, No. 2, June, 1939, P 192
- Jensen, Ove. *Battle of Horseshoe Bend*. Encyclopedia of Alabama. February 26, 2007.
- Jones, Joel D. *Old Times. The Creek War*. July 18, 1935. <http://homepages.rootsweb.ancestry.com/-cmamcrkr/crkwr4.htlm>.
- Jones, Pam. *William Weatherford and the Road to the Holy Ground*. Alabama Heritage. Fall 2004.
- Key, Joseph. Arkansas State University. "*Quapaw*." The Encyclopedia of Arkansas History and Culture.
- Leftwich, G. J. *Colonel George S. Gaines and Other Pioneers in the Mississippi Territory*. Publications of the Mississippi Historical Society, Vol. I. Centenary Series. 1904. p 442.
- Lewis, Anna, *Chief Pushmataha-American Patriot*. Exposition Press. 1959.
- Lincecum, Gideon. *Life of Pushmataha*. Publication of the Mississippi Historical Society. Volume 8-9. 1906.
- Lincecum, Gideon. *The Life of Apushimataha*, 1861, Republished as *Pushmataha-A Choctaw Leader and His People*. Introduction by Greg O'Brien. The University of Alabama Press. 2004.
- Lowery, Charles. *The Great Migration to the Mississippi Territory 1798-1819*. Mississippi History Now. Nov 2000.

- *Mobile Indian Tribe History.* <http://www.accessgenealogy.com/native/tribes/muskhogean/mobilehist.htm>.
- Moore, Sue B. *Thomas Hinds.* Jefferson County MSGenWeb Index. <http://jeffersoncountyms.org/thomas_hinds.htm>
- *Natchez Gazette.* July 8, 1820.
- *Natchez Republican.* Aug 29, 1820.
- *The Natchez Road a.k.a., the Natchez Trace.* TnGenWeb Project. <http;//www.tngenweb.org/maps/tntrace.htm
- Niles' Register. 41:480. February 25, 1832.
- O'Brien, Greg. *Mushulatubbee and Choctaw Removal: Chiefs Confront a Changing World.* Mississippi History Now. March, 2001.
- O'Brien, Greg. *Pre-removal Choctaw History- Exploring New Paths.* University of Oklahoma Press. 2008.
- O'Brien, Greg. *Pushmataha: Choctaw Warrior, Diplomat, and Chief.* Mississippi History Now. July 2001.
- Owen, Thomas McAdory. Transactions of the Alabama Historical Society 1898, Vol. 2.
- Pickett, Albert James. *Battle of Burnt Corn.* History of Alabama. 1851.
- Publications of the Mississippi Historical Society, Volume 9, 1906 p. 433.
- *Pushmataha, Choctaw Indian Chief.* Access Genealogy, Indian Tribal Records. <http://www.accessgenealogy.com/native/tribes/choctaw/pushmatah.htm>.
- Remini, Robert V. *The Life of Andrew Jackson.* New York: Penguin. 1990.
- Romans, Bernard. *A Concise Natural History of East and West Florida.* 1776. Introduction by Louise Richardson. New Orleans: Pelican Publishing Company. 1961.
- *Sister of Pushmataha.* <http://geforum.genealogy.com/pushmataha/messages/55.html>.

- Spies, Gregory C. *Major Andrew Ellicott, Esq.— Colonial American Astronomical Surveyor, Patriot, Cartographer, Legislator, Scientific Instrument Maker, Boundary Commissioner, & Professor of Mathematics*. FIG XXII International Congress, Washington, D.C. April2002.
- Spring, Joel. *The Cultural Transformation of a Native American Family and Its Tribe 1763-1995*. New Jersey: Lawrence Erlbaum Associates. 1996.
- Swanton, John R. *The Indians of the Southeastern United States*. Smithsonian Institution Press. 1946.
- Swanton, John R. *Social and Ceremonial Life of the Choctaw*. 1931.
- *Tecumseh*. Ohio History Central. The Ohio Historical Society. <http://ohiohistorycentral.org>.
- *Timeline*. <http://creekwarandwarof1812.com/timeline.html>.
- *Thomas Flournoy Papers*. William L. Clements Library. The University of Michigan.
- *Treaty of Dancing Rabbit Creek*. 1830. <http://www.choctaw.org/History/Treaties/>.
- *Treaty of Doak's Stand*. 1820. <http://www.choctaw.org/History/Treaties/>.
- *Treaty of Fort Adams*. 1801. <http://www.choctaw.org/History/Treaties/>.
- *Treaty of Fort Jackson*. 1814. <http://www.choctaw.org/History/Treaties/>.
- *Treaty of Fort St. Stephens*. 1816. <http://www.choctaw.org/History/Treaties/>.
- *Treaty of Hoe Buckintoopa*. 1803. <http://www.choctaw.org/History/Treaties/>.
- *Treaty of Mount Dexter*. 1805. <http://www.choctaw.org/History/Treaties/>.
- *Treaty of San Lorenzo/ Pinckney's Treaty, 1795*. <http://www.state.gov/r/pa/ho/time/nr/90612.htm>.

- Turner, Frederick W. T*he Portable North American Indian Reader*. New York: The Viking Press. 1974.
- Viola, Herman J. *The Indian Legacy of Charles Bird King*, Washington: Smithsonian Institution Press. 1976.
- *The War of 1812*. <http://www.gatewayne.com/history/war1812.html>.
- Wade, John William. *The Removal of the Mississippi Choctaws*. Mississippi Genealogical and Historical Research. From *The Mississippi Historical Society*, Vol. VIII, Oxford, Mississippi. 1904.
- Waselkov, Gregory A. *Fort Mims Battle and Massacre*. Encyclopedia of Alabama. March 15, 2007. <http://www.encyclopediaofalabama.org/>.
- *Washington Gazette*. December 24, 1824.
- White, Earl. *Apuckshunnubbe's Death in Kentucky in 1824*. <http://www.choctawnation.com/history/>.
- *William Cocke 1748-1828*. Tennessee Encyclopedia of History and Culture. Tennessee Historical Society. 1998.
- Wilson, Gaye. *Jefferson's Big Deal: the Louisiana Purchase*. Monticello Newsletter. Spring 2003.

PUSHMATAHA

THOMAS L. WILEY

Made in the USA
Columbia, SC
28 January 2025

52852731R00172